PAGAN
SPAIN

Books by Richard Wright

Uncle Tom's Children

Native Son

12 Million Black Voices

Black Boy

The Outsider

Black Power

The Color Curtain

Pagan Spain

RICHARD WRIGHT

PAGAN SPAIN

HARPER & BROTHERS
NEW YORK

PAGAN SPAIN

Printed in the United States of America

FIRST EDITION

A-G

Library of Congress catalog card number: 56-11091

For my friends
ALVA AND GUNNAR MYRDAL
who suggested this book and whose compassionate hearts have long brooded upon the degradation of human life in Spain.

How poor indeed is man . . .

—NIETZSCHE

I tell you the past is a bucket of ashes.
I tell you yesterday is a wind gone down,
a sun dropped in the west.

—CARL SANDBURG

PAGAN
SPAIN

LIFE AFTER DEATH

1 . . .

In torrid August, 1954, I was under the blue skies of the Midi, just a few hours from the Spanish frontier. To my right stretched the flat, green fields of southern France; to my left lay a sweep of sand beyond which the Mediterranean heaved and sparkled. I was alone. I had no commitments. Seated in my car, I held the steering wheel in my hands. I wanted to go to Spain, but something was holding me back. The only thing that stood between me and a Spain that beckoned as much as it repelled was a state of mind. God knows, totalitarian governments and ways of life were no mysteries to me. I had been born under an absolutistic racist regime in Mississippi; I had lived and worked for twelve years under the political dictatorship of the Communist party of the United States; and I had spent a year of my life under the police terror of Perón in Buenos Aires. So why avoid the reality of life under Franco? What was I scared of?

For almost a decade I had ignored the admonitions of my friends to visit Spain—the one country of the Western world about which, as though shunning the memory of a bad love affair, I did not want to exercise my mind. I had even resisted the solemn preachments of Gertrude Stein who, racked with pain and with only a few days to live, had counseled me (while nervously tugging with the fingers of her right hand at a tuft of hair on her forehead):

"Dick, you ought to go to Spain."

"Why?" I had asked her.

"You'll see the past there. You'll see what the Western world is made of. Spain is primitive, but lovely. And the people! There are no people such as the Spanish anywhere. I've spent days in Spain that I'll never forget. See those bullfights, see that wonderful landscape. . . ."

And still I had not gone. During the Spanish Civil War I had published, in no less than the New York *Daily Worker*, some harsh judgments concerning Franco; and the dive bombers and tanks of Hitler and Mussolini had brutally justified those judgments. The fate of Spain had hurt me, had haunted me; I had never been able to stifle a hunger to understand what had happened there and why. Yet I had no wish to resuscitate mocking recollections while roaming a land whose free men had been shut in concentration camps, or exiled, or slain. An uneasy question kept floating in my mind: How did one live after the death of the hope for freedom?

Suddenly resolved, I swung my car southward, toward those humped and ragged peaks of the Pyrenees which, some authorities claim, mark the termination of Europe and the beginning of Africa. The look of the world darkened; a certain starkness of mood hovered over the landscape. Gray-green masses of bald rock reared toward a distant and indifferent sky. I edged my car along in the wake of the car ahead, circling round the snaky curves of the tilting mountain slopes, glancing now and then from the narrow road to plunging precipices that yawned but a yard from my elbow.

Toward evening, under a remote and paling sky, I crossed the frontier and entered my first Spanish town—a too quiet, dreary conglomeration of squat, pastel-tinted houses: Le Perthus. Ringed by a horizon of blue-green, naked mountains whose somber hues altered with the passing hours, this border town, after the tension and rush of life in Nice, Cannes, and Paris, seemed alien of aspect, torpid, forgotten, marooned in the past. Being a national whose country had air bases on Spanish soil, the customs and immigration requirements were but a formality, yet I had to wait, and wait. Fatigued, I garaged my car and decided to spend the night in Le Perthus and take the coastal road for Barcelona the next morning.

My hotel room, with bath, cost one dollar and a quarter, as

against twelve dollars that a dingier room, without bath, would have fetched on the Côte d'Azur. My seven-course dinner, with wine, penalized me one dollar and a half, but when I learned that the waiter serving me had a salary of only one hundred pesetas (plus tips) a month, I began to understand. (A peseta has roughly the value of a large Irish potato and it would take about forty-five of such potatoes to buy the equivalent of a dollar's worth of anything.) My shower had no curtain; when I used it, water flooded the floor. There were no ashtrays; one dropped ashes upon the beautiful Moorish tiles and smothered burning butts with one's heel. The furnishings were shiny, rickety; the table sagged threateningly when I placed my typewriter upon it. My elbow collided accidentally with the thin headboard of my bed and I was startled by a deep, vibrating boom, as though a huge drum had been struck. Several times an hour the electric bulb dimmed momentarily.

Awakened by the melancholy tolling of churchbells and the strident, reedy crowing of cocks, I rose and found the morning air bracingly cool, the sky lowering and gray. The wall of mountains enclosing the town was dim and shadowy, half drowned in an ocean of mist. I pulled into a gas station and tanked up, for I'd been warned that gas was scarce. As I released my car brake and clutched to leave, a Civil Guard officer wearing a dark green uniform, a gleaming black patent-leather hat and nonchalantly dangling a machine gun at his side, confronted me, clapped his hand upon my right shoulder, and sadly blabbered something in Spanish. I blinked, understanding nothing; I was in a police state and I thought: *This is it. . . .* I extended my passport, but he waved that aside, shaking his head. The gas station attendant spoke French and told me that I was not being arrested, that the man merely wished a lift. The officer was clad most imposingly and I could not believe that one of his rank did not have a car at his disposal. I consented and he climbed in, machine gun and all.

Having no language in common, we both were prey to a curious and uneasy compulsion to talk, not to communicate but to try to let each other know that we were civilized and of good will. We chatted at random, keeping fixed smiles on our faces, furtively glancing at each other out of the corners of our eyes, and then laughing unnaturally loud and long at our inability to understand what the other was saying. I divined that he was asking me if I were an American Negro, if I liked Spain, and I also guessed that he was trying to tell me something about his family. . . . Then suddenly he touched my arm and made motions with his right foot, pumping jerkily and vigorously downward. Thinking that he was signaling for speed, I pressed the accelerator and the car shot forward. He hugged his machine gun, looked at his wrist watch, doubled his fists and again motioned with his foot for me to press down. I jammed the accelerator to the floor, feeling that if I were hailed for speeding I had an officer of the law at my side as my alibi. Finally, he grew desperate and, walling his eyes, he shook his head. I got the point: he had been urging me to step on the brake. I drew to a side of the road and offered to drive him back over the distance that I had overshot his destination, but, thanking me profusely, he would have none of it. We parted, shaking hands, waving frantically and nervously at each other, laughing uproariously, trying to fill the void that gaped between us. Head down, he lumbered off, his machine gun cradled in his arm.

2 . . .

Over reddish, undulating country the road advanced tortuously up into dark and jagged mountains whose scarred peaks soared till they blended with gray-blue mist. The day grew gradually brighter, revealing a bleak, seemingly diseased and inhospitable landscape that grudged the few patches of scrubby vegetation showing against vast humped mounds of leprous-looking rubble. Later, dainty groves of stunted, dark green olive trees clung precariously to the slanting mountainsides, their filagreed leaves glowing like silver in the deepening morning's light. The mountain road was rough and steeply inclined and the hairpin curves came sharp and unexpected and my body could feel the heavy tug of gravity as I twisted the steering wheel. Against a background of stacks of cone-shaped, yellow-brown hay, I saw a stout peasant woman dressed in bright red; she was trudging laboriously, her face downcast, her head balancing a huge earthen jug of water. Farther, I passed another peasant; he was perched atop his creaking, manure-filled cart; in his right fist he clutched a gaudy, rolled-up, frayed comic book, his dull eyes staring vacantly out across the splayed ears of his fuzzy-dirty donkey that ambled along with the slow movements of an equine sleepwalker.

Ahead, spanning the road, was a beautifully arched white stone bridge at each end of which stood a Civil Guard in gleaming black patent-leather hats and dark green uniforms, each with a machine gun nestling in the crook of his right arm. Respect for the show of power made me brake my car, anticipating my being stopped and challenged. They stared at me and I at them, but they made no sign. I drove over the bridge and rolled on, uncertain, feeling a naked vulnerability creeping down the skin of my back. I was not accustomed to armed strangers of unknown motives standing in my rear and I waited to hear *raatatatatatat* and feel hot slugs of steel crashing into my car and into my flesh. But nothing happened. I increased my speed, thankful for the distance between me and the black muzzles of those machine guns. Why were the bridges under guard? Under this calm, dreary landscape there seemed to lurk coiled tensions, fears.

Five kilometers farther I approached another bridge and, again, two Civil Guards with machine guns on their forearms stood on duty. I slowed to pass them and their black, staring eyes met mine for a split second and then they were behind me. I studied their reflection in my rear mirror, bothered, frowning, feeling exposed to danger. Another five kilometers brought me abreast of yet another bridge with its now inevitable two Civil Guards and their ready machine guns. Once more instinct prompted me to slacken the speed of my car; then suddenly an idea, or rather an impulse, came to my aid. Timidly, I lifted my right hand in a greeting, a shy, friendly salute. And the two soldiers came to attention, smiled, and waved their hands at me in return. I sighed, relieved. It had been simply a gesture, human in intent, to determine if those men who held those murderous weapons knew or understood the meaning of fraternity, if they shared my kind of humanity, if they had reactions that coincided with my own. My tension ebbed a bit.

3 . . .

Coming round a mountain, my first Spanish village arrived in a pall of heat and dust. Scrawny black goats nibbled at starved grass; stunted, barefoot boys minded dreamy sheep. A swarthy young woman at an outdoor hydrant registered bewilderment upon seeing my face; then she stared, breaking into a knowing smile. What was she thinking? Did I remind her of Moors? The irregular paving stones made my car do a nervous dance. The walls of the white-washed houses held lurid bullfight posters. This village was conspicuous for the prevalence of dogs in it; they mingled with the inhabitants on a plane of equality, sleeping in doorways, in the middle of the streets. And every dog in Spain seemed in heat; canine copulation was everywhere. Overtaking a truck in a narrow street, I started violently: a huge dog, four feet from my windshield, his great paws balancing him on top of the truck, spewed at me a torrent of ear-splitting barks, his long white fangs showing, his gleaming red tongue hanging out, flecks of foam flying from his gaping mouth. (Almost all trucks on Spanish highways carry dogs to guard the merchandise.)

The road twisted and climbed into the magnificently craggy mountains of the Costa Brava, and a blue-green sea, shimmering in a noon sun, lay on my left far below. Hours later I entered the bleak suburbs of Barcelona, then penetrated into the center of that garishly modern city, cruising along its tiny, dirty streets, its noisy, ornate boulevards, studying the neighborhoods.

At Plaza de Cataluña I located a bank whose spacious doorway was blocked by a soldier with that ever-present machine gun. I found more armed guards standing about in the dim and mute interior.

I exhibited my passport and a plump woman made me sign five different documents, gave me a tiny metal disk bearing a number, and bade me wait. I watched her staple my traveler's checks to the documents, stamp them, present them to an elderly man who leaned back in a swivel chair and studied them minutely. He signed and stamped them. The woman now took them to yet another executive who, too, lingeringly, hesitantly, signed and stamped them. Clutching the bundle of paper, the woman vanished for a quarter of an hour; she was taking the documents, no doubt, to an even higher official. Returning, she shoved the papers through a barred window to a teller who tossed them casually upon a pile. Half an hour later my number was called. Once more I signed my name, this time as proof of having changed dollars, then threaded my way past the muzzles of machine guns to the sun-drenched streets.

I was tired and my thoughts drifted toward shelter for the night. Should I put up at a modern hotel frequented by tourists, or ought I seek some small place patronized mostly by Spaniards? I was inclined toward the latter. While strolling and glancing into bars and shops, I saw two shirt-sleeved youths chatting upon a street corner. In appearance they seemed lower middle class and had the air of students.

"*Parlez-vous français?*" I asked them.

"*Oui, Monsieur. Je parle un peu de français,*" the taller, thinner boy answered proudly.

Yes, they knew of a clean and cheap pension operated by a friend and they would be glad to take me there. I sized them up; maybe they were sharpies? About the neck of the shorter and younger boy hung a silver medallion of the Virgin and I decided to take a chance. I invited them into my car and they pointed the way with shy but elaborate gestures. Five minutes later they directed me to stop before a huge cathedral; they got out and I followed.

"It's our cathedral," the taller boy told me in French.

I nodded, smiled, but I was puzzled. Maybe they had not understood me?

"But where is the pension?"

"This way," the taller boy said, taking firm hold of my arm.

They led me toward a vast, delicately wrought mass of Gothic splendor that lifted gracefully toward a hot blue sky. Where were they taking me?

"But the pension," I insisted softly.

"Yes. Later. Later," they spoke together.

Well, if they were crooks, they certainly would not be taking me into a church! I studied them; they seemed simple, honest, forthright. . . . We entered the shadowed interior and I breathed the faint fragrance of incense and caught wafted echoes of a singing choir. High overhead floated a vault wrought of fragile stonework encasing countless panes of stained glass through which soft beams of rose and blue light fell—diaphanous rays that melted into an ocean of dimness. But why had they brought me here? I walked forward between them and we came to a wall that held a jutting, hollowed-out lip of faded marble containing water. The taller boy dipped the fingers of his right hand into the basin, crossed himself, moving his lips soundlessly, then he touched his still wet fingers to the right hand of his friend who, in turn, crossed himself. Next he touched his damp fingers to my right hand. I stared, speechless. Both boys now crossed themselves anew and turned toward the interior of the church, kneeling and crossing themselves once again as they faced the Holy of Holies.

"You are not Catholic?" the taller boy asked me in a low tone of wonder.

"No," I whispered in reply.

I was deeply moved and, at that moment, a little ashamed of not being Catholic. I felt that I had somehow hurt those two boys by declaring myself outside the pale, for I could tell from the expressions on their faces that they could not conceive of anyone ever being anything other than Catholic. I began to understand now why they had brought me to the church; I was a stranger and they were taking me into their Christian fellowship even before they knew my name, their solicitude cutting across class and racial lines. And there had been no hint of conscious propaganda in them. To these boys it was unthinkable that there was no God and that we were not all His sons.

Brooding, I trailed slowly after them down a shadowed aisle whose stillness evoked in me a mood of awe; I could feel that I was feeling it; in short, I was self-conscious. Beyond iron grilles of various shrines loomed statues of saints clad in velvet and brocade, golden haloes circling their heads. The trembling glow of many candles illuminated men, women, and children kneeling, praying, crossing themselves, their lips moving silently, their sense of worshipful surrender deep beyond doubting. One shrine was dedicated to plumbers, another to electricians, another to children, and yet another to expectant mothers—no section of the population being slighted. A barefoot girl in a ragged black dress knelt at the side of a fashionably-dressed woman whose lips were rouged, whose neck was roped with pearls, and whose fingers sparkled with diamonds.

We paused before a vast basin of white marble.

"That is where the first Indians that Columbus brought from America were baptized," the taller boy informed me.

It was beginning to make sense; I was a heathen and these devout boys were graciously coming to my rescue. In their spontaneous embrace of me they were acting out a role that had been implanted in them since childhood. I was not only a stranger, but a "lost" one in dire need of being saved. Yet there was no condescension in their manner; they acted with the quiet assurance of men who knew that they had the only truth in existence and they were offering it to me.

I was then escorted through a chapel in which a life-sized statue of Crucified Jesus, carved from blackened wood, hung from a cross. Suspended from His hips was a silken skirt held in place by a cord from which dangled red tassels.

"*Santo Cristo de Sepanto*," the taller boy whispered. "He has given Spain many victories in war."

A humble woman in black rose from her knees and went forward and kissed the gnarled, wooden toes of the carved figure, planting her lips in a spot that had been worn to a much lighter shade by hundreds of thousands of people. . . . They led me through the chapel and into a small enclosure in which five or six men and women were kneeling in silent prayer with glazed, half-opened eyes. The taller boy took my arm and pointed to an oblong, transparent box toward which all eyes in the room were gazing. The light was so dim that I could not at first determine what the object was.

"What is it?" I asked.

"It's the body of one of our great bishops," I was told. "He has made many miracles."

Then I understood: in a glass coffin lay the mummified remains of a human body. I saw sunken eye sockets, yellow, protruding teeth, and a mass of sagging, gray flesh falling away from the cranial structure of the head. The main portions of the body were mercifully hidden by a silken robe, though the forearms and hands, like white, running dough, were visible, and on the shrunken fingers were diamond rings. The boys crossed themselves and we went out, wordlessly. When we were in the car, I suggested politely:

"*Maintenant, la pension?*"

"*Oui, Monsieur,*" they chorused.

The pension was on the seventh floor of a building in the center of the city and the manager spoke French. Yes, he had a room.

"But you must take full pension," he warned me. "And you must be in at ten o'clock each night. And you are not allowed to bring any women up here."

"What does full pension cost?" I asked him.

"Sixty a day," he said stonily.

Sixty pesetas made a dollar and a half for a room and three meals.

"I'll take it," I said.

"But you must obey the rules," he warned me again. "That's life in Spain."

I promised to obey. After my two young Spanish friends had helped with my luggage, I shoved some packages of American cigarettes into their hands and invited them to a bar for beer.

Both boys were swarthy, black-haired, proud in bearing, too eager in manner, pliable, and seemingly devoid of the capacity for reflection. The taller, André, was twenty-one; the other, Miguel, was twenty-six. André was a student of maritime science and was on vacation. Miguel, who carried his arm in a sling (he had fallen from his motorcycle six weeks before and had broken a bone in his hand), was a skilled woodworker and earned three hundred pesetas or about seven dollars a week. André's and Miguel's fathers had been childhood friends, and the boys were proud to celebrate their father's friendship by being friends themselves. Miguel had a brother, mother and father. André's family numbered eight and he invited me to have dinner with them Sunday.

Both were shy about women. André had a fiancée, but Miguel would not commit himself. To their minds, the feminine half of mankind was divided into two groups: "good" women and "bad" women. "Good" women were women like their mothers, sisters, and sweethearts; "bad" women were the women who could be bought, or who could be slept with for nothing. Since they had to have women and could not have the "good" ones, they frequented the "bad" ones. And since going to bed with either a "good" or a "bad" woman was a sin, it was necessary to be forgiven. Both boys went to confession regularly.

"And every time you go with a 'bad' woman, you confess it?" I asked André.

"Of course," he said.

"And how do you know when a woman is a 'bad' woman?" I asked him.

"Oh, we know where to find them," André said, laughing, misunderstanding my question. "And we'll show you, if you want to know."

I told them that I wrote books, but they could not quite grasp it. My butane gas lighter astonished them; they had heard vaguely of such contraptions, but had never seen one; they fondled it, repeatedly igniting the gas, asking questions for half an hour, exclaiming in a manner that indicated that Spanish youth was cut off from the multitude of tiny daily influences of the modern Western world. They had no racial consciousness whatsoever.

"Who is the head of your government?" I asked them suddenly in French.

"Señor Franco," André answered.

"He is like your President," Miguel said sweetly.

I squelched my desire to pry further into politics and ordered more beer, studying the boys. If André's and Miguel's reactions were genuine examples of Spanish feeling, then Spain possessed a shy sweetness, an open-handed hospitality that no other people on earth could match.

But why was Spain a dictatorship? I had long believed that where you found tyranny, such as exists in Russia, you would also find a confounding freedom secreted somewhere; that where you had a stifling bureaucracy, such as in France, there was a redeeming element of personal liberty; that where you had a police state, such as was in Argentina, you had under it, disguised, a warm comradeship; and that where you had a restrained and reserved attitude, such as is in England, you had, somewhere nearby, equalizing it, a licentious impulse to expression. *Did that principle hold true in Spain?*

4 . . .

If Spain is a police state, then it's a sloppy one; after having had my passport examined and stamped at the border, no one has asked to see it since. Though Spanish police regulations require that all private homes, hotels, or pensions report at once the presence of a stranger on their premises, no one has as yet done so in my case, for no one has bothered to find out who I am. I could be any kind of an agent, for or against them, and how would they know? Soldiers, police, and no doubt plain-clothes men are everywhere, but they do not seem to be molesting the public. Of course, I may be dead wrong about this; perhaps they have snoopers far slicker than I suspect.

My pension was a citadel of bad faith and was populated mostly by lower middle-class men and women lost in anonymity—single girls traveling in groups for mutual protection, and sad, white-collar young men, who mainly for economic reasons, were without families or attachments. The entire clientele was a damp, quiet, nervous lot whose lives were empty, who never raised their voices, were retiringly polite, and who seemed joined in a conspiracy never to mention their debased condition. My dinner was dull, top-heavy with grease and fried food.

Later that evening I went into the corridor and found a girl sitting behind the pension desk reading a thin green book. She glanced up, smiled.

"Good evening, sir." She spoke in English.

"Good evening," I said. "Please, where is the Ramblas?"

"Just three blocks left of here," she said.

"Thank you." I glanced at the title of her book: *Formación Politica: Lecciones para las Flechas.*

"If I'm not indiscreet, what kind of book is that?"

"It's my political book."

"Are you interested in politics?" I ventured.

"Well, not particularly," she said in a drawling voice. "I'm studying this for my social service."

"What kind of social service is that?"

Her face grew serious and she was silent. She rose and came from behind the desk, pushing her tiny hands deep into the pockets of her dress.

"That's difficult to explain," she began. "Are you American?"

"Yes; I'm a writer," I said.

I picked up her book and rapidly leafed through the pages, seeking clues; I saw the volume dealt with the aims and principles of the Franco regime and was in the simple form of questions and answers—a political catechism for the Spanish masses. Suddenly, desperately, I wanted that book.

"Where can I buy this book?" I asked her.

"You can't buy it," she said. "They gave it to me at school—"

"You go to school?"

"Five nights a week," she said.

"Wonderful! You're studying English?"

"We don't study English there; it's not an ordinary school," she explained. "It's a political school. . . ."

"Could you get me a copy of this book?"

She stared at me silently, then sat again behind her desk.

"What do you want with it?" she asked with feigned off-handedness.

"I'm interested in politics."

She thought a bit, then asked: "Were you ever in Spain before?"

"No. This is my first trip," I told her. (It was not until later that I understood the crucial import of her question: she was trying to determine, in self-defense, if I had fought on either the Fascist or Loyalist side during the Spanish Civil War. In other words, if I had fought with the Loyalists, her association with me might seriously compromise her.)

"Are you Catholic?" she next asked me.

"I have no religious affiliations," I said.

Her lips parted; she blinked and stared at me, then she hung her head. Had I offended her? I did not wish to presume any longer; the situation was delicate. I laid her book back upon her desk. She felt my concern and she spoke in a whisper, casting a worried glance over her shoulder: "I can't talk to you *here*. But I'm free; I've no classes. . . ."

"Let's have a drink together in a bar when you get off. There are a lot of things I'd like to ask you."

"That's difficult," she murmured.

"You can trust me," I urged her.

"It's not *that*. . . . The problem is *where*."

"I'll pick you up here—"

"No, no," she said, fear showing in her eyes. "You don't understand."

"Then where can I meet you?"

"The lobby of the Majestic Hotel," she said. "At ten."

A door opened and a bevy of girls came into the corridor.

"You'll find the Ramblas just three blocks to the left," she said loudly.

I understood.

"Thank you," I said and hurried out. I felt strongly that that girl wanted to talk about her life.

Broad and tree-lined, the Ramblas began at Plaza de Cataluña and terminated at Puerta de la Paz, and it had an atmosphere as cosmopolitan as that of Paris, London, or New York. Flanking its wide expanse were cafés, bars, restaurants, movies, night clubs, hotels, and travel agencies. One could sit at tables under the sky in the balmy night and watch perfumed and rouged girls strolling arm in arm, and black-haired young men, walking four and five abreast, marching to and fro—the girls weighing the blades with coy glances and the young men appraising the female bodies with hot eyes. The air felt like rain and the smell of the Mediterranean evoked nostalgia. Overhead tree leaves rustled whisperingly and when I looked up I saw the light of the moon glistening like water on the dark green foliage.

I counted no fewer than three policemen to the city block and no doubt there were secret police mingling with the carefree crowds. So many soldiers jammed the cheaper bars, loitered on street corners, or sauntered in groups that one had the impression that Spain was mobilized for war, had assumed a stance of military alertness to defend itself against the attack of an enemy. But, no; these troops lived in the midst of the enemy—the people of Spain. I took a seat next to a bunch of them and dawdled with a *café con leche*. Most of them were unshaven, their uniforms baggy and crinkled and of a sleazy material resembling mattress ticking, their shoes unshined, their posture slouched and bent, and their gait loose and uncontrolled, like that of a peasant lumbering over a plowed field. Were there ever worse troops? These soldiers were a caricature of a modern army.

At ten o'clock I made my way through a light rain to the Majestic Hotel and found the girl clerk of my pension waiting in the lobby with the green book under her arm.

"I'm Carmen," she said, smiling and extending her hand. "I had to phone my mother. . . ."

She was uneasy and I felt that she was, for her protection, surrounding herself with the absent members of her family. We went into the bar and sat at a table and I ordered drinks.

"And she said that you could come?" I asked.

"Since you are an *American*, yes."

"Had I been a Spaniard, you would not have come?"

"I *couldn't* have come. It's only in an American hotel that I could meet you without a scandal. You don't know what it means to be a girl in Spain."

"And what *does* it mean?"

"I'm supposed to stay home and have babies," she said, grimacing.

"Who says you must do that?"

"Tradition," she said. "I wish I were a man; they are so much nicer—"

"Why?"

"They can do as they like. They are strong. We women are nothing."

"You really feel that way?"

"After your mother, father, and the priest get through with you, you can't feel anything else," she said bitterly. "Look, I'm twenty-five, I earn my own living. Yet I can't go out at night. Here—" she gestured to the Americans seated about us—"it doesn't matter."

Carmen was a short, dark girl with large, shining eyes and an expressive mouth. When she spoke her words were charged with tense emotion.

"But doesn't your boy friend ever take you to the movies?"

"Yes, and my family raises a storm."

"So what do you do?"

"I go out anyway," she said, laughing. "And that's what is keeping my home in an uproar."

"Have you ever gone into a bar like this alone?"

"God, no! That would be the *end*. . . . Every Spaniard who saw me would insult me, publicly. They'd think that I was looking for men. No 'good' woman walks the streets alone. Only 'bad' women do that. . . . A woman alone is lost in Spain."

"How do you account for Spain being like this?"

"We're Catholic," she said, sighing. "My father's Catholic. All of my life I've heard that we were the most Catholic country in the world. What else could we be but Catholic? We've never had a choice to be anything else. I often wonder how it would have felt to have been born in England or America or some other country. . . ." She paused, staring at me. "You told me a joke tonight, when I asked you about your religion."

"I have no religion in the formal sense of the word," I told her. "I have no race except that which is forced upon me. I have no country except that to which I'm obliged to belong. I have no traditions. I'm free. I have only the future."

She sucked in her breath, sighed, and eased her glass down upon the table.

"I wish I could say that," she murmured. "Just to hear anyone say anything like that makes me tremble."

"Please, Carmen, let me see that famous green book," I said, laughing to make her forget her tension and distress.

"You're not subtle," she laughed, her mood lightening; she handed over the volume. "You're like my brother—direct."

"Neither is this book subtle," I said. "I adore catechisms."

The book was the real thing; it had been designed to inculcate the principles of Fascism in young girls ranging in age from nine upward. My Spanish was vague, but I gaped at the sentiments I saw there in cold type.

"Why are *you* studying this?" I asked her. "You can be frank with me."

"If I were not going to be frank, I wouldn't have come here tonight," she said. She drew in her breath and leaned back in her chair. "It's not voluntary," she said proudly, defensively. "It's a long story."

"I'm patient," I said.

"Well, it all begins with one fact: I wish to leave Spain more than anything—"

"Can't you just leave?"

"No. There are governmental difficulties. You see, I know four languages: Spanish, English, German, and French. I studied them in school; I can write and speak them. I can get work abroad; I've had offers. . . . But, if you're a woman, unmarried, and not a domestic worker, you must put in six months of social service to the state to prove your right to leave Spain."

"What's this social work? You mentioned it before."

"This book," she said. "I must memorize this book, line by line, the *whole* of it. I must be able to answer every question in it, just as they are written. It's one hundred and seventy-six pages of small type."

"Why?"

"I don't know," she said, gripping the edge of the table with the tips of her painted fingernails.

"Is this to make sure that, when you leave Spain, you'll remain faithful to Franco?"

"No. I'm sure that they are not that stupid," she said. "They just order you to memorize it, that's all. Oh, I've fought with my parents about this. They say that this book contains useful knowledge. But what on earth is useful in my knowing how long were the sleeves of the shirt of José Antonio? The color of his necktie?"

"I must have this book," I said.

"It's yours," she said. "People ought to know how we live." Her eyes suddenly widened. "But make sure that you blot out my name; it's written in it."

"I'll do that. But can you get another one?"

"Easily. I'll say that I lost mine." She leaned forward with purpose. "Now, I must ask you a favor."

"Of course."

"I have a brother, Carlos. . . . I told him about you over the phone. He wishes to see you. It's important. Are you free tomorrow?"

"Yes. What does he want to see me about?"

"He'll tell you that himself. He'll be at the pension in the morning at ten. Is that all right?"

"I'll be glad to meet him at ten," I told her.

I took Carmen home in a taxi through the hot, rainy night.

5 . . .

I returned in the taxi to the Ramblas, got my own car and set out to meet André and Miguel, who had solemnly promised to show me some "bad" women. They were waiting for me in a garishly-lighted café that had sawdust on the floor and dark-visaged waiters who wore aprons spotted with dirt. My two young friends, dressed in dark suits and striving to look blasé, greeted me warmly and seemed as eager and hospitable tonight as they had been this morning when they had steered me into the cathedral.

"Where are we going?" I inquired of them.

"We know," André said, nodding mysteriously.

We drank *café con leche* and the liquid looked green under the neon lights. We then set out down a narrow, smelly alleyway; from opened windows above my head poured harsh sounds of flamenco music, handclapping, stomping, and the wild, melancholy twanging of guitars.

"Just how well do you know these 'bad' women?" I asked André, trying to keep a note of irony out of my voice.

"*Assez bien,*" he replied shyly.

The rain had stopped and the hot air was moist, motionless, heavy.

"*Ici,*" André said.

We pushed through a rattling curtain made of long strings of black beads, flinging aside the strips and hearing them clack and settle into place behind us; we entered an oblong dive whose background was lost in smoke. An unshaven, Greekish face, with an unlighted cigarette stub in its partly-open lips, eyed us coldly from behind a cash register as we moved forward through fumes of tobacco smoke that stung the throat. Strips of bamboo covered the walls; I suppose that that tropical ornamentation was to make sailors feel that they were in an emotionally abandoned atmosphere. Some thirty women of all ages and descriptions and sizes sat at tables and at the long bar, their shiny black purses—the international trademark of their profession—blatantly in evidence. They weighed us with restless, surfeited eyes.

"*Nous voici,*" said André, grinning.

"*Prenons une table,*" I suggested.

"*D'accord,*" André agreed.

We sat. Miguel was staring straight ahead of him.

"Does Miguel like this sort of thing?" I asked André.

"He hasn't been here as often as I have," André said, clapping his pal on the back.

One needed no intiative in sewers like this. At least a dozen pair of dark, feminine eyes were staring at us and then a few girls began to edge forward. I ordered cognac and, as it was being poured, a tall, angular, not pretty, not ugly girl came mincing to the table; she wore the golden medallion of the Virgin between her enormous breasts. She wanted a cigarette; I passed her one and lit it. She puffed, waiting for a signal. I saw Andréa's and Miguel's eyes darting from the girl to me; than Miguel's foot kicked my leg under the table, telling me to lay off. . . .

"Drinkie *para mí?*" the girl asked in a husky tone, speaking pidgin Spanish.

I waved for her to sit. Miguel shrugged. The girl smiled, showing strong, white even teeth, then she spoke to André in Spanish.

"She wants to know if she's met you before," André told me.

"Not a chance," I told her through André.

"You no man from sheep?" she asked, thinking that I was a sailor.

Her name was Pilly and she had learned a few words of English from soldiers and sailors.

"No possibility fuckie?" she asked me with the brutal directness of a professional.

"Not tonight, Miss Pilly," I told her.

Another girl, older and harder than Pilly, came slowly toward the table, moving her hips exaggeratedly in her tight green gingham dress. I waved for her to sit and offered her a cigarette.

"Drinkie?" she asked.

I ordered her a beer. Through André I learned that her name was Isabel, that she had traveled in France and Germany. She did not smile and her eyes were like green agates.

"*Pesetas para los niños,*" she begged me. "Money for my children."

I gave her five pesetas. She wore a silver medallion of the Virgin.

"Catholic?" I asked her.

"I no Catholic," she growled.

"*Por qué ça?*" I asked, mixing languages and pointing to the medallion. "Why that?"

She shrugged. André and Miguel were furious; their faces darkened with displeasure.

"*Vilaine fille!*" André spat. "*Sale fille! Va-t-en!*"

Isabel understood and tried desperately to hang on to me.

"You *mí* telephone, *sí?*" she suggested.

I extended my notebook and indicated that she should write down her name and telephone number.

"Me no write," she said, looking at me as though I had accused her of a crime.

Pilly, who had been hovering in the background and overhearing what had been said, now came forward and exhibited her golden medallion of the Virgin.

"*Mí Católica,*" she said proudly.

"*Bon,*" André approved.

Pilly and Isabel glared at each other; then André, over my protests, waved Isabel away from the table. Both boys shook their heads, indicating that they would not tolerate Isabel's anti-Catholic attitude. To be a prostitute was bad, but to be a prostitute who was not Catholic was worse. . . .

The atmosphere was getting more and more strained. André and Miguel were feeling that the tables had been turned; in one half hour I had plunged my hands into Spanish life and had brought up poverty, fear, prostitution, illiteracy—and all of this was but half a mile from the bishop's rotting body in the glass coffin, the white marble basin in which Columbus's Indians had been baptized. This morning I had been the lost heathen standing in the need of being civilized and saved; now it was I who was feeling the tissue and texture of their lives and they were ashamed and angry.

I drove slowly toward my pension. Poor, "bad," illiterate girls . . . I glanced at the tall, dark middle-class apartment buildings and hotels that loomed to left and right of me; they were filled with respectable Catholic families in which all the women were "good." The sailors, soldiers, the men who were married to "good" women and the young sons in "good" families became the clientele of "bad" girls. . . .

I undressed, washed, and stretched out to sleep. Carmen's green book! I bounded out of bed and got it and opened it to page one and began to read slowly:

First Lesson

SPAIN

WHAT IS SPAIN?

Spain is a historical unit with a specific role to play in the world.

WHAT DOES THIS MEAN?

That destiny has constituted all the people of Spain, varied as they may be, for all time into a unit in the natural order of things.

WHAT IS A UNIT?

The union in one body of a number of distinct parts.

WHAT DOES DESTINY MEAN?

The purpose assigned to everyone in life.

WHAT IS MEANT BY THE NATURAL ORDER OF THINGS?

Something which concerns not only the Spanish but all nations.

WHAT THEN IS MEANT BY SAYING THAT SPAIN HAS BEEN FORMED BY DESTINY INTO A UNIT IN THE NATURAL ORDER OF THINGS?

Because it is a whole constituted from the various peoples who are united by the common destiny they have to fulfill in the world.

IS SPAIN OUR MOTHERLAND?

Yes.

AND IS IT OUR MOTHERLAND BECAUSE WE WERE BORN IN IT, OR BECAUSE WE FEEL OURSELVES INCORPORATED IN ITS DESTINY IN THE WORLD?

It is our Motherland because we feel ourselves incorporated in its destiny in the world.

ARE THERE THEN PEOPLE WHO WITHOUT BEING BORN IN SPAIN ARE SPANIARDS?

Yes; all who feel themselves to be incorporated in the destiny of Spain.

AND CAN THERE BE PEOPLE BORN IN SPAIN WHO ARE NOT SPANIARDS?

Yes; childen of foreigners and those who disassociate themselves from the destiny of the Motherland.

THEN, DO YOU SEE CLEARLY THAT FOR US THE MOTHERLAND IS NOT THE LAND IN WHICH WE ARE BORN BUT THE FEELING OF FORMING PART OF THE DESTINY OR AIMS WHICH THE MOTHERLAND MUST FULFILL IN THE WORLD?

Yes.

WHAT IS THIS DESTINY?

To include all men in a common movement for salvation.

WHAT DOES THIS MEAN?

Ensure that all men place spiritual values before material.

WHAT ARE SPIRITUAL VALUES?

Firstly, religious values derived from our Catholic religion.

AND WHAT ELSE?

Those which concern human dignity, honor, service, culture, etc.

AND MATERIAL VALUES, WHAT ARE THEY?

Those which refer to economic advantage, money and other things.

HOW WILL SPAIN ACHIEVE ITS DESTINY?

By the influence it exercises over other nations and also by conquest.

WHAT DO YOU MEAN BY INFLUENCE?

Making others do something because they see us doing it.

WHAT DO YOU MEAN BY CONQUEST?

To take possession by force of arms.

SINCE WHEN HAVE WE KNOWN THAT SPAIN HAS A DESTINY TO FULFILL?

Since the most remote ages of its history.

GIVE SOME EXAMPLES.

When the Roman emperors such as Trajan, Theodosius and Hadrian were Spanish.

When Roman philosophers were also Spaniards, like Seneca.

When Spaniards led by Don Pelayo, began to clear the Moors from Spain.

When the Catalans carried their conquest as far as Greece.

When the University of Salamanca was the most important in the world.

When the Catholic sovereigns succeeded in ejecting the Moors by the conquest of Granada, and later discovered America.

When the sovereigns Isabel and Ferdinand began, through the Universities and the Spanish missionaries they sent there, to civilize the whole of America.

AND FURTHER?

By the conquest made by Charles I in Europe and Africa to defend Christianity.

By the struggle carried on by Philip II against the Protestants of all Europe and Spanish participation at the Council of Trent.

When Don Juan of Austria, sent by Philip II, defeated the Turks at Lepanto.

When the troops of Philip II conquered Portugal.

I was staring at the mouth, at the veritable fount of Western history. I was tired. I went to sleep thinking of poor Carmen's tense and rebellious face. . . .

The aspect of early-morning Barcelona that impressed me most next day was the strident quality of its noise, lifting that city into a class of the noisest cities on earth. Huge trucks careened through the thoroughfares, causing the pavements to tremble; streetcars, their steel wheels grinding loudly upon steel tracks, crashed past, their bells clanging deafeningly; the bellowing shouts of children shattered the air; motorcycles roared thunderingly down the streets; shrill auto horns sounded insistently; and over and above it all was an indefinable din that created a mood of unrest.

Remembering that I had urgent letters to post. I inquired in my clumsy Spanish the way to the main post office. I entered and found the window at which I could dispatch airmail. The black-haired woman clerk behind the counter was busy, bent over with her head down; her fingers, sparkling and glittering with two diamond rings, shuttled with the dizzy speed of a machine as she counted peseta notes. Patiently, I watched her finish, clip the bills together into a pack, and toss the pack into a drawer. Then she looked up and saw my face; her lips parted, her expression became blank, and she quickly crossed herself. I handed her my letters and she nervously occupied herself with them. But why had she seemed so shocked to see me? Had it been that the sight of my heathen face, which she could tell at a glance was most probably not a Catholic one, had made her cross herself?

Heading toward my pension, I reached a street corner and found my path blocked: a vast flock of sheep was ambling down the broad, modern avenue. I stared, doubting my eyes. Yet, there they were, mincing along slowly in the center of the city, occasionally bleating. A boy with a long staff was leading them. I watched them until they were out of sight, then I became aware of the pavement vibrating under my feet from the rushing force of a subway train. Barcelona was so sophisticated that one was likely to see anything.

At the pension Carmen introduced me to her brother, Carlos. He was taller than Carmen, but he had her driving intensity. His face was florid, his mouth thin and determined. He was high-strung, restless, and had a habit of pacing the floor as he talked.

"Let's talk in your room," he suggested abruptly.

I led him inside my room and he closed the door and looked around; he had the air of a disturbed man, a hunted man, a man who had the habit of regarding his enviroment warily.

"My sister told me that you're a writer and that you're looking at Spanish life," he said.

"That's right. . . . Say, your English is fluent. Where did you learn it?" I asked.

"At school," he said, sitting. "I've traveled in England, France, and Germany."

"What do you do?"

"I'm a horticulturist. . . . I was almost a priest once," he told me with a wry smile. "I attended a Jesuit school in Paris."

"What a background. Just what do you grow or cultivate?"

"Orange trees," he said.

"Spanish oranges are good," I said.

"Nothing's good in Spain," he said emphatically.

If Carmen was rebellious, Carlos was bitter.

"Are you free now?" he asked.

"Yes."

"Then we're going to Valencia. I want to show you something."

"Fine. My car's downstairs."

"No. Your car's French. We'll go in mine. The French are not popular here. And we must not be too conspicuous," he said.

We went down and I got into his car. We rolled in silence through the suburbs of Barcelona.

"Why are the French disliked here?" I asked him.

"There are many reasons. . . . There was Napoleon; then there was the Civil War; the Spanish believe that the French are immoral; and, too, there is a conflict of French and Spanish interests in North Africa." He switched quickly back to his main concern. "I've a large orange-tree nursery. I've one hundred and forty thousand orange trees. Everything I have in the world is tied up in them. But I can't sell them."

"Why?"

"The government prohibits it," he explained.

"Why is the government pursuing such a policy?"

"It's to protect the exporter's trust," he told me, screwing up his eyes. "Not only do they stop my selling my trees, but there are regulations against the planting and exporting of orange trees. The rich men who control the exporting of oranges make the political and social policies of the country. They have the approval and support of the Church. The orange industry is controlled by the state in the interests of the rich, who, in turn, are backed by the Church. That's the gist of it."

"When was this law—against the selling, planting, and exporting of orange trees—passed?" I asked.

"Passed?" he scoffed. "Laws are not *passed* here. The government issues decrees. This particular decree was issued on June 26, 1953, and it was retroactive, covering orange trees already planted and growing in the nurseries. That's what caught me. And no indemnification was given to those whose sole means were tied up in such trees."

"Have you protested this? Are you allowed to?"

"No effective protest is permitted," he told me. "Sure. I protested, but it was no use. I got nowhere. All of my letters and petitions went unanswered. And they talk of the evils of Communism! *This is Communism!* I live in a religious Communist state!"

We were speeding past groves of olives and oranges.

"How does the government enforce this law?"

"They have their spies. . . . If you plant an orange tree without authorization, you're liable to a fine ranging from one thousand to fifty thousand pesetas, depending upon how much they dislike you. And the government confiscates all of your trees.

"Now, a worker earns about twenty pesetas a day. Oranges cost from three to four pesetas a kilo. Poor people can't buy them. Yet the government says there are too many orange trees in Spain. What they mean is that if more orange trees were planted, the price of oranges in the world market goes down and the men who control the orange export industry would make less money."

"Why don't you publicize your problem?" I asked.

"Who would dare publish this in Spain?" he demanded. "The first newspaper telling the truth about this would be forced out of business and the editor would be jailed. An explanation of the most innocent economic processes, publicly printed, is a criminal offense. If I wrote a letter to a newspaper about this, the paper would turn my letter over to the police and the next day I'd be arrested."

When we entered Valencia, he said tersely: "We're going through without stopping." He glanced at me and grinned. "You're highly visible, you know. If you are seen with me, and if you wrote something about this, they can easily put two and two together and know who told—"

"Is it that bad?" I asked.

"It's bad. I've a brother in exile. He's a Freemason. I'd like to get out of Spain, go to America, perhaps. But how can I?"

"So Franco is not only against Communists?"

"You don't know! This government is against Communists, Radicals, Socialists, Anarchists, Protestants, Liberals, Freemasons, Atheists, Agnostics, Existentialists, Surrealists, Vegetarians—"

"You're joking! Why Vegetarians?"

"Because many Anarchists are Vegetarians," he explained. "Only recently they closed down a Vegetarian restaurant in Barcelona. Anarchists are mystics and many of them won't eat meat. So, if you shut down a Vegetarian restaurant, you defeat Anarchism. Simple."

As Carlos sat hunched tensely over the steering wheel of his car, I studied his reddish, strained face and a fear for him entered me. This man would blow up someday and they would kill him.

"Try and get out of Spain," I murmured.

"I'm trapped!" he cried, his eyes hard upon the road ahead.

I saw his jaws swell as he clamped his teeth together. We entered the countryside of Valencia and came to the grounds of his nursery.

"Do you own this land?"

"No. I rent. Look, one hectare of rich Andalusian land, well irrigated, costs eighty thousand pesetas. Planted with orange trees, it costs four hundred thousand pesetas. That same hectare here in the vicinity of Valencia would cost more than a million pesetas. How can I get hold of such sums?" he poured it out bitterly.

We stopped amidst a sea of dark green trees about two and three feet high. We got out of the car.

"There they are!" he shouted, waving his arms wide. "What can I do with them? They are worthless! Men take the place of God and condemn me! They ask me nothing! They just tell me one morning: 'You have nothing!' "

His lips were open and he breathed heavily. He grew conscious of my presence and controlled himself. He reached down and tenderly plucked a leaf from a young orange tree and crushed it in his palm and smelt it, then tossed it away with a gesture of disgust. I did the same and the pungent odor made me look wonderingly at the dark fecund earth from which the plant had sprung, at the high blue sky overhead that had watered and warmed the plant, and then at the tight, bitter, baffled face of Carlos—a man alienated from his dark rich earth, from his sea of green, prolific plants, from his deep blue sky, yet silhouetted against the darkness and the greenness and blueness that he so obviously loved.

"Why didn't you become a priest?" I asked him impulsively.

My question startled him. He looked at me, smiled, then slowly shook his head.

"The roads to salvation are many," he murmured.

I felt something incongruous in him. This man was a kind of scientist, using empirical methods to control the causes and effects of the external world. Yet in his life he was vainly trying to function in an impossible situation. I was curious to know why his hot bitterness had stopped at a certain point.

"What methods are you using to produce these orange trees?" I asked him.

"The most modern," he answered readily. "I'm in touch with the most advanced farming methods used in American and England."

"I saw the dead, rotting body of a bishop in the Barcelona cathedral—"

"Oh, that," he murmured.

"Do you believe in that?" I asked him directly.

He smiled sadly, compassionately at me; he advanced and placed his hand in a brotherly manner upon my shoulder.

"I told you I once studied to be a priest," he said. "Well, I'm not going to discuss religion with you. You're intelligent and I like you. And there's no point in arguing. There's only one thing: *You must believe*. If you believe, the rest is simple. *I believe*. That's all."

"But all this poverty, this cheating, this prostitution, this ignorance—"

"That has nothing to do with it," he spoke vehemently. "You MUST BELIEVE! That's all."

"I think I understand you," I sighed.

As we drove back to Barcelona, he told me of his life. With the exception of a few foreigners, he had no friends or contacts. He had seen the world and he knew what was wrong in Spain and he had not been afraid to speak out. He was, therefore, shunned, regarded as a dangerous man.

Back in Barcelona, he suggested that we stop for a cup of coffiee. I was glad, for I wanted to talk to him some more.

"Carlos, why didn't you become a priest?" I asked him softly. "You haven't answered me yet."

He was stirring his cup and he glanced up and grinned for the first time.

"It was hard. To be shut away from life . . . Brother, I couldn't keep women out of my mind. I was going crazy," he said ruefully.

"And you gave it up for that?"

"Yes. My body was stronger than my will."

I told him of the "bad" women I had met last night and he said promptly: "They're hungry. It's economic."

"Then you don't believe in sin?"

"Not that kind of sin, no."

"Why not?"

"Sex is no sin," he said. "That's why I couldn't be a priest."

"Brother, you're remarkable," I said. "You get out of Spain."

"How? Tell me how!" He began to seethe again.

I let him cool off; I knew that as long as he felt his own plight, he could talk of nothing else. Then, when he had burnt out, I asked him: "How are the general economic conditions?"

"There are but a few real figures," he sighed. "We Spaniards don't believe in statistics. Figures hurt our pride."

"Yes. But just a few simple, obvious facts. You're a horticulturist. What is produced here?" I asked.

"Not too much. Cereals, fruits, and garden produce; add oranges, grapes and olives and you've almost covered the agricultural side. Otherwise, we have a little coal, iron, and steel. But, you see, our whole economic structure is lopsided. Our agriculture is still mainly primitive. We have but little power and less transport," he recited. "No matter what they tell you in Madrid, our production is below that of 1935."

"Your facts tally with what I heard from United Nations people in Geneva," I told him. "What has been the effect of Franco's freezing of wages?"

"It has worsened matters," he argued. "Wages are stationary, but prices rise. Our population is slowly increasing, but production lags. Our people do not have enough to eat. Over half of the active people in Spain are either farmers or farmhands, and we have over two million and a half surplus agricultural laborers. You can guess what that spells in terms of economic misery."

"Carlos, en route here from France, I was amazed at the aridity of the Spanish landscape—"

"Not enough water," Carlos summed it up. "Irrigation is one of our biggest problems. Officially it is known that there are large areas in Spain where crops are perishing and there is plenty of water at a depth of three meters. It's maddening. We don't have enough water; we don't have enough fertilizers. Just say we *lack*, *lack*, and *lack*. . . ."

"Carlos, you have to do with the soil. What is this chronic agrarian ulcer in Spain that no government seems able to cure?"

He took a deep breath, laughed, shook his head, and said:

"We've got twenty-eight million people living on one hundred twenty-five million acres of land. Now, we are cultivating between fifty and sixty million acres; another fifty or sixty million acres are allotted to pasture and woodland. There are fifteen million acres that are more or less barren. Now, that does not seem to be so bad a picture until you begin to examine what happens. First, two-thirds of all the land in Spain needs water; the need is worse in some section than in others. At this point, social conditions—the class structure, the attitude of the Church, and tradition—complicate matters.

"For example, in Extremadura, Andalusia, and La Mancha about seven thousand absentee landlords irrigate their land and operate farm factories and keep wages down to starvation levels. Take the province of Cordova: about half of it is owned by big operators. The same is true of the province of Seville. In the province of Cádiz, big estates dominate more than half of the economy, in some instances accounting for ninety per cent of the land, the best land. Now, when you realize that the landless population in these areas make up three-fourths of the population, you can see what we are up against. There are more than a million people in Spain who earn less than ten pesetas a day.

"Now, I'll divide this problem up into two sections. In the center and the north of Spain the land holdings are too small to support the people who cultivate them. In the south, the holdings are too big.

"The problem is: How to take the surplus population out of the south and west and north and colonize them upon newly irrigated land. Well, the government has some lovely plans. I won't go into them. All I'll tell you is that, between 1936 and 1948, only a quarter of a million or so acres of land were brought under irrigation. The people who live on that productive land amount to one-fifth of the increase in the rural population. You see, they are pecking away lazily at the problem and it will never be solved like that."

"But aren't they worried about it?" I asked. "This is what made for the Civil War."

"Yes; they worry in a lazy sort of way," Carlos said, laughing cynically. "But they are depending more on the Civil Guard and the Army to keep down trouble than upon any scientific plans. We don't believe in science or plans down here."

"But, Carlos, hasn't the government timed or scheduled their colonization program?"

"No," he said. "We live under the eye of eternity. They are more concerned about the restoration of the King than about irrigation."

"But didn't the Republic rectify this problem of land distribution?" I asked.

"Yes; but Franco and the Falange reversed all the work of the Republic."

"So those dead died in vain?" I asked.

Carlos shrugged.

"How much foreign exchange has Spain?"

"Not too much and official stealing cheats the nation out of most of what little we do have," Carlos was relentless. "Take my oranges. When I sell them abroad, the government fixes the price of the dollar I am to receive. But they have their own personal, private price for the dollar which is higher than the price they give me. I'm paid in pesetas. I never see a dollar.

"Take another example; it's claimed that in 1952 we had a tourist trade of forty million dollars. One and one-half million tourists spent that amount here. If we attracted that many tourists, we should have had more than a measly forty million dollars. But Spanish official fingers are very sticky. There's corruption at the very top."

"Then your civil service is no good," I said.

"Civil service?" Carlos exclaimed, laughing scornfully. "That phrase describes the opposite of the Spanish character. Our corruption is the only really human quality we have left."

"You sound hopeless," I said.

"I'm just realistic," he maintained. "Listen," he said, changing his tone. "Carmen and I have been discussing your accommodations. That pension is no good for you. I know of a Spanish home; they have a room free. They speak both French and English."

"I'd welcome a change," I said. "When can I see it?"

"I'll take you by tomorrow afternoon," he said.

6 . . .

Next morning I was blasted out of my dreams by a sound so gratingly brutual that I emotionally took it to be the trumpet of Gabriel blowing for the last judgment. I lay still and listened, calling upon my memory to help me to identify it. It continued and I could tell that it was not human, but I'd never heard a beast give forth such a discordant bellow. Maybe it was a bull on the loose? Or maybe it was a fire engine with a newfangled siren . . . ? I rolled from bed, opened the window and the sound now smote my ears so directly that I winced. I looked down. It was a donkey, seven flights below, and he was braying his damned head off, not stopping, it seemed, even to catch his breath. I sighed, looking wistfully and unbelievingly at the tall, clean skyscrapers gracing the Plaza de Cataluña, then turned to wash and dress with mechanical movements, mulling over this strange Spain.

While drinking my *café con leche*, a dirty, frightened-looking urchin with blinking eyes entered the pension dining room and shuffled to my table and, with downcast head, began a long, low, complaining mumbling that I could not make head nor tail of. Finally, the manager rescued me; the boy merely wished to wash my car, which was parked down in the street below. Having debated and decided the price, I told him to go ahead. He ducked out to do the job.

I felt listless and, when back in my room, I picked up Carmen's green book and pored over the Spanish view of the world, reading:

Lesson II

LA FALANGE (THE PHALANX)

WHAT IS FALANGE?

A political movement set up by José Antonio to save Spain.

WHY HAD SPAIN TO BE SAVED?

Because Spaniards had lost the consciousness of their historic destiny.

WHAT IS MEANT BY LOSING THE CONSCIOUSNESS OF THEIR HISTORIC DESTINY?

Forgetting that Spain had something very important to accomplish in the world.

AND WHY HAD THEY FORGOTTEN IT?

Because Spain, between 1648 when it lost Holland and 1898 when it lost Cuba and the Philippines, was successively defeated by stronger nations so that Spaniards believed their mission had come to an end.

WHAT CONSEQUENCES DID THIS HAVE?

The loss of the Spanish Empire.

WHAT ELSE?

The breaking up of the territorial unity of Spain through the Catalan and Basque separatist movements.

WHY DID THIS OCCUR?

Because, as Spaniards from the various regions lost the consciousness of their common destiny, they had no reason to remain united.

WHAT THEN IS IT THAT UNITES THE DIFFERENT PARTS OF SPAIN: GEOGRAPHICAL BORDERS, LANGUAGE, CHARACTER OR DESTINY?

Destiny.

WHY?

Because the Basques do not talk like the Catalans, nor the Catalans like the people of Castile; Andalusia is not Galicia; nevertheless all are united by a common destiny.

WHAT OTHER CONSEQUENCE HAD DEFEAT FOR US?

Economic misery for most Spaniards.

WHAT THEN IS THE FUNDAMENTAL MISSION OF THE FALANGE?

To give Spaniards back their faith in themselves and in the destiny of the Motherland and ensure through the revolution that all live better.

HOW SHALL THIS BE DONE?

By teaching Spaniards a doctrine which will make them live always up to certain ideals.

WHAT IS MEANT BY ALWAYS LIVING UP TO CERTAIN IDEALS?

Making our conduct conform to certain principles which will make us better.

WHEN WAS THE FALANGE FOUNDED?

On October 29, 1933, in the Comedia de Madrid Theater, with the title Falange Española (the Spanish Phalanx).

WHO FOUNDED IT?

José Antonio.

WHAT GROUP JOINED IT LATER?

The J.O.N.S., founded in 1931 by Ramiro Ledesma Ramos.

WHAT DOES J.O.N.S. MEAN?

Juntas de Ofensive Nacional Sindicalistas (National Syndicalist Commando Groups).

WHO ALSO FORMED PART OF THE MOVEMENT?

The Juntas Castellanas de Actuación Hispánica (Castillian Spanish Action Groups), set up by Onésima Redondo, and the forces which were united in the Conquista del Estado (Conquest of the State) also founded by Ramiro Ledesma Ramos.

WHAT WAS "LA CONQUISTA DEL ESTADO"?

A review founded by Ramiro, where the first signs of the rebellion of Spanish youth against the degenerate country in which we were living appeared, and about which was formed the first group which later became the J.O.N.S.

WHY DID THE J.O.N.S. JOIN UP WITH THE FALANGE?

Because they and the Falange desired the same things for Spain.

WHEN WAS THE UNION?

February, 1934.

WHAT WAS THE FALANGE CALLED FROM THEN ON?

Falange Española de las J.O.N.S.

WHO WAS ITS CHIEF?

José Antonio.

WHAT IS IT NOW CALLED?

Falange Española Tradicionalista y de las J.O.N.S.

WHY?

Because on April 19, 1937, it joined up with the Comunión Tradicionalista (Traditionalist Confederation).

WHAT WAS THE "COMUNIÓN TRADICIONALISTA"?

A political and military organization which had fought for a century against the liberal monarchy.

WHO IS HEAD OF IT?

Since José Antonio, Franco.

I started violently. There had come a hard, urgent knock upon my door. I leaped up.

"Who is it?" I called out, wondering if the door was locked.

"It's the police!" It was Carmen's voice calling.

With a reflex gesture I tossed the green book under the covers of the unmade bed. I opened the door, glancing to make sure the green book was out of sight.

Three police officials in dark blue uniforms confronted me.

"*Sí, Señor,*" I said.

I stood blocking my doorway so that they could not enter unless they asked or pushed me aside. But they seemed to have no wish to enter. Behind the three officers I could see Carmen's tense face. The officers had papers and pencils in their hands.

"Ask them what they want, will you, Carmen?" I asked her.

She spoke to them, then relayed their question to me:

"Is your car numbered 8323-BL-75?"

"Yes. It's downstairs. What's wrong?"

"They want to know if you are French. Show them your passport," Carmen instructed me.

"*Je suis Americain,*" I told them exhibiting the document. I realized that I should have spoken in English, but it was too late.

They were taken aback when they saw the passport; I watched them leaf slowly through it.

"They thought you were French," Carmen whispered.

The officials consulted among themselves, then spoke to Carmen who told me: "They want you to come downstairs."

"Okay."

The policemen stepped aside and let me lead the way. Carmen followed close.

"They're treating you with dignity," she whispered.

"Why?"

"You're American. When they knew that you were American, I thought that they'd let you off. But they've gone too far now to drop it."

"What am I guilty of?"

"I don't know," she said. "They never tell you that until they are ready."

All of us rode silently down in the elevator, crossed the narrow lobby, and went out upon the sidewalk. Two more policemen stood guarding my car and a small crowd had collected. The ragged boy who had been washing my car stood, wet rag in hand, beside a zinc pail, and he looked alternately at me and at the pavement, his face full of apprehension. The police spoke to him and he replied with alacrity, pointing to me and saying:

"*Señor!*"

Do they think that my car is a stolen vehicle? I wondered.

"Carmen, ask them what's wrong?"

She did and they replied by demanding my *carte grise* (official certificate of ownership), my driver's license, and the *carnet de passage* (the right to take the car across national boundaries). I surrendered the documents, begging Carmen: "Ask them what I'm guilty of?"

When she asked this time, the answer came: "You have committed a public nuisance."

I blinked. Was it illegal to leave my car parked upon the street? Or had I forgotten to conform to some regulation?

"What nuisance?" I asked.

"You are bathing your car in public," I was told.

"But I'm not bathing my car, as you call it," I defended myself. "*He's* washing it." I pointed to the boy who shrank back from me.

"Bathing and washing are the same thing," they said.

"But a car's not a person," I argued. "And the boy was washing it—"

"No matter. You violated the law."

"I was ignorant of the law. I'm a tourist."

"Ignorance is no excuse."

"That boy should have known better than ask to wash the car in a public street," I contended.

A long confab took place between the assembled policemen and Carmen conveyed me their decision: "They said that you asked him to bathe it."

"No! He asked me to let him wash it," I told them.

"But the car is yours; you are responsible," it was pointed out to me.

It was a vicious circle. All right; I'm guilty. And I thought of all those desperate prostitutes who were permitted to ply their trades, of the flocks of sheep who dropped their excrement upon the asphalt of the ornate boulevards, and of the donkeys who were allowed to bray when and where they damn pleased. . . .

"What's the fine?" I asked with a sigh.

Carmen spoke to them at length and I could tell from the sense of her words that she was making a plea for me on the grounds that I was a writer, a visitor, a guest. But it was no use. I was guilty. I was fined fifty pesetas. I nodded. Sure, I'll pay. I fished in my pockets for money but was told that I'd have to pay the fine in the traffic court.

"They get a percentage of all fines that they impose," Carmen whispered to me.

"Oh," I breathed, understanding it all.

I looked at the boy, whose guilty eyes avoided mine, and the whole game became clear. That boy was working with the police, finding victims for them. The boy was now glaring at me with defiant eyes, and I knew that he knew that I knew. I was handed a summons; I tossed the boy a few centavos and he vanished, rag, pail, and fearful face. The police walked away and the crowd began to disperse. I gave my poor French car a pitying look and rode up in the elevator with Carmen.

"You got off easy," she said. "Had you been French, they would have fined you more and made you pay on the spot."

"Why were they light on me?"

"You're American," she said, smiling ironically. "You're our friend and ally."

"The hell you say," I said.

Carmen bent double with laughter.

7 . . .

Returning to my room, I pored over my notes, projecting an itinerary for the hinterland. Through the partly-opened window and the cracks in the door there seeped the scent of frying, rancid olive oil and I knew that I would not eat in the pension at lunchtime; my stomach was in rebellion against the food. Toward mid-afternoon hunger decided me to grab a quick lunch somewhere and return in time to meet Carlos. But when I entered a restaurant I found, to my despair, that the lunch hour had passed and almost every dish I asked for could not be had.

"*Donnez-moi une paella,*" I ordered.

No; it was too late to cook rice.

"Then give me anything you've got; I'm hungry," I said.

There was only one other customer in the restaurant; he turned from his plate and stared at me. He was short, swarthy, Spanish-looking. He rose, came to me, and asked: "Would you mind sharing my *paella?* There's enough here for two and I can't eat half of this."

"Well, to tell the truth, I'd love it," I said. "But let me pay for half of it."

"If you like," he said. "Would you join me, or shall I join you?"

"It's more convenient for me to join you," I said, rising and sitting at his table.

"My name is Pardo L.," he said.

I identified myself and we shook hands. He seemed a man of great reserve and dignity. He was graying a bit at the temples and had an almost sardonic manner. He hesitated before speaking, as though searching for the right word, and his eyes would widen and light up with what he was about to say.

"American?" I asked.

"Yes. You?"

"Yes."

"Do you like Spain?" I asked.

"I'm enjoying it immensely," he said slowly. "My parents were Spanish, you know. One of the ambitions of my life has been to visit the birthplace of my parents. I came here with them on a visit when I was six years old and it is strange how unchanged everything is—"

"You remember it?"

"Clearly."

"By the way, are you with the government?" I asked.

"No," he drawled, a smile hovering about his lips.

"I don't mean to be indiscreet," I murmured.

"Not at all," he assured me. He frowned while still smiling, then said in a manner that gave full value to his words: "Not civil government, at least. I work for a religious government."

I stared at him.

"What do you mean? A religious government?"

"I work for the Vatican," he said after a pause.

"My Lord," I said. "Oh, excuse me. I didn't mean to be profane."

"That's all right," he said, laughing.

"Here on religious business?"

"No. Just a tourist," he said.

"You're stationed in Rome."

"Naturally."

"Has your service there been of a long duration?"

"Since 1946," he said.

We were silent. Just how did one talk to a man who worked for the Vatican? God's representative on earth was there; yet this man seemed mundane, blasé even. None of the transcendental qualities that were supposed to be in evidence in the Vatican had rubbed off on him; at least I couldn't detect any.

"What do you do there, if I may ask?"

"I'm an official translator."

"You must see some interesting documents," I commented.

"No. It's the most prosaic work imaginable." He spoke in measured, deliberate tones.

"Just how aware are those in the Vatican of what is happening in the world today?" I asked.

"The Vatican is not very much aware of anything," he told me. "Tradition rules in the Vatican. I wished I could say otherwise."

I was overwhelmed by the quality of his frankness.

"How did you get the position?"

"They just asked me if I wanted to work, and I said I did," he told me, shrugging.

"They didn't investigate you?"

"No, thank God," he said.

There was so much that I wanted to ask him that I didn't know where to start.

"Have you visited any of the religious shrines here?" I asked.

"A few. But I intend to see many of them."

"I want to see the Black Virgin of Montserrat," I told him. "It's reputed to be the most famous of all the religious shrines in Spain."

"I was told to see that too," he said. He paused, then added in an odd tone of voice: "Spain bothers me."

"In what way?"

"I'm Catholic, but . . ."

His voice trailed off. He chewed his food. He had given me an opening, but I wanted to proceed with caution. He was expressing himself about vital matters with more frankness than I had thought possible, and I did not want to make him defensive.

"My approach to religion—by the way, this doesn't bore you, does it?"

"Not at all. I'm passionately interested."

"—my approach is more spiritual than what I've seen here so far," he said cautiously.

"Did you see the bishop's body in the glass coffin in the cathedral here?" I asked.

"Yes." He laid aside his knife and fork and I saw a shudder pass through him. "That offends me," he said flatly.

"An offense, a stumbling block, eh?" I asked gaily.

He laughed and stared at me.

"You know your Bible," he said.

"I was weaned on it," I told him.

"By the way, are you going to see the Black Virgin?" he asked.

"Yes; I intend to."

"Then, let's see it together," he suggested.

"I'll have to move today, maybe. It'll have to be tomorrow—"

"Tomorrow morning?"

"Good."

"How shall we go?"

"Let's take one of the tours. In that way, we can see how the tourists react."

"That's an idea," he said, accepting. "All right; we will each buy our ticket and we'll meet on the bus. There's a ten o'clock tour given by the big agency on the Ramblas."

"Fine."

Later we shook hands and parted. That ought to be something, I told myself as I hurried to my pension to meet Carlos.

And Carlos was there, nervous, his thin lips pursed determinedly, striding up and down in front of the street door of my pension.

"I'm sorry if I kept you waiting," I told him.

"It's not me that matters," he muttered, taking my arm and guiding me toward his car. "It's Dolores. . . . She's the youngest daughter in the family and she works. She's taken time off to pass on you as a prospective guest."

"Let's roll then," I said.

Carlos was silent as the car moved through heavy traffic. The sky darkened and fine slanting strings of rain washed the air of dust, bringing a smell as of wet clay. Flecks of water peppered the car windows; the windshield wipers wobbled to and fro. The car stopped in front of a tall apartment building.

"It's on the sixth floor," Carlos said, "and sometimes the elevator doesn't work. Not enough electric power. That's one drawback."

"If the room pleases me, I won't mind," I said.

"They're good people," Carlos muttered. "They've been put through the mill."

"You mean the Civil War?"

"Yes."

"What does the father do?"

"There's no father. He was killed—"

"By Franco or the Loyalists?"

Carlos pulled down a corner of his mouth.

"All of the supporters of Franco who were killed were killed by Communists; and all of the supporters of the Loyalists who were killed were killed by Fascists," he explained in a jeering tone.

"And who killed the father?"

"The Communists, they say."

"Oh, so these people are supporters of Franco?" I asked.

"It's better to say that they're traditional Spanish Catholics." Carlos suggested.

"And how many are in the family?"

"There's a mother; then there's Dolores who works and supports the family; and there's another daughter. Nice people," his voice trailed off.

We crossed a spacious lobby and when Carlos pushed the elevator button, he exploded: "Damn! The elevator's not working; it had to be now—"

"Let's walk up," I said. "Tell me more about this family."

"What do you want to know?"

"What are they like?"

Carlos was so long in answering that I thought that he had not heard; when I looked at him he was frowning and I sensed that something was bothering him. He mounted a full flight of steps before replying.

"The older daughter . . ." he began and broke off. He paused and looked at me meaningfully and put the forefinger of his right hand to his temple and twisted it round. "Understand?"

"You mean she's off?" I asked.

"Somewhat."

"Why don't they institutionalize her? They keep her at home?"

"Yes. But she's harmless. She bothers nobody."

"Yeah," I breathed softly.

Carlos was puffing heavily from his climbing and his face was so red that it had a tinge of blue.

"There's a maid," he said. He stopped and smiled bitterly at me. "And a dog . . . That's all."

It was the kind of apartment building that the Americans had hurriedly and cheaply thrown up during the false prosperity of the twenties: thin walls, commodious hallways, façades of make-believe luxury, tiny panes of stained glass, and large zigzagging cracks gaping in the concrete.

Reaching the sixth floor, Carlos pushed a bell whose metallic trilling seemed a signal, for the strident barking of a dog burst forth from somewhere deep within the apartment and advanced, rising in volume as it neared the door.

"The dog," I said.

"Oh, you'll learn about him," Carlos said significantly.

"Is he dangerous?" I asked.

"Noooo; I don't think so," Carlos drawled.

I heard the dog's paws scampering over the wooden floor inside and then I heard the impact of his body smashing against the door facing us, making it rattle on its hinges, and from a rasping throat came an awful growling and snarling.

"How *big* is that dog?" I asked.

"He's just a little dog," Carlos said.

"Yeah, but he's got a hell of a lot of spirit," I said.

A woman's cajoling voice sounded behind the door and the furious barking ceased. Silence. Sounds of retreating footsteps. Silence again. Then echoes of approaching footsteps. The door opened and a stout woman of middle age stood facing us, grinning. The mother, I thought. The first thing that I noticed about her was that she was so horribly self-conscious that she made me feel somewhat the same. She greeted us in Spanish and I vaguely remembered that a dog had been barking savagely and had stopped abruptly, but he was not now in sight. Carlos and the woman exchanged a few words in Spanish and finally the woman turned to me, extending a pudgy hand, laughing and turning her head away in embarrassment. I shook her hand, saying in French and English that I was glad to meet her, then followed her and Carlos into a large, neat living room. I saw at once a photo of the dead father of the family: a dark, angular face staring from a huge frame bordered in black atop the piano—the kind of face that looked out upon the world with such deliberate self-consciousness that I knew that only a man with an old-fashioned and sentimental conception of life would have dared have a photo of himself taken in so obviously unnatural a pose.

Carlos and I sat. The mother smiled sweetly at us and left.

"She's calling Dolores," Carlos said.

"Where's that dog?" I asked Carlos.

"Are you scared of a dog?" he asked me with a hard stare.

"No."

"Then forget him," he said.

About ten minutes later a small, dark, tense girl who looked about twenty-six years of age came into the room. Her crown of wavy hair, her long and arching brows, her large and luminous eyes, and her severe but stylish skirt were all dead black; her smooth skin, her nylon blouse, and her even teeth were startlingly white. She smiled, stood a bit aloof from us and spoke in flawless English, all the while radiating a kind of defiant virginity. She always looked straight in your eyes as she talked, but gave the impression that she was thinking of another subject, a subject which, had it been broached, would have made her recoil in shame and moral loathing.

Yes; there was a room available; yes, I could see it; she was sorry that she had read none of my books, but, as she worked, she had very little time for reading; her dear, dead father had been a great and avid reader. . . . They were not in the habit of letting rooms to anybody, but, for a friend of Carmen and Carlos, they would be glad to do so. She was, she told me, rarely ever home during the day and her sister "was not well," but her mother (who now hovered grinning in the background) and the maid, Rosario, would look after me. Yes; it would be all right to move in that evening; the maid would help me to bring my things up. She was very sorry, but she could not do any better about the price; after all, it was a home atmosphere; I would be like one of the family. . . . She asked to be excused now, as she had to rush back to her job. We shook hands all round and we all walked down the stairs together, silently; when we reached the street, Carlos offered to drive her to her job, but she exclaimed:

"No. It's not far. I'll walk." And, unsmilingly, she strode briskly off, her head erect.

En route to the pension, Carlos said: "She's a plucky girl. She's the man in the family. She carries the load."

"What did the father do?"

"He represented a British telegraphic agency here."

"Why did the Communists kill him? Was he mixed up in intelligence?"

"Who knows?" Carlos said.

"Well, that family can feel that it made a sacrifice for this new order," I observed.

"What new order?" Carlos asked bitterly. He changed the subject. "You think you'll be all right there?"

"Sure. Why not?" I said, masking my emotions.

"I hope so," he said.

I thanked him warmly for his help and went to my room and lay upon the bed. I picked up Carmen's political catechism and began to pore over it. Lesson five read:

Symbols Representing Spain and the Falange

WHAT ARE SYMBOLS?

Visible or palpable representations of things we cannot see.

SUCH AS?

Religion, the Motherland, and political ideas, chiefly.

SO WE DON'T SEE ANY OF THESE THINGS?

No. Our understanding of them comes through reason.

BUT DON'T WE SEE THE MOTHERLAND IN WHICH WE LIVE?

We see it graphically in maps and physically with our senses, but we perceive its mission, the goal it has to reach, only through symbols.

SO, WHY DO WE NEED SYMBOLS TO STAND FOR THESE THINGS?

Because when we perceive them with our senses we can render them the homage they deserve.

WHAT IS THE SYMBOL OF RELIGION?

The Holy Cross.

WHAT ARE THE SYMBOLS OF THE MOTHERLAND?

The Flag, the Arms, and the National Anthem.

OF OUR POLITICAL IDEAS?

Banners, the Yoke and Arrows, and the song "Face to the Sun."

ARE THESE SYMBOLS ALWAYS VISIBLE?

No. They are sometimes visible like the Banners and Arms, sometimes heard like the Anthems.

WHAT DO THE BANNERS AND ARMS REPRESENT?

The history of the country, with its victories and losses.

AND WHAT DO ANTHEMS RECALL?

The poetic feeling which is always present at great historical occasion.

Just what kind of attitude did these lessons seek, I asked myself, to instill in children? Frowning, I turned the pages; I came to lesson nine, which read:

The Yoke and Arrows—Origin and Significance

WHY DID THE FALANGE CHOOSE THE YOKE AND ARROWS AS AN EMBLEM?

Because they link our task today with the most glorious years in our history.

WHO USED THE YOKE AND ARROWS BEFORE THE FALANGE?

The Catholic Kings.

WHY DID THEY CHOOSE THEM?

Because of gallantry, and perhaps for their symbolic value.

WHAT DO YOU MEAN?

Because when each sought a personal emblem, the King sought one with Y in homage to the Queen, and the Queen one with F in honor of the King.

WHO WERE THE CATHOLIC KINGS?

Isabel I of Castile and Ferdinand V of Aragon.

WHAT OTHER SYMBOLIC VALUE MAY THE YOKE AND ARROWS HAVE?

The bond between hard and disciplined daily toil, as represented by the yoke, and the capacity to undertake ambitious and world-wide enterprises, as represented by the Arrows.

ANYTHING ELSE?

Perhaps the final union of the kingdoms of Spain (the sheaf of Arrows) joined by the bond (the Yoke or knot).

WHAT IS THE SIGNIFICANCE OF THE FALANGE'S CHOICE OF THIS PARTICULAR EMBLEM?

Because of the last centuries of our failure, we want to bind our times with those of the Catholic Kings.

WHY?

Because we want Spain to achieve a glory similar to that which she achieved during their reign.

WILL THIS BE POSSIBLE?

Yes, with adaptations to the era in which we live, of course.

WAS THE EMBLEM OF THE CATHOLIC KINGS LIKE OURS?

No. They had the Yoke and Arrows separated; with us they are joined. Moreover with them the number of arrows varied; with us there are always five.

WHAT ELSE?

Theirs did not have a definite color and ours is red.

HOW ARE THE FALANGISTS TO USE THE YOKE AND ARROWS?

On a blue shirt, as a distinguishing mark, and embodying it in all that they do of importance in life.

WHAT ELSE?

On our Flag, as already said, and on our whatever it may be, to show our Falangist faith.

HOW WOULD YOU LIKE TO SEE OUR EMBLEM?

Cut in stone as a symbol of our age.

WHY?

It would manifest proof of our intention to endure.

WHAT DOES "ENDURE" MEAN?

Survive this age.

WHAT DOES "SURVIVE" MEAN?

That our ideas and deeds should outlast our own lives.

I sighed and closed the book. As yet I had not encountered a single practical idea. One thing was certain: something was bothering these Spanish. . . . If Spain wanted to be great again, what I had read so far was the best guarantee that it would never happen.

Later I packed, settled my bill, bade Carmen good-by, and set off in my car. I was about to enter a strange home. I could feel it.

When I rang the bell, I did not hear the dog's greeting. The maid admitted me, deferentially, with lowered eyes and a downcast mien.

"*Yo,*" she said, pointing to herself, "*yo, Rosario.*"

"*Sí, sí,*" I said.

She was silent, with a full, broad, flat face that had high cheekbones. Her hair was profuse and jet black; her skin was a very pale copper and she had a body that resembled a Sherman tank. Peremptorily, she forced my heavy bags out of my hands and walked blithely with them down the hallway, as though she were sauntering to a picnic. I followed her, conscious that there was no sign or sound of the dog. Ten minutes later I was installed in a neat, cool room that had two large windows overlooking an imposing sweep of the rooftops of Barcelona.

Toward six o'clock I was seated at a table, writing, when I felt the need of turning on the light. I rose, then whirled, sensing a presence near me. A woman of about forty stood with a twisted smile on her face in my partly opened doorway. She was hatless, had on a street coat, but a long, dirty, crumpled nightgown hung from under it. She wore tattered house shoes and her blond, touseled hair crawled over her head in all directions. Peeping out from behind the woman's billowing street coat was the dog, whose nose and eyes only were visible. His shaggy tail waved indecisively now and then. Had she opened my door or had I left it open . . . ?

"Hello," I said.

"Good evening," she said, speaking perfect English. "I hope I'm not disturbing you."

"No. Not at all," I managed to say, wondering if I should invite her in or call her mother. I knew now, without doubt, that this was the older sister, the crazy one. Not knowing what to do, I did nothing; I stood there and studied her.

Neither did she move; she stood there tugging aimlessly at the lapels of her coat. The dog now advanced timidly into my room, poking his nose at my suitcases; then, sniffing my shoes, he began to wag his tail in earnest. He seemed friendly enough and had none of that air of viciousness that I had heard in his barking earlier that afternoon.

"My name is Lola," she said. "And that—" she pointed to the dog— "is Ronnie, my little dog." She had the manners of a well-brought-up child of six.

"Hello, Ronnie!" I called cheerfully.

Ronnie was a mongrel, covered with white, brown, and black spots; he now rose on his hind legs and waved his front paws at me. Hesitantly, I took hold of one and he nestled a cold wet nose into my palm.

"He's such a sweet darling," the woman singsonged. "Really, he is. He never bothers anybody." She frowned suddenly and narrowed her eyes at me. "The maids used to beat him. That's why he misbehaves sometimes. He doesn't know *who's* his friend." She advanced into my room and, stooping, swept the dog up into her arms, folding him to her breasts, closing her eyes and nuzzling her face into his shaggy hair. I was standing next to her now and I noted her appearance: her neck was ringed with dirt; her mouth was large and her gums were blackened with stumps of rotted teeth. She had put on so much powder, rouge, and lipstick that she seemed to be wearing a mask; her deep-set eyes, a clear brown in color, were shadowed with long eyelashes drenched in mascara. She was kissing the dog, mussing his hair, and he responded with strange, subdued growls, but made no attempt to bite her.

She impressed me as having had a genteel background and education and she bore the faded manners of one who had moved in an international milieu. Intuitively I felt that, to escape scenes of unforgettable terror, she had fled her life and was wandering disconsolately in the dark bogs of her childhood memories.

"Do you love music?" she asked me suddenly.

"Oh, yes," I said.

"Oh, I'm so glad," she crooned, smiling toothlessly, her eyes shining. "I have a piano and I love to play. It's therapeutic for me, you know. When I get nervous, I play and it helps me. But Mama was afraid that I'd disturb you with my music—"

"No; no; you must play just as you always did," I told her.

"Oh, thank you." She sighed like a child being reprieved, still fondling and caressing the dog. "Isn't he wonderful?"

"He's a wonderful dog," I agreed.

"You see," she began in plaintive, honeyed, but doleful tones, "he *knows* that we won't go home till father returns. He *knows* I'm waiting." She spoke directly of herself now. "And I won't leave till he comes back. . . ."

Nonplused, I managed to smile and murmur: "Yes, I see; I understand."

"We'll stay right here, won't we, Ronnie?" she asked the dog as he licked her neck and chin.

"Your father?" I sounded a tentative question.

"*They* took him," she told me readily, her eyes showing astonishment and indignation. Her eyes widened and she glared at me silently for a moment. "*You*, you are not a Communist, are you?"

"Oh, no!" I said and took a step back. The dog let out a growl that trailed off.

"They took him and I refuse to go back home until he comes," she said emphatically. She looked longingly and soulfully at the dog. "We won't, will we, Ronnie?"

Ronnie trembled in her arms; his mouth opened and he stared at the girl's face, then barked anxiously. The rest of the apartment was quiet. I wanted to talk to her, but feared posing questions that might touch off reactions leading to violence.

"I don't understand about your father. What happened?"

"But don't you *know?* Didn't I *tell* you?" she asked with incredulous eyes.

"No," I answered.

"But didn't I show you the photos of our house by the sea?" she asked, her lips hanging open.

"No; no. I'd like to see them," I said.

"Wait. I'll get them!" she cried. She dropped the dog and ran out of the room. The dog rushed after her.

She returned with Ronnie switching at her heels. Her street coat had worked loose and her bosom was partially bare. Her hands were full of photos.

"See," she said, pointing. "That's our home. . . ." She put the photos in my hands.

I saw a lovely little bungalow set amidst sand dunes.

"Isn't it beautiful?" she asked, smiling. "I was happy there and he was there with us and—"

"Your father?"

"Of course," she said. "But we can't live like that now. Life was wonderful then. But it wouldn't be right for us to go back there without him, would it?" Without waiting for an answer, she went to my window and stared wistfully out. "But he'll come back. They'll find out that he's a good man and they'll let him go—"

"The Communists?" I asked.

"Yes; *they* have *got* him," she explained. "I'm waiting for father. . . ." She turned to me with fearfully large and luminous eyes. "I won't go back until he comes back. I swore that and I'll keep my promise." She waxed suddenly tearful. "I hope that you won't be like all the others who come to live here. They go away. Always, they go away." She grew aggressive. "I don't like that. Why do people always leave?" She beamed a sudden smile upon Ronnie, who sat watching her face. "We don't like that, do we, Ronnie?" she asked. Then she lifted appealing eyes to me. "But you'll stay, won't you?"

"Oh, I'll stay," I said heartily, at last sensing a vague drift to the woman's concerns.

"*You must stay*," she said, her voice desperate. Then brightly to to the dog: "Ronnie would like that. Wouldn't you, darling?" She was suddenly worried for Ronnie. "Ronnie, come here?" The dog ran and leaped into her waiting arms, giving a little bark of anxiousness. "We'll stay, won't we, darling?" She sighed, looking at me. "They say you write books. Do you have a book you've written that you could show me?"

"Yes; I think I have," I said. "There ought to be one in my suitcase."

Until that moment I had moved but a few inches. I turned and started toward my suitcase and Ronnie erupted a bark and shot like a bullet from the girl's arms and came at me, snapping, snarling. I turned and faced him. He was crouched low on the floor, his teeth bared, his growl a low, vicious snarl, his body tense and ready to leap.

"What's the matter with 'im?" I asked her.

"Ronnie!" she was screaming. "Ronnie!"

The dog snapped at me and I lifted my shoe to ward off his attack. The dog continued to growl.

"Ronnie, no!" she screamed.

She got to her knees and grabbed the dog, gathering him to her bosom. He quieted suddenly, but still glared at me.

"He thought you were *leaving*," she explained. She looked at Ronnie reprovingly. "He's not *going*. See?" Then she smiled at me. "He's a good dog, really."

"Yes, I see," I agreed, edging to my chair to sit down, wanting to let Ronnie know that I was harmless, would remain, was not leaving the apartment, and was no Communist. . . .

"He's staying, Ronnie," she cooed to the dog, who still watched me, growling occasionally.

I heard the front door opening. Ronnie sprang from her arms and tore down the hallway, barking.

"Excuse me," she said.

She rushed from the room and I stood listening. It was the mother and the maid, Rosario. They had evidently been out shopping together. I closed my door softly and sat on the edge of my bed. The Spanish Civil War had been over for eighteen years, yet its black shadow still lay upon the minds and feelings of the people. For Lola there had been no peace, no armistice. The bullets had long since stopped whining, and the bombs were bursting no more, but memories of violence and horror lived on and kindled mental and emotional pain. A timid knock came at my door.

"Come in," I called.

The door opened and the mother peered in, grinning, her eyes avoiding mine.

"Are you all right?" she asked me.

"I'm fine," I said in a voice that was strange even to my own ears.

She laughed and then said, apropos of nothing that I could determine: "Dolores will be home soon."

"Thank you," I murmured, not knowing what I was being grateful for.

She lingered on in my doorway, then she advanced into my room. "You have enough cover? Is there anything you need?"

"No; everything's all right," I said.

She impulsively caught hold of the jamb of the door, as though for support; then she was serious, unsmiling.

"I'm sorry Lola bothered you," she said, shaking her head. "You must have a lot of work to do. . . . You see, sir, she has been through a lot; she has seen terrible things. . . ." She came close to me, clasping her hands, and she half whispered: "She saw them kill her father. *She saw it happen!* That's why she's like that."

"She was a witness?" I asked.

"They killed him right in front of her eyes," she explained. "It was night. They took the both of them from the house and out into the countryside. They told her: 'We are taking your father. We'll bring him back soon.' And they took him off a few feet and shot him.

She saw that, but she does not wish to believe it. She says that they'll bring him back. That explains why she is like that."

"That's horrible," I breathed, understanding it all now.

"*C'est la vie*," she smiled bitterly.

"Life in Spain!" I exclaimed softly.

I saw her jerk a bit; her eyes roved restlessly about my room.

"It's life everywhere," she said. "It's the same everywhere. Father Rubio was telling us that only last week. It's the same all over the world. . . ."

I understood. To negate this horror, the Church had had to make it the normal lot of men. If this horror were the heritage of all men, then rebellion was senseless, was sinful.

I lit a cigarette and sat down. A few moments later another knock came at my door. It was Dolores. Her pale face was tense and serious.

"Pardon me," she said. "But do you plan to go out tonight?"

"Well, I'm going out to eat dinner," I told her. "Why?"

"Then, listen," she said and paused. Her eyes were defiant. "When you are ready to go out, you'd better call the maid and ask her to lock up the dog."

"What?" I knew what she was hinting at, but I wanted her to spell it out; I wanted to understand it.

"When you leave the apartment, the dog must be locked up. Or he'll attack you, seriously," she told me.

"Why? Have I made him afraid—?"

"No," she said and sighed. "Ronnie's just that way; that's all."

"He seems friendly enough," I said, wishing she would be still more explicit.

"No. He's friendly only when someone *comes* to the apartment," she explained. (Her eyes were tortured and suffering.) "But when someone tries to *leave*, he becomes dangerous."

"Why?"

"He just acts like that," she said vaguely. "He doesn't want anybody to leave the apartment. When you are ready to leave, just open your door and yell: 'Ronnie, *por favor!*' You understand?" She stared at me, wondering if I caught it all. "And Rosario will lock Ronnie up. Then you can leave."

"Has he really attacked people leaving the apartment?" I asked.

"He has ripped people's legs open," she told me.

"All right," I agreed. "I'll call out whenever I wish to leave. . . . But is someone always there?"

"My mother or the maid will always be there," she said.

"Good."

"I'm sorry," she said, smiling bitterly.

"Not at all."

"Thank you."

"Good night."

"Good night."

Well, Ronnie or no Ronnie, I was hungry and I was going out to eat. I got ready and went to my cracked door.

"Rosario!" I yelled.

"*Sí, Señor!*" her voice came distantly from deep within the apartment.

"Ronnie, *por favor!*"

A wild barking sounded. Running footsteps. A door opened and slammed roughly. More running footsteps. Another slamming of a door and Ronnie's savage barking was now faint. Rosario came rushing with a sheepish grin on her broad, bland face, and said breathlessly:

"*Sí, Señor!*" She spread her arms wide to let me know that the coast was clear.

"*Muchas gracias,*" I murmured, walking nervously into the hallway.

Lola was standing in the door of her room and her large eyes were stony with apprehension as she watched me pass.

"*Buenas noches,*" I said.

She did not answer. Her dazed expression hit me harder than a blow or a scream. I increased my pace and when I reached the front door, I was almost running. I opened the door and ducked out, then pulled it shut behind me. I waited. There came a furious rushing of paws over a wooden floor and a cataract of barking spilled forth; then I heard Ronnie's body landing against the door, shaking it violently. It seemed that he could tell that I was still there and he whined and barked and leaped, ramming his body against the door again and again.

"My God," I breathed.

8 . . .

Returning after dinner, I let myself into the apartment and Ronnie ran in circles of gladness, walking on his hind legs and waving his paws at me in gestures of greeting. Lola was playing the piano in the living room. Hearing my footsteps, she stopped and stood in the doorway, smiling her welcome. Dolores sat sewing at the dining-room table, her legs crossed, her bent head framed in a cone of yellow light cast by a floor lamp; she glanced up, smiled and nodded. The mother went rushing grinningly ahead of me and offered her services by opening the door of my room. Rosario hovered nearby, dumpy, cold-eyed, placid, observing with a detached and ironic air, then went off to the kitchen, lifting her voice in a raucous flamenco ditty.

Before going to bed, I dipped again into the Falangist catechism, reading lesson ten:

The Blue Shirt—Origin. The Red Cap

WHAT DO THE FALANGISTS WEAR TO DISTINGUISH THEM FROM OTHERS?

A uniform.

WHAT IS A UNIFORM?

That which equalizes and distinguishes all those who belong to a group or organization.

GIVE SOME EXAMPLES.

The uniforms of various schools, military uniforms, and, in another sense, the religious habit.

WHAT IS THE FALANGIST UNIFORM?

The blue shirt with the Yoke and Arrows embroidered on the left pocket.

WHY IS THIS OUR UNIFORM?

Because José Antonio decreed it at the first National Falangist Council in Madrid, October, 1934.

WHAT WERE HIS MOTIVES IN CHOOSING IT SO?

He wanted a uniform that showed the Falangists as militant, resolved to bring about the social revolution which was represented by the blue of our shirt—a proletarian color.

WHAT DOES THAT MEAN?

It is the color workmen wear for their hard labors.

WHY HAS THE SHIRT ALSO GOT THE YOKE AND ARROWS?

Because, besides the social revolution, the Falange wants to emphasize the national character of our movement.

HOW IS IT TO BE WORN?

Without a coat and with rolled-up sleeves.

WHAT ELSE IS THERE IN THE UNIFORM?

A black tie, since the death of José Antonio.

WHAT ELSE?

A red cap, since the Unification of April 19, 1937.

WHAT IS THE ORIGIN OF THE RED CAP?

The Carlist wars. It was the distinguishing sign of those who fought against the liberals, and remained forever the true sons of Spain.

IS THERE ANYTHING ELSE THAT IS NECESSARY FOR THE UNIFORM?

No. I have described the uniform proper. Other parts are according to circumstance.

WHAT IS THE WOMAN'S BRANCH UNIFORM?

The same, but without a tie.

WHAT UNIFORM DOES THE YOUTH ORGANIZATION HAVE?

A similar one, but without the blue shirt or red arrows, as they are not yet militant members of the movement.

WHAT MUST A YOUNG FALANGIST MAIDEN DESIRE ABOVE ALL?

To wear one day the Falangist uniform and serve Spain with her comrades.

TO WHAT DOES THE UNIFORM OBLIGE US?

To behave so that we set an example to all.

WHAT ELSE?

To remember always that Falangists are "half monks, half soldiers" and so their life must be courageous, austere and ordered.

Next morning I hurried to the tourist agency on the Ramblas, bought my ticket, climbed aboard the waiting bus, and walked down the aisle, looking for Pardo.

"Here," he signaled me, half rising. "I thought you weren't coming."

"I barely made it," I said.

The bus pulled away and we were Montserrat bound. The tourist passengers were in a quietly gay mood, chatting and commenting upon the landscape of bald mountains that loomed hazily through blue mist ahead.

"Well, what do you know about this Virgin we are going to see?" I asked Pardo.

He shaped his words slowly, as though seeing the pages of history that documented what he wished to say.

"It is claimed that St. Luke carved this statue from his memory of the Virgin Mother of Jesus. It is further claimed that it was brought to Spain by St. Peter himself in A.D. 30. In 717, to save it from the Moors, it was brought to Montserrat and hidden in a cave. It was discovered in 880. . . ."

"And since then?"

"It has become famous because of the adoration showered upon it by the Catholics of Europe and the world. Hermán Cortés came here to ask blessings from the Black Virgin. Even Columbus made a pilgrimage here," he said in a slow, soft voice.

"And what do *you* think?" I asked.

His eyes looked out of the bus window to the lifting, scarred walls or rock.

"I don't *think*," he said, laughing.

The ascent to Montserrat was breath-taking. We climbed, spinning and circling slowly round the naked mountain peaks on tiny roads that skirted the sheer edges of cloud-filled chasms whose depths made the head swim. There was scarcely a moment when we were not tilting downward, upward, leftward, or rightward while pulling round hairpin curves. The air grew thin, its pressure lessening so much that one had to swallow repeatedly to clear one's ears. And the higher we went the bleaker was the look of the world.

We were now traversing veritable kingdoms of desolation, vast continents of perpendicular columns—immense in their dimensions—of clustered, grayish rock, seemingly numberless in extent and imposing in their grandeur, all standing delicately balanced on their ends, side by side, adhering one to the other as though glued together by some miraculous substance, many of them rearing up and into the white clouds. The sense of the defiance of gravity of these forests of upthrusting series of columns evoked a hint of the mystical, of the impossible, and one understood why this locality had lent itself so readily to the establishment of a religious shrine.

The tourist passengers grew silent as we slowly but continually lifted ever upward, rounding mountain bends. More and more nations of seriated granite phalluses, tumefied and turgid, heaved into sight, each rocky republic of erections rising higher than its predecessor, the whole stone empire of them frozen into stances of eternal distensions, until at last they became a kind of universe haunted by phallic images—images that were massive, scornful, shameless, confoundingly bristling, precariously floating in air, obscenely bare and devoid of all vegetation, filling the vision with vistas of a non- or superhuman order of reality.

"What on earth could have prompted the first man to climb up here?" Pardo asked in a tone of wonder.

We were now all of some three thousand feet in the air, and the city of Barcelona and its vast configuration of dwellings could not be seen. Geology had it that at some remote period in the history of the earth a volcanic upheaval had tossed up these gigantic masses of round, oblong rock out of their ancient ocean beds, had stood them on their ends, and that some odd chemical reaction of the rocks, sea slime, and atmosphere had enabled them to cling uprightly together during eons of time in so astonishing a manner.

Veiled by haze, the numerous buildings, the chapel, and the monastery of Montserrat rose ahead of us. The bus slowed and stopped and I saw candy bars, cigarettes, postcards, pennants, banners, clay replicas of the Black Virgin, brochures, rows of bottles of cognac and Coca-Cola arrayed for sale. At a sidewalk café coffee and ice cream and sandwiches were selling briskly. The guide now took over with rough authority and shepherded us onto a funicular railroad which lowered us far down into a deep ravine out of which we could see the tips of looming mountain peaks. Many tourists took out their cameras and began snapping pictures.

After being dragged for what seemed an eternity over stony acres to look at sundry marvels, we were at last informed that we could see the Virgin; we queued up and began filing toward the chapel.

It was a small chapel, but one of the most beautiful, simple, and tastefully decorated I had ever seen. Narrowly rectangular in shape and with a remote and quietly luminous vault, it was filled with a soft, almost golden light that floated down from high windows. A choir of young boys clad in black and white chanted in piping, virginal tones. Pardo genuflected before the Holy of Holies, then crossed himself. I stood discreetly in the background. Inch by inch the queue moved forward and we mounted steps of white marble flanked by walls of glowing alabaster. I looked at those in the queue around me and saw the features of many racial stocks: Chinese, Japanese, Hindus, Negroes, Frenchmen, Germans, etc.—all of them awestruck by the nearness of the Virgin. We rounded a bend of steps and there it was. . . . Bathed in an effulgence of indirect golden light was a wooden image of a woman seated upon a throne of gold. The right and left sides of the statue were bounded by two phallic-looking uprights with oblong, smooth, extended heads. The statue was about three feet high, gracefully carved, black of face, and held within its plastic ensemble a kind of quiet, expectant tension. The facial features seemed a blend of the Roman and the Oriental; the nose was aquiline. Seated upon the woman's lap, and seeming to gaze in the same direction that the woman was gazing, was a baby whose features resembled those of the woman. The infant possessed that same attitude of quiet, tense expectancy.

From under the woman's queer headpiece—it was a cap or a hat or a crown—fell a shawl-like garment whose ripples flowed down well past her shoulders. The robe, regal and simple in design, draped her body in a modestly clinging fashion, descending in soft folds down to her feet, which rested upon something resembling a cushion. The child, a scaled-down duplicate of the mother, was garbed in a like manner. In the woman's right hand—her hands were strangely large and strong, as though she had not been unacquainted with rough or heavy labor—was a ball or globe, which, perhaps, symbolized the world—no one knew exactly. The child's left hand held something that looked like a pine cone, the significance of which was never alluded to in the literature that I consulted. Surrounding the statue were walls of gold and silver partly covered with priceless religious paintings.

The queue moved on and we found ourselves in a dim corridor lined with long glass cases filled with masses of jewels: watches, rings, necklaces, brooches, bracelets, earrings, clips, pendants, diamonds, pearls, etc., gifts donated to the Black Virgin by those who had received aid from her in the crisis periods of their lives.

We emerged by another stairway into the chapel and the majority of the tourists knelt at benches, crossed themselves and began to worship. Pardo and I wandered to the rear of the chapel.

"I need a drink," Pardo said. "You want a cognac?"

"Sure. Let's go. We'll cut this tour."

We summoned a waiter and ordered brochures explaining the genesis and history of the Black Virgin. We settled down to read. (I found later that the apologists at Montserrat were far more modest than the *Encyclopedia Britannica* in accounting for the history and reality of the statue.)

The few ascertainable facts were about as follows: In 880 a group of boys, wandering and playing amidst the ravines and rocky columns of Montserrat, were astonished by hearing strains of wonderful music coming from a cave. Approaching to investigate, they saw flickering lights as from many candles and smelled sweet odors. They grew afraid and retreated; later they reported their findings to the proper authorities, among whom was Gondemar, Bishop of Vich. The bishop, accompanied by others, was determined to have a look at the cave and he discovered exactly what the boys had reported: unearthly strains of music, beguiling scents, and the glimmering lights of innumerable candles. Taking courage, reports the legend, the bishop ordered the cave to be entered. The statue of the Black Virgin holding the Baby on her lap was found.

The bishop directed that the image be brought forth and a group entered the cave and came out with it. At that juncture strange things began to happen. The men carrying the statue suddenly found that it had grown so heavy that they were obliged to stop; they were anchored down; they could not move forward, backward, or sideways. This immobility that gripped the men was interpreted as being a sign indicating that a chapel should be erected on the spot.

That was the gist of the story. In comparison with the famous miracles claimed by the partisans of the Black Virgin, it was not much.

Pardo and I continued to drink our coffee and sip our cognac.

"Would you deprive people of that statue?" he asked me suddenly.

"No," I assured him. "If people feel that they *need* it, then, by all means, let them *have* it."

We pored over postcards showing the Black Virgin in color, depicting the many odd aspects of the shrine.

"Forget I'm Catholic. What do you really think of this?"

"Pardo, my attitude is complicated," I began slowly. "I'll tell you my objections to this statue, but you'll see that my objections won't mean much. In the first place, Jesus and His Mother were Jews. Now that statue does not seem to me to be Jewish either in features or dress. I definitely do not accept the vague statements about its origin.

"I'm convinced that that statue is either Roman or Oriental. My guess is that it represents a mixture of both influences.

"The concept of the Virgin Mother antedates Christianity by some two thousand years. Maya, the mother of Buddha, was supposed to have been a virgin. Chinese temples have long had their images of the Holy Mother sitting with the Child on her lap. The Egyptians worshiped Isis, mother of Horus, as a virgin, and she was called Our Lady, the Queen of Heaven, Mother of God.

"I'd say that that statue had once been used in pagan religious ceremonies, either by Romans or Eastern colonial subjects residing in Rome long before the time of Christ.

"We know that the black color of the statue does not come from paint. Neither is its blackness racially representative. It is highly likely that that statue turned black from the smoke of incense that pagans burnt before it.

"Now, to brand the Black Virgin a pagan relic plays right into the hands of the Church. Indeed, the apologists of the Church have long contended that pagan practices are *proof* of Christainity! As you know, Pardo, the Church's theory is that the pagans, without the aid of revelation, blindly groped their way toward a confused idea of Christianity long before Christianity came upon the scene. So the Black Virgin stands, from the point of view of the Church, no matter how she came to Spain—whether she came from some Eastern religion or was transported by St. Peter.

"Though but little of an objective nature can be proved about the Black Virgin, the existence of that statue proves a lot about man. Some men need that statue and others like it. The image of the Virgin symbolizes how man likes to feel about how he came into this world. That statue is one of the ways in which the Church can accept sex, the most prevalent, powerful, emotional, and factual experience in human life. Man senses that if there is anything at all really divine or superhuman in us, it is linked to, allied with, and comes through sex, and is inescapably bound up with sex. In worshiping the Black Virgin, men and women are worshiping the female principle in life, just as they have always done.

"Now, Pardo, don't you see at Montserrat the complementing male principle of life?"

"What do you mean?" he asked me, frowning.

"The male principle is represented here too," I told him. "In fact, the presence of that male principle is why they built a shrine here around the Black Virgin."

He stared at me and blinked.

"I can't say that I follow you," he said.

"Come here," I called to him, rising and going to the door. He followed and stood at my side. I pointed to the round, erectile, swollen clusters of stone lifting their bare heads defiantly skyward. "Pardo, don't you see that conglomeration of erect stone penises? Open your eyes, man. You can't miss. I'm not preaching the doctrines of Freud. Let the facts you see speak to you—"

Pardo leaped back from me and his face registered a strange combination of mirth and shock.

"*You are terrible!*" he said.

9 . . .

In my room I sat and pondered upon the mystery of the two Spains I had so far seen: the official Spain and the human Spain. How far they were apart! The sheer distance between them spelled danger. This nation had been brutally and bloodily wrenched from the slender democratic moorings it had had during the days of the Republic and had been set upon another course. But what was that course and where was it leading? Because what I had seen so far had failed to provide a satisfactory answer, I applied myself once again to the Falangist political catechism, turning to lesson fourteen, reading:

Juvenile Heroism—Jesús Hernández—The Young Falangists of the Baleares

WHAT IS HEROISM?

A noble impulse which makes us perform outstanding deeds.

ARE CHILDREN CAPABLE OF SUCH DEEDS?

Yes, just like adults and with even more disinterest.

WHY?

Because they cannot set a false value on life.

ONLY FOR THIS REASON?

And because in their tender years they have a greater capacity for admiration of heroic deeds and greater generosity for giving themselves.

DO YOU KNOW OF ANY CHILDREN WHO GAVE THEIR LIVES FOR SOME GREAT CAUSE?

Yes, religious martyrs.

DO YOU KNOW THEIR NAMES?

Yes, some. St. Tarcisius, St. Pancras, St. Just, St. Pastor, St. Pelayo, St. Ivez, St. Eulalia, and many more.

MUST CHILDREN ALWAYS DIE TO BE A HERO?

No. There are children who are heroes without giving up their lives.

DO YOU KNOW OF ANY?

The drummer boy Bruch.

WHAT DID THIS YOUNG CATALAN DO?

By beating his drum, he made a whole regiment of Frenchmen flee from Montserrat.

ARE THERE SUCH CHILDREN NOWADAYS?

Yes, the young Falangist Jesús Hernández, for example.

WHO WAS HE?

A boy of fifteen who wanted to fight in the Falange like the grownups, though, on account of his age, they would not let him.

WHAT HAPPENED TO HIM?

He died from a wound in the back on March 27, 1934, when he was doing liaison work for the Falange.

DO YOU KNOW OF ANY MORE?

Yes. That of the young Falangists on the cruiser Baleares.

WHAT DID THEY DO?

Nine of them embarked to help the crew and when the ship sank they went down stoically, singing "Face to the Sun."

WHAT DOES "STOICALLY" MEAN?

Without moving, without fear, despite their years.

DEATH AND EXALTATION

10 . . .

IT WAS one of those unsolicited and dubious letters of introduction pressed upon me by friends in Paris that provided the chance for me to meet a Spanish nobleman, the Duke of A.—I shan't identify him more precisely. His name, though illustrious, is not important. It was the Duke's attitude, gracious but brutally disconcerting, that held my attention.

One morning, accompanied by the Duke, I visited one of the city's exclusive clubs. Ensconced in comfortable leather chairs in a quiet corner, we nursed tall, sweating glasses of Scotch and soda. Heralding each of the Duke's sententious utterances were prolonged, noisy clearings of his throat, then, with an arrogant tilting back of his white head—he was over sixty years of age—would come a squinting of his gray-blue eyes at the ceiling as he let go a smooth, nasal stream of Oxford-accented English:

"Harrrrumph . . . I don't wish to shock you, but I must tell you exactly how I feel. I'm sick and tired of this survival of the unfit. And that's all that our modern life means today—coddling the unfit. . . . Harrrrumph . . . None of these modern ideas for me. Maybe I sound hard on the individual, but it is the race that I'm thinking of. The hell with plumbing, sanitation, and modern medicine! I say, the hell with it all! These damned antibiotics, what have they brought us? Nothing but the survival of millions who ought not exist. Now you may think Spain is backward. Years ago we had hardly any sewerage system in this city. Today, we have one. They call it hygiene. When we had no sewerage system many people died, but the strong survived. You had to develop resistance in those days. Harrrrumph . . . Now the weak are saved. I don't like it.

"The ruling classes of the world today are decadent; they have grown too soft. In the past the nobility created the Church, the State, the social classes—all the values of life. But they have let things slip out of their hands."

"But isn't Franco trying to restore all of that for you?" I asked.

"Franco?" he snorted. "That man . . . Harrrrumph . . . He's nothing. He's not nearly hard enough. He lets himself be pushed this way and that. We need a few excellent people, not millions of the botched, the unfit—"

"But how do you define 'fitness'?" I asked him.

"The ability to survive without help," he answered. "Harrrrumph . . . Go and look out of that window. See those people. . . . What do they mean? Nothing. They have no right to this earth. In the old days we gave them their duties; their lives had a meaning and they were happy. Now they suffer and plot revenge against their betters.

"Ah, the old days . . . Harrrrumph . . . Ha, ha! Diseases carried them off like flies. We didn't have to worry about them then. Nature settled the score. And those who survived were *good* and *strong*. . . . This has nothing to do with democracy. We accepted men coming far down, but they had to be endowed by nature with the will to live and rule. . . .

"Harrrrumph . . . This cutting of man off from nature has made all the mischief. We've got to reverse it. And where do you find these denatured men? In these terrible cities. Do you know I hate cities? I only come into town when I have to, and then I scoot back to my place in the country as soon as I can. Harrrrumph . . . Ah, I see that I shock you, don't I? Ha, ha!"

I did not try to answer the Duke's arguments; I was sure that no words of mine could have ever reached him. And thereafter, wherever I went in Spain, I saw either the consequences of the Duke's attitude or heard echoes of his words; for most of the life that I saw in Spain was a distorted protest against the Duke's philosophy. The Duke and his class had instilled in the hearts of the Spanish masses an instinct for revenge, an impulse toward hot rebellion, a tortured desire to have done with the Duke and his class. But these insurgent instincts were feeble, afraid, and ashamed of themselves; they were laden with guilt and sought to hide, and whenever they did emerge into the light of day, they were disguised, deflected, shrinking from frontal attack. I was not long in learning to detect, under a thousand varied masks, the all-pervading, substitutive, and symbolic nature of most Spanish reactions—reactions that ranged all the way from the offering of the mass to bullfighting.

11 . . .

One sweltering afternoon, upon leaving the American Express, I saw one of those faces that tease the memory: I knew that I'd met the young woman who was coming smilingly toward me, but, no matter how frantically I tried, I could not recall when, or under what conditions I'd last seen her.

"Hi," she greeted me familiarly, extending her hand. "What on earth are *you* doing in Spain?"

"Hello," I hailed her, shaking her hand, searching desperately for a clue. "I'm just nosing around. What're *you* doing here?"

"Writing articles," she answered. "And studying dancing." She smiled. "Look," she chided me with a touch of superior aggressiveness, "I hate seeing you trying to hide that baffled expression in your eyes. You don't really remember me, do you?"

"Frankly, no," I replied, laughing.

"I'll make it easy for you," she said. "We met casually about a year ago in G——'s bookshop in Paris. The name's V.L."

She was a woman of about thirty, a native-born American. Self-possessed, intelligent, she was dressed in a stylishly Continental manner and wore some becoming jewelry. We continued standing and confronting each other. She spoke first, and I'd known that she would, for she had been studying me with a peculiarly speculative air.

"What are you doing at the moment?" she asked me suddenly.

"Nothing. Why?"

"Let's have a *café con leche*," she suggested.

"Sure."

Ten minutes later we were seated in a café over steaming cups of coffee. After a few moments of small talk, she leaned forward and said: "I want to ask a favor of you."

I raised my brows and looked at her.

"I'm listening. I'll do what I can," I said.

"If you don't want to do it, or if you don't have the time, then just say so." She spoke hesitantly.

"What is it?"

"Would you mind coming with me to my pension?" she asked. "Just for half an hour—"

"Hunh?" I blinked and laughed. "Is this a gag?"

"I'm truly serious," she told me. "I'm scared."

She was suddenly mute, tense. Was she playing a game? But she sat there, an image of just what she said she was, that is, scared. Her eyes showed it.

"What are you scared of?"

"That *man*," she whispered, her eyes squinting at me. "My landlord . . . I want to move from my pension and I'm scared stiff."

"What are you so frightened about? Do you owe him any money?"

"No. I—I can't explain it. Look, I'm not a nervous person. . . . I walked the streets for two hours today, looking for somebody who would come with me while I packed my things. I'm terrified—"

"Have you had anything to do with this man? I'm no moralist; you can be frank with me."

"No, no," she said, shaking her head. "It's nothing like that."

"Then what's *wrong?*"

She stared at me and sighed.

"How long have you been in Spain?" she asked.

"Just a few days."

"Then you don't know what it means to be a woman alone in Spain," she said.

Holy Moses. Here it was again. I remembered the terror that had come over Carmen's face when I had suggested that she meet me in a bar. She had reacted as though I had proposed a trip to perdition.

"But you are an American," I told V.

"It doesn't matter. I'm a woman and I'm alone. . . ."

"Why did you choose this particular pension?" I asked.

"It's cheap; I can't afford a big hotel," she explained.

She covered her face with her hands and shuddered. Was she overdoing it?

"Is it that bad?" I asked.

"You have to see it to believe it," she sighed.

"All right. I'll come with you. I want to see this," I said. "Now, just do you want me to do?"

"Nothing. You just stand there. If a man is there, he'll act differently."

There was no doubt in my mind now of her terror. But how could such a thing be? Who had the right to throw gratuitous terror into lonely women? We finished our coffee and headed toward her pension. It was on the seventh floor of a fairly new and modern building. The elevator worked. The whole atmosphere smacked of cleanliness, respect, of quiet, secure living. She opened the pension door with her key and we went down the hallway to her room. As she unlocked her door, I asked her:

"Will they object to my coming into your room?"

She turned a pair of hopeless eyes upon me.

"It doesn't matter now; I'm leaving." As we entered she said: "Oh, they think I'm a whore, all right. All women alone are whores. I'm worse; I've no official card."

"What do you think makes them act like that?"

"They're just Spanish," she said, summing it up. "Now, just stand by while I pack," she said, rushing breathlessly to her wardrobe and pulling out clothes by the armfuls. She worked feverishly, opening suitcases and dumping clothing into them, stuffing papers and books into cartons.

"Take your time; I'm here," I said. I sat on the edge of her bed and lit a cigarette.

In half an hour she had packed her belongings and arranged them in a group along a wall. She stood looking appealingly at me.

"Would *you* tell him that I'm leaving and ask for the bill?"

"Sure. But my Spanish doesn't exist."

"He speaks French."

"Where is he?"

"Back there in his office," she said, pointing.

"Okay, sister," I said, rising. "Stay here."

I went out and down the hall and rapped upon the door of the office, opened it and went in. Behind a small desk sat a large man, pale copper in color, with a shining bald dome of a head. He had a wide mouth with full, determined lips.

"*Buenos días, Señor,*" I said.

"*Buenos días,*" he sang, smiling whitely.

"The American lady is my friend," I explained softly in French. "She's checking out. Would you please prepare her bill?"

He stared at me a moment, then winked knowingly, smiling.

"Of course. When, *Señor*?"

"Right now," I said.

"*Sí, Señor.*"

"*Gracias,*" I murmured, gritting my teeth.

"*Nada,*" he sang softly.

I went back to V.'s room

"It's all right," I told her.

"What'd he say?"

"Nothing," I said. I didn't want to mention his lascivious wink. "He'll bring the bill in a moment."

We were silent. She moved nervously about, touching this item and that one. Finally a knock came at the door.

"*Entrez!*" I called.

The landlord entered with the bill in his hand. He poked it at V. with a sardonic air, then stepped dramatically back and waited, his lips pursed. As V. studied the figures, her eyes widened.

"He's charging me for three months of baths," she told me. "I didn't take them."

"She's objecting to the charge about the baths," I told him.

Then it came. He leaped into the center of the room and towered over her, bellowing like an enraged bull.

"*Monsieur!*" I chided him sharply. "*Vous n'êtes pas correct!* That's no way to speak to a woman!"

He checked himself, turned to me, smiling an apology, sighing.

"It was understood that she was to pay ten pesetas a day for baths—" he began.

"But I didn't take them!" V. blazed. "And you know it! The water was never hot. Ask the maid."

He insisted that she pay; she insisted that she was not going to pay for what she had not gotten. She argued that she had not asked for the baths and, therefore, was not liable for them. He stood over her, lifted his clenched fists, and screamed.

"*Monsieur!*" I called to him.

He ignored me and began jumping up and down, stomping both feet on the floor. I rose.

"*Vous m'étonnez beaucoup!*" I said. "You shock me!" I appealed to him, spreading my palms. "You cannot reasonably expect her to pay for what she didn't get."

He sighed again and fronted me, spreading his hands in a gesture of helplessness. He smiled and explained in a sort of murmur that we were men, that men were not, perhaps, superior to women, but they were certainly more intelligent. His air was one of cynicism and his manner asked me to join him in his masculine game of domination.

"She says she didn't take those baths, didn't ask for them, and she's not going to pay," I explained.

"She said she wanted a bath every day," he sneered.

"I asked if I could *take* a bath every day," she corrected him.

"Look, knock off the bath charges," I asked him softly.

He sighed and spread his hands again; I felt that he would have loved to wrap them around my neck.

"*No, Señor,*" he was adamant.

"But she didn't ask for them; the water was not heated for her—"

"She *asked* for them when she came here," he insisted.

"Let her pay for the baths she took, for those for which water was heated," I insisted.

He stared at me for a long time, then breathed despairingly: "*Sí, Señor.*"

We had won. I told V. to pay for the baths she had taken. I watched her figure it out with him; she paid. He turned wordlessly to the door, and, as he left, he slammed it so hard that the room shook.

"You see?" V. said, her eyes round with shock.

"He's crazy," I said.

"Now, watch," she warned me. "He's going to cut the lights, cut the water, and lock the bathroom door—"

"No!" I laughed.

No sooner were the words out of my mouth than the lights winked out, plunging the room, which faced a dim court, into semidarkness.

V. was so angry that her lips were rigid. I understood her now. She had never in her life endured such treatment and she could not imagine taking it without some form of retaliation.

I rose and tried the water faucets in her sink; a trickle of water came through, then there was a sucking of air through empty pipes.

"You see?" she asked, driving her point home. "You have to *see* it to believe it. He wanted that bill paid just as he had drawn it. They simply can't resist humiliating a woman who's alone."

"How do you stand it?"

"On the street it's not so bad," she said resignedly. "They insult you as you pass. But the public protects you from their going too far. But when they get you alone in front of them, they let you have it."

"Are you ready? Let's get out of here."

"I'll call the maid," she said. "She'll help with the luggage." She went out and came rushing back, her face scarlet. "He won't let the maid help. He says she's busy!"

"I'll take 'em down," I said.

We struggled down with the luggage, placing it upon the sidewalk.

"Wait, I'll get my car—"

"No! You've done your share. I'll get a taxi," she insisted.

She hailed a taxi and we loaded the luggage. She climbed in and slumped back against the seat and burst into tears.

"I could kill him! I could kill him!" she cried in a nervous rage. Her humiliation was complete.

"Take it easy," I said. "You're out of there now."

"I could rip his windpipe out with my hands!" she shouted, clenching her fists and grinding her teeth.

I took hold of her shoulder and shook her roughly.

"Stop it! You're getting hysterical!" I yelled at her.

The taxi driver was staring at us incredulously. I nodded to him and said: "*Un momento, Señor.*"

"*Muy bien,*" he said in a worried tone.

"Can I *help* it if I'm a woman? Why *do* they act like that? It makes me mad clear through!" she spoke in fury.

I looked at her wavy locks of hair, at her white skin, her brown eyes.

"You are acting like a Negro," I told her.

That shocked her.

"What do you mean?" she asked wonderingly.

"Raging and wailing and crying won't help you." I argued. "Negroes do that when they are persecuted because of their accident of color. The accident of sex is just as bad. And crying is senseless."

"But they *treat* me senselessly," she contended.

"And crying *compounds* the senselessness," I said.

She dried her eyes. She straightened up suddenly, then looked at me with a demanding stare.

"You must write about this. People ought to know."

"No. This is your story," I said. "It happened to you."

"No. Nobody'd believe it," she said. "A woman's word would be doubted."

"Okay," I said. "I'll tell your story. Now, calm down. And tell this man where were going."

She gave directions to the driver and the taxi moved off. It stopped before a big hotel.

"It looks civilized," I commented.

"That's why I took a big one," she said. "For my own protection, I want to be where other Americans are."

The luggage was unloaded and porters were taking it inside. I stood watching her.

"You'll be all right?"

"Sure." She smiled. "Maybe I can do as much for you someday."

"So long and take it easy," I said.

I walked away. Yes, you had to see it to believe it.

I went back to Carmen's Falangist political catechism with renewed interest. Somewhere there was a clue to all this. Maybe this funny book of questions and answers could tell me. I turned to lesson sixteen and read:

Feminine Heroism

DO WOMEN ALSO HAVE OPPORTUNITIES FOR HEROISM?

Yes, though for them heroism consists more in doing well what they have to do every day than in dying heroically.

WHY?

Because women haven't so much occasion to risk their lives.

ONLY FOR THIS?

No, also because their temperament tends more to constant abnegation than to heroic deeds.

BUT ARE THERE SOME WHO HAVE GIVEN THEIR LIVES FOR THEIR COUNTRY?

Yes, because women do not shun their daily tasks even if they cost them their lives.

WHAT DOES "SHUN" MEAN?

Flee, abandon one's obligations.

CAN YOU QUOTE SOME CASES?

For example, María Paz Uncita, the Chabas sisters, Sagrario del Amo, María Luisa Terry and many others.

BUT WHAT WAS THE DUTY THEY WOULD NOT LEAVE?

Helping prisoners and in various front-line hospitals and wash houses.

DID THEY KNOW THAT THEY MIGHT BE KILLED?

Yes.

AND YET THEY DID IT?

Yes, for this was what Spain at war demanded of them.

HOW DID THEY DIE?

María Paz Uncita and the Chabas sisters were murdered by the Reds; Sagrario del Amo and María Luisa Terry while helping wounded soldiers at the front.

ARE THERE CASES OF WOMEN DYING WHILE FIGHTING LIKE MEN?

Yes, in the War of Independence against France, but it is unusual.

SO WHAT IS THE REAL HEROISM OF WOMEN?

Giving up the pleasures of life when we feel we have to do a duty over and above them.

WHAT DO "PLEASURES OF LIFE" MEAN?

All that is pleasant in life, beginning with life itself.

AND WE CAN DO ALL THESE THINGS?

Yes, for they were done before by creatures of flesh and blood like ourselves.

12 . . .

My fairly woolly hair had made me hesitant for a long time about testing the racial reactions of Spaniards in terms of their giving or withholding tonsorial services. Finally, overcoming my qualms, I entered a small barbershop and asked for a haircut, making elaborate signals with my hands to indicate what I wanted. A thin, dark-complexioned little barber in a soiled white coat waved me readily to a chair. It was directly after lunch and I was his only customer. He spoke a little French.

"You are American, are you not?" he asked me as he gently tucked a white cloth into the collar of my shirt.

"Yes, I am," I answered. "But I live in Paris."

He wanted to know how life was in France, if this was my first trip into Spain, by what route I had entered the country, what my profession was, had I found a hotel, and what did I think of Spanish food.

"Do you like Spain?" he continued, arching his brows.

"I love the people," I said diplomatically.

"We are poor," he sighed. He picked up his comb and scissors and paused, staring off. "We were a great nation once. Now we are something like Roumania or those Balkan countries. I know; I know. . . ." He nodded and pursed his lips. "Most Spaniards won't admit it, but it's true. One time we were the foremost nation of the world, but now we are nothing."

"Nations rise and fall," I said philosophically. "The thing that worries me about Spain is the suffering—"

"Ah, you have *eyes!* You can *see,*" he congratulated me. "Most tourists come here because it's cheap, no? But they do not see; they do not care to see." He breathed asthmatically and began snipping the blades of his scissors as he clipped my hair.

"I hesitated about coming into your shop," I confessed to him.

He stood off from me and gaped in astonishment.

"Why?"

"Well, you know . . ." I began slowly, "some people have very strong racial feelings."

He lifted both of his hands and looked at the ceiling; one of his hands held the comb and the other the scissors.

"But that's insane!" he exclaimed. "You are a man, a human being. Why should I refuse to cut your hair? The cutting of hair is my profession. I've heard that in some countries such things happen. . . . Look, sir, the sun made your hair crinkly; the cold made mine straight. All right. Why should that make such a difference?"

"It shouldn't," I said. "But it all too often does."

"I don't think it does very much with the Spanish," he said. "You know," he smiled knowingly, "Spanish blood is all over the world. We don't shrink from dark skins. We created new races in South America; you know that, eh?"

"Yes, I know it," I said.

"Racial feelings are insane," he said with final judgment.

"Maybe the Spanish mixed *too* much?" I suggested, smiling.

"What do you mean?" he wanted to know.

"Well, they married everybody they came in contact with, but they didn't do much developing—"

"They took the gold, didn't they?" he asked me.

"Yes."

"*Muy bien*," he said, accepting my judgment with such aplomb that I was suspicious. He paused and confronted me, his small eyes fanatic and unblinking. "I'm *not* Spanish," he said. "Yes, I live in Spain. I was born in Spain. I speak Spanish. I speak a little French too. But I'm *not* Spanish." He put the backs of his hands on his hips. "*Monsieur*, I'm Catalan. We are Catalans here; understand?"

"Yes."

"We are an occupied people; understand?"

"Yes," I said. He was preaching Catalonian nationalism.

"We Catalans didn't colonize very much," he explained. "We were not allowed to. We have been oppressed for centuries. Not many of our people were in South or North America. That was the way they oppressed us, by keeping us out—"

"Why did they oppress you?" I asked.

"Because we are better men and they know it," he said stoutly. "The men in Madrid forbid our language. They won't let us hold high offices. They ram their orders down our throats. Understand?

"*Monsieur*, Catalans would not have behaved as the Spanish did in those colonies," he told me. "We have certain types of personalities in this country who feel that they must have something for nothing. They feel that they are agents of God. *They* were the people who colonized and who have oppressed us. We Catalans have a language, a literature, a culture. But, now, we are buried."

This man felt that to live in Spain under what he called the "men in Madrid" was an insult to his humanity, yet, since there was nothing concrete that he could do about it, since he could not altar matters or redress his grievances, he had embraced the dream of nationalism. That part of him that had been unfulfilled had been projected out in a hunger for an independent national existence, and someday he hoped that he could fight for it. He could not have been more than twenty-five; he owned his little shop, was married and had two children.

"Your parents?" I asked him.

"Dead," he said. "My father died in the war. My mother died soon after."

"If I'm not indiscreet, what side did your father fight on?"

He looked at me in astonishment.

"For the Republic, of course," he told me proudly.

"Are you bothered or hounded because of what your father did?" I wanted to know.

"That *could* happen," he said slowly, "but it hasn't."

"How are conditions around here?"

"Not so bad," he said. "But you know we are overrun with the unemployed from other areas. That is what causes our poverty. In Andalusia and Extremadura there is much, much misery. And those poor people come here. . . . *Les gens la-bas ont faim, Monsieur.* The men in those areas are hungry."

"What can be done?" I asked him.

He was silent for a long time. His scissors went *clip-clip-clip*. . . .

"Someday we'll heave them off of us," he predicted finally. "This *can't* last. It's not in the human heart to support things like this—"

"Does the Church play a strong role in this?" I asked, trying to push him into other areas.

"Listen, it's all *one* thing: the State. The Church is only a facet of it; that's all," he analyzed it. "Those men in Madrid go too far, too *far*! There'll be an evening of the scores one day; understand?"

"Why do you say that Catalonia is different from Spain?"

"We Catalans work hard. Look at Catalonia and you'll find it different. See our farms. Our factories. We are an industrious people. We are not like the Spanish, who are lazy, arrogant, and always wanting someone to work for them while they rule. Understand?"

"But the central government is powerful," I reminded him.

He lathered my temples with a big white warm brush of soft bristles and began lining the razor down the side of my head.

"Ah, *Monsieur,* we are patient," he said with a knowing smile. "We have a saying in Spain. I don't know if I can translate it into French. But it means that, though hungry, I am my own master, my own dictator. It means that I do with my life what I want. . . . *En mi hambre mando yo.*"

"I don't understand," I said.

In a variety of ways he explained what he meant; it boiled down to this: I AM THE MASTER OF MY HUNGER. It was a bitter way of taking life. It was a flight into a fierce and burning pride.

"*Nous ne bougerons pas, Monsieur,*" he told me, his voice quivering with fervor. "We won't move. We stay put. We stay put till death." He looked at me and smiled. "And *he* knows it."

"Who?"

He turned and pointed his lather-stained razor to the faded image of Franco's face on the wall.

He finished shaving my neck and asked me: "You've seen the soldiers and the machine guns?"

"Yes."

"They are not there for nothing," he observed.

"You mean that *he* needs them?"

"He couldn't rule without them," he said.

"Naked force?"

"*Oui, Monsieur.*"

He gave me a tiny mirror in which to look at myself, then smiled proudly. I paid him and then shook his hand warmly.

"*Bonne chance, mon frère,*" I told him.

I left, marveling. He was by far the most anti-Spanish Spaniard I had yet met. But I could not escape the impression that he was still basically Spanish, for he had denounced Spain in terms that were so emotionally Spanish! He had boasted that he was the master of his hunger and his misery, and that nothing could alter his attitude of insurgency. He was the emperor of a bleak empire indeed. He would refuse to repress his instinct for freedom even if faced with starvation. In fact, he would take starvation and death and make of them a kind of victory. Somehow, in his outlook, he had substituted the objective for the subjective and was clinging to it with all the passion of his heart. Proud, sensitive, knowing no practical way out of the morass of his shame and degradation, he had made a monument out of his black defeat.

13 . . .

My first Sunday afternoon in Barcelona was spent in André's home with his family. He lived on the lower and more commercial end of the Ramblas in a vast, dreary tenement that looked much better from the outside than it did on the inside. Armed with a bouquet of red roses for his mother, I trudged up four flights of winding, dirty, dark stairs and saw André, a murky shadow in the watery beams of a distant skylight, framed in the doorway of his apartment. As I approached him, I was aware of whitish blobs of faces, members of his family, no doubt, floating behind him in the background.

I was kindly, even elaborately welcomed and I was sure that André must have coached them not to be too demonstrative or forward in their reactions, for they stood about in attitudes of silent expectancy, waiting. One by one they shook my hand, allowing me to advance into the living room. André held my left forearm in a firm but brotherly grip, guiding me gently but surely, signifying that he was my sponsor and protector here. He translated and interpreted for me, an act which gave me time to hover and observe.

They were all got up in their Sunday best and their awkwardness and embarrassment were touching. The woman I intuitively knew to be André's mother waddled forward; she was swarthy, short, fat, with jet-black hair streaked with gray. Toil had aged her prematurely. After she had shaken my hand, I presented her with the bouquet of roses. For a moment she was taken aback, gaping at me as though she was sure that I had made a mistake; her bewildered eyes circled the family group, then she grabbed me and kissed me on the cheek. She gazed wistfully down at the flowers and began a soft, silent weeping. André patted her shoulder and gave me a wink that begged my indulgence for his mother who, his expression implied, was a weak and irrational creature. Slowly the woman detached a rose from the bunch and tucked it into her hair; there were exclamations of "Ah!" and "Oh!" as all the women in the room followed suit, and they looked uncommonly pretty with the red roses glowing darkly against their somber tresses. It was amazing (and it was not to be the last time that I was to notice this) how simply and cheaply a Spanish woman could effectively decorate herself.

André's father was a squat, bald, hefty man and, when he crushed my hand in his, I found the calluses of his palm as hard as stone. He looked at me directly with lips that were always partly opened; I had the feeling that he was waiting for me to issue him some command which he would instantly execute, and it was impossible for me to glance at him without his giving a slight, vibrant, nervous start in response. He worked in the shipyards and had a blunt, honest face and a pair of dark, deep-set eyes that stared out at the world with a certain degree of mild self-distrust. A big black cigar holding an inch of ash was in his left hand and he puffed at it now and then. With a slow gesture he pulled another from his vest pocket and tendered it to me. I was about to refuse, but felt the pressure of André's hand, indicating that I should take it. I did, slipping it into my inner coat pocket.

"*Gracias, Señor,*" I said.

"*Nada,*" he murmured, smiling.

André's sister, a little mousy, self-effacing, black-haired girl, was presented to me next; she shook my hand, bowing with ceremony, her eyes fastened in fascination upon my face, my hands: my color seemed to hypnotize her. At her side, clinging shyly to her skirt, was her tiny, three-year-old daughter, at whom I smiled brightly and paid compliments. The mother prodded the child to offer me her hand and I bent and shook the sticky little fingers, wondering at the dirt that smeared her features so much that she resembled a rag doll that had been left too long out in the rain. André's mother swooped across the room and swept up the tot and whisked her away amidst the general laughter of the family.

"*La petite est sale*," André explained, guffawing.

André now led me up to his brother-in-law, who was the tallest of the family. He seemed somewhat sophisticated, urbanized even; he worked in an office. At once he offered me another long black cigar that went into my inner coat pocket.

As though in response to some signal, or maybe from custom, all the women gravitated toward the other women and edged slowly from the room, leaving the men alone. I noticed that there was always an attempt to herd the men with the men and the women with the women; it was as though they wanted to protect the men from the women and the women from the men, even in public, and it made one conscious of sexual differences when normally such notions would have been far from one's mind.

An awkward silence prevailed, during which André pulled me to the balcony from which I could see a plunging perspective of the crowded and noisy Ramblas. The doorbell pealed and there was a scurrying of footsteps, then exclamations of greetings. A tall, well-made girl swept into the room and paused; she was sensual, olive-skinned, and had the kind of personality that made you watch her and wonder what she would do next. She had presence. André rushed forward and kissed her chastely on both cheeks, standing a little off from her while doing so. Behind the girl, smiling and shrinking, stood a woman whom I took to be her mother—a morbidly timid creature who was not presented to me.

"*Ma fiancée*," André said.

I shook her warm, pliant hand and bowed and smiled. She had large, dark, shining eyes and she gazed at me with so mute, melting, and stricken an expression that I had the feeling that, if I had said:

"All right, now, pull off your clothes and lie there on that couch!" she would have been momentarily shocked, but would have obeyed at once. The girl was the living personification of sexual consciousness; one could have scraped sex off her with a knife. She whispered something to André, who turned to me and, laughingly, asked:

"She wants to know if you are married?"

"*Sí, Señorita,*" I said.

She sighed. Her full, moist lips were rouged; her eyes were dewy with a dim, smoldering sparkle. Unconsciously her left hand rose slowly and tenderly cupped her left breast as she backed away from me till she was safe in a corner of the room. But she kept her eyes riveted upon my face and her lips hung open.

"She's a virgin," André whispered proudly to me.

"Oh!" I said. André was clearly waiting for me to make some kind of response to this announcement, but I was at a loss as to what to do or say. Instinct urged me to reach out my right hand. He had been waiting for it and shook it solemnly.

"*You are lucky,*" I told him, nodding my head gravely.

"Yes, yes," he agreed readily.

By sheer accident my reaction had been the right one and I could feel myself rising in André's estimation.

"When are you getting married?" I asked him. He shrugged and pulled down the corners of his mouth while he rubbed the fingers of his right hand together.

"I've no money," he said. "Maybe Papa'll help me as soon as I'm out of school."

"What does your fiancée do?" I asked him.

Dumbfounded, he stared at me.

"She's a virgin," he repeated.

"Oh, yes, I understand," I said, nodding my head still more gravely.

Being a virgin, evidently, was a kind of profession in itself. It seemed that she stayed home with her mother and was never allowed out except in the company of the immediate members of the family, a situation that constituted proof of her virginity. I understood now why she had been so wonder-struck by me; she had not had an opportunity to meet many men, and I was, moreover, a different sort of man: brown. . . . Her being a virgin was all in the world she knew, felt, and thought about. Hence, each man that she saw she regarded as a possible agent of defloration, an agent which, no doubt, she longed to meet and embrace. Her living the role of a virgin had steeped her personality with an aura of sex and she unconsciously attracted men to her body with more definiteness than even a professional prostitute. Her entire outlook was one of waiting to be despoiled, longing for the day when she could shed her burdensome and useless role, when she could live a free and normal life like the older women about her.

Suddenly something became terribly clear to me: André was aware that he was sacredly pledged to marry this girl whose sole value was centered in her virginity. When in her presence he could not help but be conscious of her longing to be deflowered, and he responded emotionally and psychologically to this ardent wish of hers, but he could do nothing about it. He had to worship her from afar and wait until he had money enough to marry her with the ceremonial blessings of the Church. And that was why he had to go so often to seek the "bad" women in the dark and fetid alleyways, and it was why, in his confused and embattled heart, he hated those women and yet had to be with them. Those prostitutes were the iron-clad guarantee that his fiancée was and would remain a virgin until marriage. But it was a torturous emotional and psychological price that André had to pay for so dubious a value.

The apartment was bare, poverty-stricken. There were not even carpets on the floor; it was not, I think, that they could not afford them; I doubted if they had ever thought of putting any down. In fact, the home was shabby and dirty. One wall of the living room boasted a loud and vulgar print of the Last Supper; another wall was claimed by a huge calendar showing a laughing, pretty girl, her head flung wantonly back, her merry eyes contented and mischievous and watching you as you moved about the room—and all the while she was about to take a sip from a cold, sweating bottle of Coca-Cola. There was not a book or a magazine in sight; there was no attempt at all toward aesthetic embellishment.

There was something missing here. There was not enough psychological food in this home to sustain a genuinely human life. What was there that linked this family with the modern world? Nothing that I could see. Was it possible that they were that much cut off from life? No! Ah, I had it. *They had the Church!* The Church alone was their link with the world, with other men; and they felt no need for other links—no books, no magazines, no love of art beyond the traditional ecclesiastical. I recalled that magnificent cathedral and realized how weighty and meaningful a role it played in the emotions of people living so naked and bare a life. Indeed, the cathedral was the only bright and colorful thing on their whole horizon; without it their existence would have been senseless. If the Church were taken away from them, the displacement left would have plunged them mentally and emotionally into a void.

But even the decisive value that I assigned to the Church in their lives did not completely satisfy me. I felt that there was still another element lacking here, another dimension unaccounted for. But, for the moment, I could not place my finger upon it. (I was far closer to discovering what that element was than I imagined.)

The women now came into the living room to set the table for lunch. André and his brother-in-law crowded about me as though to shield me from the women, or to distract me from their presence.

"Do you like bullfighting?" André asked me.

"Oh, yes," I said.

"Have you seen many?" the brother-in-law asked me.

"A few . . . But that was years ago in Mexico," I told them.

"There's a bullfight this afternoon," André informed me.

"Then you and your brother-in-law will come as my guests," I invited them.

"But we have no tickets," André moaned.

"Can't we get some?" I asked.

"Sure. But they are expensive," André said.

"What do they cost?"

André shook his head hopelessly, gloomily.

"Sixty, seventy, and up to one and two hundred pesetas."

I pulled a thousand-peseta note from my billfold.

"This ought to take us with something to spare," I said.

André was undecided. I could see from his eyes that he wished hotly to go. But would it be right . . . ? André and his brother-in-law consulted together, then stared at the note and shook their heads. André's father came forward and spoke disapprovingly in a low voice, his eyes looking at the note in awe. I guessed that he was telling André that it was not correct for me to spend so much money to take them to a bullfight.

"It's nothing," I assured them. "It's a pleasure for me."

The old man slowly nodded his consent. André was wild with excitement. He took the note and handed it to his brother-in-law, who rushed out of the apartment to buy tickets. André could not contain himself; he danced for joy, literally. He ran to the balcony and I followed him; we watched his brother-in-law disappear toward a bullfight ticket office. Ten minutes later the brother-in-law returned, panting and sweating, holding three bright-red tickets in his hand. It seemed that the father had instructed them to buy two cheap tickets for themselves and a ticket of one hundred and sixty pesetas for me.

"You won't mind sitting alone, will you?" André asked me. "We couldn't pay that much of your money for seats for us. It wouldn't be right; Papa said so."

"Who's fighting today?" I asked.

"CHAMACO!" they all chorused gleefully.

"Who's he?"

"You'll see," André promised me.

He snatched the freshly ironed tablecloth from his mother's hands and got in the center of the room. He held his feet close together, his chest out, his buttocks in, his head tilted at an arrogant angle. His right arm extended and dangled the tablecloth. His eyes were fastened with contempt upon the horns of an imaginary bull. He twisted his wrist, making the tablecloth tremble ever so slightly.

"Ha!" he shouted, shaking his body, trying to cite the bull of his fancy.

"André," his mother pleaded, laughing.

André's eyes widened to indicate that the bull was charging; he swept his arm gracefully upward, lifting the cloth with a flowing sweep, his eyes glowing like coals and his voice, hoarse and filled with a tremor of danger, sang out: "*Ole!*"

Every voice in the room echoed him: "*Ole!*"

When the room was quiet, I asked André: "Do you know the meaning of the word, '*Ole*'?"

"It's just an expression," he said.

"It's a Moorish word," I told him.

"Really?"

He informed his family of the origin of the word.

"What does it mean?" they wanted to know.

"It means 'For God's sake!' "* I told them.

They all stood frozen and stared at me with open mouths. They had been uttering the pagan religious phrases of the Moors and had never known it!

14 . . .

The talk of bulls and bullfighters swamped a long, heavy luncheon that swam in olive oil. The afternoon was torrid and, though we were in our shirt sleeves, I sweated as I ate. Spain being a man's world, we men were served first by André's mother; the women had to wait meekly for their turn. No nonsense here about the priority of women, of the mothers of the race, not even if they were certified virgins. The women ate silently with one eye cocked in the direction of their men, ready at a moment's notice to drop their knives and forks and refill the half-empty masculine plates.

We began with *paella*, then moved on to fried fish, followed by steak, after which came salad; the dessert was canned peaches, a

* See Américo Castro's *The Structure of Spanish History*, Princeton University Press, 1954, page 113.

universal favorite with the Spanish. I gave up after the *paella* and begged for mercy, much to the astonishment of André's mother, who promptly predicted that I would collapse upon the streets if I didn't eat more.

With his napkin tucked efficiently into his shirt collar, and speaking while masticating mouthfuls of food, André's father held forth about famous bullfighters—Belmonte, Manolete, Joselito. Under the impact of potent red wine and excited talk of bulls, the men's faces reddened, grew mobile, inspired almost. Everybody ate a dreadful lot, including the yearning virgin, who loaded her fork, packed the food into her sensual mouth, and wolfed it down with open relish. She would take a long swig of red wine, swish it about her gums for a moment to clean up, and would swallow while her eyes roved the table, appraising the men. Perhaps she was storing away a reserve of food for the children she hoped someday to have. Anyway, she was not troubled with delicacy; maybe she was resigned, knowing that she was undoubtedly destined for fatness, and fairly soon.

After lunch we men sat, grunted, sighed, stretched out our legs while the womenfolk cleared the table. I put one of André's father's big black cigars in my mouth and let the old man have the pleasure of lighting it.

"*Muchas gracias, Señor,*" I murmured, pretending to smoke.

"*Nada,*" he sang, grinning with delight.

He patted André on the back and nodded approvingly toward me and said: "*Simpático.*"

André and the son-in-law chuckled in agreement.

A few moments later the old man's eylids began to droop, then his chin sagged slowly to his chest. André urged his father to take a siesta. Laughing sheepishly, the old man rose, shook my hand, excused himself, and lumbered off to bed. I relaxed and let my cigar go out. . . .

No one felt like talking; in fact, there was nothing to talk about. André kept glancing at the clock on the mantle and the long, dull afternoon wore on. The voices of the women wafted musically from some rear room. I was bored. At four o'clock André leaped to his feet and announced with a whoop:

"*C'est l'heure! Partons!*"

"*Ole!*" I cried.

"*Ole!*" they chimed in.

We came to life, bade the women a lingering good-by, thundered down the dark, smelly stairs, and went out upon the street to my car. André and his brother-in-law were so excited that they were speechless; they sat silent, hunched tensely forward, their eyes wide and unblinking. The traffic was heavy; everybody was bull-bound. We came in sight of the arena and even I began to succumb to the contagion of bull fever.

One glance at the straggling throngs converging upon the circular stadium was sufficient to disclose that all social, class, and political lines were melted here; but, wherever I looked, I saw armed members of the Civil Guard, their machine guns ready.

"*Por qué ça?*" I asked André, mixing languages and pointing to the machine guns. "Why that?"

"*Nada, nada,*" he mumbled, frowning.

Flocks of girls and boys scurried about with earthen water jugs they had tiny spouts from which water would jut into your mouth if you held them up and out at arm's length and aimed the thin stream of water accurately; they threaded their way through the throngs, calling:

"Water, fifty centavos!"

I parked my car. André and his brother-in-law went off to find their seats. I saw upon the façade of a massive brick building fronting the stadium a gigantic emblem of the Falange: a batch of red arrows held together by a red horizontal bar, the symbol of the Yoke and Arrows dating from the time of Ferdinand and Isabel.

The yokels from the hinterland, wearing dull brogans and sleazy, crumpled trousers, mingled with the sleek members of the nobility, and one could see the absoluteness that cleaved Spanish society, the working class and the nobility, in twain. I was quickly hemmed in by men wishing to sell booklets in English describing bullfighting, photos of matadors, and brochures detailing their exploits. Others peddled combs, cigarettes, canaries in cages, paper hats of many colors to shade the head from the sun, pocketknives, wristwatch bands, dolls, rings, and a sprawling welter of other cheap and flimsy trinkets. Beggars were universal, eagerly exhibiting the stumps of arms and legs, their outstretched palms beseeching centavos; they would follow you for minutes, jabbering plaintively, their eyes humble and desperate.

Hawk-faced gypsy women offered bits of colored paper upon which your fortune was printed; others, a little better dressed, had elaborate astrological charts showing loops and whorls that traced the influence of the stars upon your life. Excited, black-eyed teen-age girls passed arm in arm, their painted lips spewing out words so rapidly that their voices sounded like the spluttering ends of dangling electric wires emitting blue sparks.

Suppressed emotion filled the air; all about me eyes glittered with the expectation of seeing something loved and believed in. Several working-class women carried tiny babies in their arms; in a quiet, shaded nook of the stadium wall one young woman was giving the swollen, veined teat of her breast to her infant and crumbly milk drooled from the tiny mouth as it suckled, and the mother, her eyes dreamy and vacant, stood oblivious of passers-by. To me she was a spectacle far more moving and beautiful than the ancient, wooden Black Virgin seated among the rearing stones of Montserrat. . . .

I surrendered my ticket and followed the stream inside, renting a tiny pillow that was thrust upon me, the significance of which I did not appreciate until I saw the bare slab of concrete that was to be my seat for more than two hours. Up a short flight of steps and some thirty thousand people magically appeared in a vast sun-drenched circle, the tiers of faces rising like a wall toward the hot blue sky. The scene leaped with color and noise. The heat was like steam and there was scarcely room to move. I was jostled in front, in back, and from both sides by pushing, sweating, panting people. An usher grabbed the stub of my ticket and beckoned me to follow him; he pointed to a seat in the shade at the barrier, with no one directly blocking my view of the wide circle of red sand that formed the bullring. But, when the usher indicated a span of bleak concrete ten inches wide and jammed in between two other people, I thought that surely a mistake had been made. But, no, that was my seat. In order to possess it, I had to straddle my legs so that my kneecaps, when I eased down into a sitting position, touched both of the hips of a fat woman sitting directly ahead of me on a lower tier; and I could feel the fleshy legs of a woman behind me cushioning my back. I smiled bitterly. The fantastically elaborate pains to which Spaniards went to segregate the sexes were annulled here in a manner that more than wiped out all of their other moral efforts. I could not crook my elbow or reach for my pack of cigarettes without colliding intimately with female anatomy.

The women were dressed to the hilt and everybody was edgy, nervous; some were biting their fingernails and others were pulling absent-mindedly at the lobes of their ears. Friend greeted friend and the ushers shoved rudely, seating people, their faces bathed in sweat. Uniformed men sold beer, Coca-Cola, candy bars, advertising their wares in singsongy wails. The Civil Guards were stationed at intervals of about ten feet and they had their machine guns handy. Though there was a bubbling din of voices, I had the impression that the vast crowd was very quiet.

Suddenly I was aware of whispers and snickers coming from the people around me; my ears caught the word: "*Americano . . .*" I grew self-conscious, feeling that someone was commenting upon my national identity. I looked cautiously at the faces near me, but they were staring off intently in another direction. Then I spotted the object of their bemused curiosity: I saw that it was a Protestant clergyman looking awfully out of place in this splendid pagan setting and a long way from his home and his ideas. He was aware, I felt sure, that he was a minor sensation and now and then he ran the forefinger of his right hand deep in and around his white turned-about collar. He kept his eyes dead ahead and he held a fixed smile that did not look genuine.

Momently the crowd thickened. The bullfighters and their

assistants began to make their appearance in the space, about a yard wide, between the barrier and the bullring. The matadors were dressed in flashy, tight-fitting costumes that were known as "suits of lights"; their aids were less gaudily clad. Reporters and photographers began to circulate among the bullfighters, who went about arranging their capes and swords and other paraphernalia in a tight-lipped, matter-of-fact manner. Their faces were drawn, their eyes holding dull glints of apprehension.

A band began to play on the far side of the arena and a roar of voices filled my ears. The spectators about me began moving with nervous starts, their lips hanging open. I noticed that the pressmen and the photographers behind the space of the first barrier kept looking up at the tiers of human bodies in such a queer and self-conscious fashion that I felt compelled to turn my head and seek out what was interesting them so intensely. I discovered that they had an amazingly graphic view of many women who, enthralled and excited, had allowed their legs to spread, offering froglike visions of white flesh. The men would march to and fro, with nervous expressions on their faces, then they would pause and glance up, their eyes stony with lust. Now and then they would form a knot, jab one another in the ribs, whispering, laughing with taut lips, then resume their pacing and looking furtively upward. One enterprising photographer attached a telephoto lens to his camera and, with his comrades crowding about him so as to screen his actions, pointed his camera upward and began snapping photos. . . .

15 . . .

The tempo of events quickened. As with one prompting, everybody now turned toward the ornately decorated box where sat the president of the bullring and official referee. His signal for the commencement of the drama came when his fluttering white handkerchief showed over the top railing of his box, and a highly synchronized, dazzling, and bloody game got under way, at first slowly and with touches of studied ceremony, but later becoming more desperate, fatalistic, and beautifully horrendous as the grappling with danger grew more and more intimate and mounted to a determined and inevitable climax of life or death for man or beast—but surely *death* for something or somebody.

A bugle sang a clear, golden note and the band began to play the dolorously lively bullfighter's *pasodoble.* From out of a wide opening on the far side of the blindingly bright red ring a score or more of brilliantly costumed men, led by a lone black figure astride a gracefully prancing horse, fanned out slowly and evenly over the scarlet sand and advanced with solemn steps toward the presidential box, looking like glowing pawns as they moved in the sunlight. They halted, facing the presidential box, and lifted their dark eyes grimly upward. The lone, mounted black figure now doffed his hat to the president; the others—the matadors, banderilleros, and picadors—following tradition, pressed their black hats firmly upon their heads, waiting. The president now rose and tossed a key that traced a swift downward arc and fell into the hat of the black, horse-mounted figure who, whirling his horse, galloped across the ring of sand and handed the key to the doorkeeper of the bull pen. Meanwhile, the matadors and their entourage were bowing to the president, then, with hurried, tense steps they scampered behind wooden, protective barriers at three points in the circumference of the ring.

Again came the sound of a bugle, higher, clearer. A huge gate was thrown open by a man who fled to safety. A gaping black hole yawned and all eyes peered expectantly into it. Then out thundered a wild, black, horned beast, his eyes ablaze, his nostrils quivering, his mouth open and flinging foam, his throat emitting a bellow. He halted for a second, amazed, it seemed, at the spectacle confronting him, then he settled squarely and fearlessly on his four hoofs, ready to lower his head and charge at the least sign of movement, his sharp horns carrying the threat of death, his furious tenacity swollen with a will that would brook no turning aside until all movement about him had been struck down, stilled, and he alone was left lord and master of the bloody field.

16 . . .

It took but thirty seconds of contemplation of that black bundle of bounding fury for my feelings to declare in me the definite conviction that, though that raging bull was indubitably and dangerously real, he was, at the same time, a complement of a subjective part of almost everybody in the stadium; he was, though an incontestable and charging beast, a creature of our common fantasy, a projected puppet of our collective hearts and brains, a savage proxy offered by us to ourselves to appease the warring claims that our instincts were heir to. And all the swift and decisive moves on the part of the matadors and their assistants that I saw in the ring that hot August afternoon served but to deepen and inform my original intuitive impression.

There was no doubt but that this beast had to be killed! He could be allowed to linger along; he could be played with, teased even, but he had to go, for there was no possibility of coming to terms with him. One could not live with him, yet one could not run away, could not leave him alone. This beast had not only to be slain, but *ceremoniously* slain—slain in a manner that would be unforgettable. And when one faced his wild and wayward presence, one knew that one's every act had to be suffused with the implacable resolve to put him out of life, or he would put one out of life.

From behind the three wooden, protective barriers of the ring the bullfighters now ventured cautiously out into the sandy arena, each group converging from a different angle, waving their scarlet capes to lure the bull into making repeated charges so that they might study his modes of attack, his manner of hooking with his horns, his predilection for tossing his head to left or right; in brief, in a frantically short space of time they had to familiarize themselves with the aggressive tendencies of that restless beast.

And that crashing hump of a black bull that they had sworn to kill was deeply loved; no mistake must be made about that. The long, secluded, and attentive rearing that had been lavished upon him to bring him into this ring virginal and pure, in terms of his having had no previous experience in fighting men afoot, had been much too expensive and elaborate to fit merely into a design of assuaging the desire to kill for the sake of killing. That bull had been so tended, fed, supervised that he was beautifully, wonderfully, innocently, and miraculously bad, evil, ungovernable—the hallucinatory image of the undistracted lust to kill.

That starting black hair, that madly slashing tail, that bunched and flexed mountain of neck and shoulder muscles, that almost hog-like distension of the wet and inflated and dripping nostrils, that defiant and careless lack of control of the anal passage, that continuous throbbing of the thin, trembling flanks, that open-mouthed panting that was so rapid that it resembled a prolonged shivering, that ever ready eagerness to attack again and again that was evidenced by those fluid shiftings of his massive and mobile weight from hoof to hoof, those unreserved lunges that sometimes carried him far past the elusive capes and sent him pitching and sprawling into the dirt until his flaring nostrils scooped up sand, that single-mindedness of concentration that would never allow his turning his head away from his enemy, that instinctively imperious pride that told him that he and he alone was right, that superb self-forgetfulness that made him make of his body an expendable projectile to hurl at and annihilate his adversaries, that unheard-of ability to fight on even when rigor mortis was slowly engulfing the tottering limbs, that total and absolute dedication of life to defend life at any cost—all of these qualities made of that murderously leaping monster in that red ring a bull that was obviously something more than a bull. He was a substitutive instinct, a careening impulse, a superhuman image to contemplate for an awful hour in the hot sun buttressed by the supporting presence of one's neighbors—something to look at and then forget with a sigh, something to be pushed into the underground of one's feelings till the overmastering need to experience it again would arise. Yes, the mystery and the miracle were here: the mystery resided in why the human heart hungered for this strange need; and the miracle was in the heart's finding that a rampaging bull so amply satisfied that need.

The matadors worked tensely with their capes. This beast had to be known, tamed—that proud and insurgent head had to be lowered, that wild lunging had to be calmed—in sum, this beast had to be educated quickly so that he could serve human ends, human purposes. The bull's desire to kill had to be harnessed so that those sharp horns could graze, when guided by the skillfully held cape in the hands of a man who was master of his fear, the chest with an inch to spare and death would not come! *Death must serve as a secular baptism of emotion to wash the heart clean of its illegal dirt. . . .* And the matador in his bright suit of lights was a kind of lay priest offering up the mass for thirty thousand guilty penitents. I sighed, realizing that, in Spain, all things were Spanish.

17 . . .

Exclamations of admiration for the bull now filled the stadium. It could be seen at once that he was a fighting bull, the ever-charging kind, the sort that moved as though he had rails under him to make him come at you like a thundering train. Once again the bugle sounded through the hot, golden afternoon sunshine. The bull had now been sufficiently observed by the matador and his assistants and the moment had come to attack the beast directly by planting barbed hooks of steel deep in the center of the mound of knotted muscles on the hump of his monstrous neck, the ultimate object being to wear him down, to tire him and make him lower his defiant head so that, at the moment of killing, the matador could, while luring the bull in one direction, move his body in another and reach across those ever-moving horns and plunge the sword hilt-deep into the vital area of his body.

Also the matador had to check the beast's leaping lunges, had to slow down his unearthly pace so that he could be played with the muleta, the small yard-wide, yard-long stretch of red cloth attached to a stick which the matador would use in his final and finest stages of playing the bull. The bull had to be so conditioned that, when he chased the muleta guided by the supple wrist of the matador, his horns would sweep past the back, the side, the stomach, or the chest of the matador with but an inch or a fraction of an inch to spare, sometimes leaving smears of blood from the bull's sticky mane on the matador's uniform. This was the dreadfully delightful climax that could evoke the scent of death in the nostrils, the taste of death on the tongue, and the feel of death in the blood—which was a way of experiencing death vicariously.

The matador and his assistants now took up positions to be ready in case they were needed to coax the bull with their capes into a stance where the banderillero could make his approach and jab home the darts of steel. The panting bull now stood alone, looking from man to man, waiting for some move, not knowing from what direction action would come first. Then, on the far side of the ring, from behind a protective wooden barrier, a man stepped forth and stood erect, bold, holding a stick about two feet long in each hand. The sticks were gaily decorated with frizzily cut, colored paper and were made of slender rods of hardwood tipped with sharp, short spears of steel barbed and forged like fishhooks. Once sunk into the body, they could not be withdrawn without shredding the flesh.

The bull and the man were now alone in the red ring. The stadium was silent. The sun beat down pitilessly. The man now proudly lifted the brightly-colored banderillas high above his head, straightened his shoulders and stood poised, then began to ready himself by flexing his muscles as he lifted his body first on his heels and then on his toes. The bull watched, then slowly began to move closer to the man. Man and bull were still far apart and the distance between them burned with tension. Still lifting and lowering his body on his heels and toes, the banderillero began brandishing the sticks at the bull, shouting hoarsely with full lungs, his pelvis jutting forward, his chest reared back:

"Ha! Ha! Ha!"

The bull lowered his horns for attack. The banderillero began advancing, step by step, teasingly twisting his body from side to side, all the time nearing the bull. The bull advanced. The man advanced. Now both quickened their pace. Then man and beast rushed headlong at each other, both at a dead run. The bull had reached the speed of an express train, his horns lowered and aimed at the man's stomach. The banderillero held his barbed sticks high, slanting a bit downward, and his body was leaning forward at an angle, the steel tips in his hands ready to fly over the onrushing horns to the hump of neck of the black, hurtling body. Then, at the point of what seemed an inevitably bloody juncture of man and beast, the man swerved to one side and leaped into the air, and, at the same time, plunged the steel darts home into the hot and quivering flesh of the back of the bull's knotted neck, then skipped aside, avoiding the seeking horns, leaving the sticks dangling and flopping as the bull still moved. The man escaped free and the bull now stopped in his tracks, searching for the missed target and feeling searing fire blazing in his gashed flesh.

A quick sigh went up from the audience. There was some handclapping. Then came cries of:

"*Muy bien! Muy bien!*"

"*Bravo hombre! Bravo hombre!*"

The bull galloped in circles, heaving his massive shoulders, trying to dislodge the steel hooks that ripped him the more he moved. His target had eluded him and now he sought it again, determined, undaunted. He trotted this way and that, thrashing his gigantic body about to rid himself of those hooks in his flesh, and the candy-looking sticks bobbed and flapped like circus pennants waving in the wind, shaving the tissues anew, causing tiny streaks of scarlet to ooze down his forelegs each step he took.

As though crazed, the bull loped into the center of the ring, snorting, flinging his body to toss away those splinters of steel that bit ever deeper into his muscles and the red streaks of blood turned to broad, gleaming patches of scarlet that matted the black, bristling hair of his back.

Then, to his right, another man appeared. The bull turned to face his adversary, settling solidly on his four hoofs, then advanced. The man advanced, holding two more red and green and white sticks tipped with steel. Pained, the bull pawed the sand, lowered his horns, sighting his target, and moved forward with quicker momentum, and the two steel tips tore and widened the gash in his neck. On he came and on came the man, and, at the point of meeting, when the horns of the bull seemed about to gore the intestines and you could hear the bull's vast lungs expelling a mighty breath, the man rose into the air, shooting the steel-tipped darts downward and into the gaping, bloody wound. The man was in the air when the sticks left his hands, and, upon landing lightly upon the sand, he leaped aside, veering from the searching horns, escaping to safety.

The bull now stood and lifted his head and bellowed, raging, looking about for the vanished target, heaving his vast black shoulders and feeling the steel slashing his flesh and the streaks of blood now turned to rivulets. The peak of muscle back of his neck gushed blood. That was the way it had been planned. The means were cruel; the ends were cruel; the beast was cruel; and the men who authored the bloody drama were cruel. The whirlpool of discordant instincts out of which this sodden but dazzling drama had been projected hinted at terrible torments of the heart. Anyway, the results were being attained; the bull was now forced to hold his head a bit lower.

The goaded animal now careened into the middle of the sandy ring, bellowing, whirling his head in agony, his glaring eyes seeking vainly for a moving target. It appeared; the banderillero stood arrogantly some distance from him, again waving two beautifully deadly bright sticks capped with hooks of shining steel, making dainty, capering steps, yelling disdainfully:

"Ha! Ha! Ha!"

The bull studied the target. The man advanced mincingly, edging closer. Slowly, head down, horns ready, the bull came, shaking his body to loose those four arrows of steel that had now built a roaring fire in the muscles back of his neck; he came, dripping blood, his mouth shedding viscous gobs of white foam and saliva, his anal passage emptying, his urine spraying the red sand. The man stopped and motioned the two sticks at the bull, then stepped forward again.

Then they both rushed at each other; the man again left the earth, his arms outstretched, his feet close together, and then he flung his arms forward, the pointed steel tips shooting downward and sinking into the shaking flesh as the horns passed an inch away from the stomach and the man skipped off to safety. Maddened, the bull charged about the ring at random, his eyes hunting something to hurt, to kill, the sticks flinging limply about his bloody shoulders. He lifted his head and bellowed to the hot and empty skies.

The bugle sounded yet again and the ritual marched relentlessly on. I settled back to watch the work of the picadors. Two men were leading a blindfolded and padded horse, atop which sat the picador, cautiously alongside the wooden barrier when the bull, spotting them, tore snorting across the ring to attack before the picador and his horse could get set.

The matador and the banderilleros rushed out with capes flaring and flapping, calling to the bull, trying to distract him. The uproar checked the bull in his flight; he now stood, turning his head in a wide semicircle, looking from the waving capes to the mounted man. A cape fluttered high and the bull charged; another cape flashed and the bull altered his charge, changed his direction and went for that last beckoning cape, twisting his gigantic body in a swift arc almost in midair, hooking and snorting as he followed the fleeing and weaving cloth, yet, as always, missing his adversary. Yet another cape rippled and taunted him and again he was off upon another charge, and, once more, the goal that his horns sought evaporated. . . . When the bull now came to a standstill, he was facing the picador, who had ranged his horse lengthwise along the wooden barrier. The picador reined his blindfolded and quilted horse tighter and made the horse prance as he forced the blindfolded animal to sidle toward the bull, all the while readying his pick, pointing it toward the bull's back. He motioned the pick toward the bull, goading him with heavy, throated grunts:

"Huh! Huh!"

The bull, head down, shot forward, his two horns striking the horse's padded belly frontally, and, in the same instant, the picador's steel-tipped pick was rammed with brute force into the already mangled mass of oozing blood and hair of the bull's neck. The picador bore down, his face twisted with effort, and he screwed the pick in, piercing deep and turning it viciously left and right, jabbing downward, leaning his weight upon it. But the bull never wavered; he lifted both horse and man into the air, toppling them to the red sand that was already stained with redder splotches of blood.

A wild melee of men and beasts ensued. The bull was the center of the affray, following the frantically kicking horse, seeking the inert picador, butting ceaselessly, avid to sink his horns and kill. The matador and the banderilleros now converged upon the bull, coming within a yard of him, flapping their capes in his eyes. Momentarily blinded, the bull halted and looked about. Then he rushed after the floating and dissolving capes, snorting, hooking to left and right until he was in the center of the ring.

The picador was on his feet and was pulling his horse up; a stain of blood showed on the horse's belly. Quickly, the picador remounted, grabbed the long pole whose steel tip now dripped drops of blood, and ranged the horse's padded body parallel to and almost touching the wooden barrier; the picador knew that he needed support for the bull's next rush.

Once more the bull was seduced with trembling capes toward the picador and the padded horse. The banderilleros and the matador now retired to a distance and the bull, without hesitation and as though having suffered no wounds, lowered his head and attacked the horse once again, sending both man and horse slamming violently against the wooden barrier. But the picador's steel pick had again invaded that inferno of churning flesh and blood on the bull's humped back. The picador was off balance, but he leaned and threw his weight behind the pole, grinding it into the pulverized tendons; yet the bull rammed his head forward again and again. The bull reared; for a split second the picador was lifted off the horse, clinging to the pick like a pole vaulter, then he was pitched far and wide.

The crowd began to howl, protesting, disapproving, fearing that the bull was being punished too much, would be too weak to fight well. And, as thousands rose to their feet, shouting, the bugle sounded, signaling the end of the picador's work and the beginning of the artful drama of the bull and the lonely matador.

The men began to lead the picador and his blindfolded and limping horse away, but the bull was too roused to stand idle. He bellowed and went for the picador, who was now afoot, and the horse. Again the swirling, circling scarlet capes flapped in front of the bull, and the bull spun round and round, going for first one cape and then the other. He finally singled out a fleeing cape and chased the man who was manipulating it to the wooden barrier which lay but three yards directly below me. The man leaped the barrier to escape the bull, dropping the cape. The bull hooked the cape, tossing it on his horns, snorting, then, when the cape fell, he bent and sniffed it, then lifted his head. While the bull was standing baffled for that moment, I could see a tiny fountain of blood bubbling up out of the confusion of flesh of his humped neck—a tiny geyser of red that jutted up two inches high while a sheet of scarlet flooded down the bull's left side, coagulating in soft, tiny, irregular lumps in the bright sunshine. The bull now reared, lifting his two front legs, and tried to hurdle the barrier, his eyes glowing like the lights of hell and his distended nostrils flaring like a scream too terrible to be heard. The reporters and the photographers ducked for cover, scurrying left and right, seeking exits. And the people around me rose, screaming, shouting—already beginning to push and shove in panic. The bull's front hoofs were now resting atop the railing of the wooden barrier. The matador and his aids ran forward, yelling, shouting, hurling their capes at the beast, trying to bait him into turning and charging again.

I had stiffened when the bull had reared and placed his hoofs upon the barrier's railing, but I could not have moved had I tried, for the fat woman who sat directly in front of me and a few inches lower down had twisted her body about in convulsive terror and had flung her hands to her face, covering her eyes, and had pushed her face down into my lap, shuddering in horror. Stupefied, I stared down at her tumbling, glistening black locks and did not move.

A moment later she lifted her head and peeped out toward the ring, seeing that the bull had been enticed back from the barrier. She straightened, gave a little orgiastic moan, and turned her body toward the ring again, not saying a word. I doubt if she really knew what she had done. I sat awhile, filled with wonder. And then I felt as though I needed to go to confession. . . .

18 . . .

The matador was Chamaco. The bull now stood in the center of the ring, winded, his head down, his eyes balefully watching the vague movements of the men at the barrier. Across the red sand came a slender figure carrying a muleta and a sword under his left arm. The sun glinted softly on his suit of lights and his step was solemn, slow. With his chin almost on his chest, he walked toward the presidential box, stopped, looked up, bowed, then, following tradition, tossed his black hat to the red sand, and turned. He strode slowly along the barrier, his assistants following at a respectful distance.

Many people stood to get a full view of him. There was some handclapping. He gave a swift, enigmatic glance at the circular wall of faces and I was stupefied to see how young he really was; the contours of adolescence were still upon his dark, brooding face. Impulsively, I turned to the man who sat on my left and asked him in French:

"*Quel âge a-t-il?*"

"*Dix-neuf*," he said.

"*C'est un enfant*," I said.

"*Oui. Mais il est brave*," the man said, smiling at me. "You are American, yes?" he asked in English with a clumsy accent.

"Yes," I answered.

"I could tell by your clothes," he said. "America and Spain are friends, yes?" He patted my forearm.

I looked out to the red ring, pretending that I did not understand or hear him. Politics was the last thing on earth that I wanted to discuss at the moment.

"Friendship is a great thing, no?" he said.

"Tell me: why are all those machine guns here?" I asked him.

He was startled by my question, then laughed.

"For protection," he said.

"Whose protection?" I asked.

He looked at me and winked, then we both laughed.

"That boy is too young to risk his life that way," I said, bringing bullfighting to my rescue.

The man leaned toward me and said in a whisper: "Pain caused by a bull's horn is far less awful than pain caused by hunger. Understand?"

"Yes; I understand."

"That boy comes from a poor section of Spain, a town called Huelva, in Andalusia. He has a large family, many brothers and sisters. Two years ago he was starving; now he is almost rich."

"Yes."

"*C'est la vie*," he summed up, laughing.

"*Peut-être*," I murmured.

I resumed watching Chamaco, who was now strolling with downcast head toward the bull. The bull turned and faced him, eyeing him, immobile. I had seen that boy Chamaco rushing about the ring with the others; I had even noticed that he wore a suit of lights, but I had refused to believe that one so young was a full-fledged bullfighter. (In fact, technically speaking, Chamaco was not a full-fledged bullfighter. He was what was called a *novillero*, that is, a fighter of young bulls. But he had been fighting full grown bulls for a long time now and he was slated to take his *alternativa*, that is, his formal inauguration as a regular bullfighter, in the ring in Madrid, perhaps in 1956.)

He strode across the bloody sand and stopped at a spot about ten yards from the bull, who regarded him tensely, not moving. Then, without once glancing at the bull, Chamaco unfolded his muleta and took out his sword, as though he were at home pulling off his hat and coat to hang them up. He put the end of the spread muleta between his thighs, like a boy straddling a broomstick, making believe that it was a horse. The other end of the muleta now extended out, about a yard from his knees, the red folds dangling. His right hand held the sword, which he now inserted under the cloth so that the tip of the sword terminated at the point where the muleta ended and fell toward the sand. Until that moment he had been facing the bull; now he turned his left side to the bull and stared straight ahead, acting as though the bull did not exist.

The thousands of onlookers were profoundly quiet, watching. The bull advanced a step, lifting his head imperceptibly, studying this new phenomenon. Then, for the first time, Chamaco looked at the bull, his chin still on his chest. The bull trotted closer, looking, watching for movement. Chamaco's right hand now jiggled the sword ever so slightly and the outer fringes of the muleta fluttered a bit. The bull's head lifted sharply. He had seen that movement. Despite all the punishment he had taken, he was still able to send his horns through a man's body with a mere casual toss of his mammoth head; he could still kill.

The bull was at Chamaco's left. Chamaco was fronting the crowded stands, his slight figure draped in an attitude of indifference. Once more he twitched the far end of the muleta with the sword, making the folds in the cloth tremble. Chamaco was citing the bull's left eye, and was so gauging and calculating the bull's angle of attack that he knew exactly where the bull's right horn would pass and how deadly close.

The bull flew forward full tilt, seemingly certain now that he had at long last gotten his hated target on the beam. As he thundered forward, Chamaco moved the far end of the muleta slowly, slightly, lifting it, and the bull's right horn swept past, within inches of Chamaco's chest, his body rearing, and, as the muleta continued to float upward into the air, the bull finished his wild lunge with his head high, horns pointing skyward, both of his front legs extended, slanting upward in midair, and his entire mass was one vast ensemble of taut black muscle covered with bristling hair. Other than lifting his arms to raise the muleta, Chamaco had not moved.

As with one voice, thirty thousand throats sang out in a soft, slow burst: "*Ole!* (For God's sake!)"

It had been beautiful and awful and horrible and glorious, and ought to have been forbidden, for there had been something undoubtedly criminal about it. I shifted nervously on my slab of concrete to watch and wait for what would come next. My mouth hung open; I was revolted, but hungry for more. I was indignant, but bewitched, utterly.

The bull's wild leap ended and he settled to earth, turned; he now stood on Chamaco's right. Chamaco, without moving from his tracks, held the muleta in his right hand, waist high, about two feet from him, and the bull, without ceasing to move, came in for another charge, his horns this time sweeping past Chamaco's stomach, and, following the muleta, the bull rose to the height of Chamaco's shoulder, the force of the beast's effort making his forelegs shoot into the air while the muleta floated above his head.

"*Ole!*" the crowd sang with bated breath.

Man and beast had now become fused into one plastic, slow-moving, terrible, delicate waltz of death, the outcome of which hung upon the breath of a split second. The bull, now to Chamaco's left again, was turning, his tail swishing, readying himself to resume attack. Chamaco, still rooted to the spot, lowered the muleta till it dragged in the sand, the handle of the stick of the muleta being held close to his thigh. He held the muleta this time in his right hand and, as the bull came in, he swept it gently, slowly backward, round to his side. The bull, head down, hypnotized by the cloth, followed, hooking his horns past Chamaco's kneecaps. While the bull was in this low charge, Chamaco, pivoting slowly, advancing his left foot and pulling back his right, turned, still moving the muleta ahead of the bull's nose, luring the beast around him so that, when he whipped the muleta out of range of the bull's vision, the bull's horns were almost touching his knees, the beast having made a full circle around the man.

"*Ole!*" the mass chanted with fearful glee.

There was a dramatic pause. Chamaco hid the muleta behind him;

he was now two feet from the bull, looking directly down at it, not moving, his right hand lifted high into the air. The bull stared, outwitted, baffled.

Chamaco now stepped aside, disclosing the muleta which he now held in his left hand. The bull lowered his head, then looked at Chamaco, then at the cloth, at Chamaco, then at the cloth.

The stadium filled with murmurs. Everyone knew that the bull was now trying to choose between the man and the cloth. Had the beast learned the difference so quickly? Then the bull hurled himself at the cloth and a sigh went up. Chamaco swept the cloth gently around him until he was facing the middle of the bull's body, while the bull rushed until his horns were in back of the man. Chamaco shifted the cloth from his left to his right hand, and the bull was bound to his waist, still whirling, and at last his horns were almost scraping the back of Chamaco's calves.

"*Ole!*" the crowd sort of whispered its reaction, waiting.

Two feet out of line with the bull, Chamaco now stood with his back to the bull's horns. The muleta was held in his right hand, about a foot from his body. The bull moved. The cloth moved. Head and horns lifted violently, viciously, sweeping under Chamaco's elbow and into the air.

"*Ole!*" rolled from the tiers of jammed seats.

Chamaco now draped the cloth over the bull's nose and lured the beast toward his feet, then, as the bull, head down, followed, the cloth moved to the side and then to the rear of Chamaco. Chamaco's left hand now reached behind him, taking the cloth from his right hand, keeping it moving all the while, and the bull circled him once more, his head and horns at Chamaco's feet.

"*Ole!*" It was barely heard now.

With the muleta still in his left hand, Chamaco drew the bull round past him, floating the cloth, his back leaning backward over the bull's back. The bull's horns, ever seeking the cloth, now thrust past the retreating cloth and into the blinding sun, rushing past Chamaco's chest and his lifted arm, the beast's forelegs kicking skyward and his eyes round pools of frustrated fury.

"*Ole!*" It came crisp now; the crowd was sure that the man had mastered the bull.

Chamaco faced the bull, planted his feet in the sand, holding the muleta at his left side. The bull brushed past his left hip, his lunging head and horns lifting the muleta, his forelegs pawing the air.

"*Ole!*" the crowd sang.

The bull turned, always charging. Chamaco now extended his right arm behind his body so that the muleta jutted out from his left side. The bull leaped at it again, its horns grazing Chamaco's left side, rising in the air past Chamaco's shoulder, and the man stood gazing calmly at the madly lashing tail of the bull which was now directly under his eyes.

"*Ole!*" The voices now sounded like a prolonged sob.

Man and beast confronted each other. Chamaco, holding the muleta in his right hand, began a kind of slow, creeping movement with his feet, standing upright all the while, one toe thrusting out before the other, then the other. Standing still, the bull turned his head, his eyes following the ever-elusive cloth. Chamaco, shuffling one foot ahead of the other, completed half a circle about the bull, and his back was now to the barrier. Had the bull charged, he would have been killed, for he could not have escaped.

A sigh swept the stands. Men closed their eyes and moaned: "*Bravo hombre . . . !*"

On and on Chamaco turned, shuffling his feet in the sand; and the bull's eyes followed the cloth, his massive black and bleeding body turning. Chamaco returned to the original spot from which he had begun his creeping movement. The bull was mastered.

Soft handclapping swept the stands.

The bull now stood facing Chamaco, his eyes dazed, his four feet directly in line with his vast, heaving body, his head down. Chamaco was about six feet away. Suddenly you knew that the moment for the kill had come. (They call it "the moment of truth.")

Chamaco's left hand now grasped the muleta firmly; he turned away from the bull, looking at him sideways, letting the red cloth drop below his left knee. He now lifted his gleaming sword chin high and sighted along the length of it, pointing its sharp, steel tip at the tormented and bloody mound of wounds on the bull's back. Chamaco's left hand twitched the cloth, citing the bull. The bull saw it and charged. Chamaco charged, meeting the bull. But, as he moved toward the bull, his left hand swung the muleta farther leftward and his feet moved sharply to the right. The bull's horns rushed past his stomach as Chamaco tiptoed, leaning in and over the driving horns, and sent the sword to its hilt into the correct spot in the bull's body.

The bull halted, swayed. Chamaco stood watching him, gazing gently, sadly it seemed, into the bull's glazed and shocked eyes.

An uproar broke out in the stands. Almost everybody stood up, pulled out white pocket handkerchiefs and waved them, making the looming, circular stadium resemble a ripe cotton field being lashed by wind.

I watched the bull. He sagged, his eyes on his tormentor. He took an uncertain, hesitant step forward, and then was still. Chamaco lifted his right hand high above the bull's dying head; it was a gesture that had in it a mixture of triumph and compassion. The bull now advanced a few feet more on tottering legs, then his back legs folded and his hind part sank to the sand, his forelegs bent at the knees. And you saw the split second when death gripped him, for his head nodded violently and dropped forward, still. A heave shook his body as he gave up his breath and his eyes went blank. He slid slowly forward, resting on his stomach in the sand, his legs stretching straight out. He rolled over on his back, his four legs already stiffening in death, shot up into the air.

The man-made agony to assuage the emotional needs of men was over.

19 . . .

The dead bull's mutilated carcass was being hauled away over the sand by a team of galloping horses while thousands stood, applauding, marveling, waving handkerchiefs. An avalanche of gifts—ladies' handbags, men's hats, flowers, cigars, and packages of cigarettes—

rained down into the ring. Most of these were scooped up by Chamaco's aids and tossed laughingly back to their owners, only the flowers being kept.

For the daring manner in which he had played the bull and in recognition of the determination of his kill, Chamaco received an honorable award of the tail and a hoof of the animal who had died so bravely. With the tail in one hand and a hoof in the other, he trotted slowly around the ring to acknowledge his homage, his adolescent face still solemn and his black eyes holding a soft, inscrutable expression. I had the feeling that the boy did not quite believe in the value of what he had done, or maybe did not thoroughly understand it, and harbored some rejection or doubt about the Niagara of applause that deafened his ears. Anyway, he seemed detached from, and consciously outside, it all.

Contrary to popular belief, which has it that bullfighters are something like ballet dancers, bullfighting does not demand much muscular exertion, physical fitness, or strength, and its practice does not develop the body as football, basketball, baseball, or cricket does. Indeed, some of the most memorable bullfights ever witnessed in modern times were executed by a man almost too ill and too weak to stand upon his feet. That man was Juan Belmonte, perhaps the most intelligent, courageous, and perceptive of all the men who ever entered a ring to kill a bull. Belmonte has characterized bullfighting as being "fundamentally a spiritual exercise and not merely a sport. Physical strength is not enough."

But what is this mysterious "spiritual exercise" of which Belmonte speaks? It there something hidden here? If there is something hidden, why are bullfights enacted out in the open, before thousands of spectators? The answer is not often recognized even when one is directly confronted with it. It is the conquering of fear, the making of a religion of the conquering of fear. Any man with enough courage to stand perfectly still in front of a bull will not be attacked or killed by that bull. It has been known for a man to sit in the bullring in a chair reading a newspaper in front of the bull-pen gate. The gate was thrown open; the bull thundered out, stopped, gazed at the seated man, and trotted away. But to remain immobile when a beast of more than a thousand pounds is hurtling toward you is usually beyond human capacity.

Back in my room I dutifully performed my daily stint of reading Carmen's political catechism; I read lesson seventeen, for girls aged twelve to fourteen.

José Antonio

WHO WAS JOSÉ ANTONIO?

The founder of the Falange.

WHERE AND WHEN WAS HE BORN?

In Madrid, April 24, 1903.

WHAT WAS HE IN THE FAMILY?

The eldest of six.

MIGHT THE OTHERS HAVE BEEN INFLUENCED BY HIS CHARACTER?

Yes, perhaps, for due to his father's long absences, he was the leading light among his brothers.

WHERE WAS HIS FATHER?

Fighting the Moors.

WHAT WAS HE?

A soldier like his forebears.

MIGHT JOSÉ ANTONIO HAVE BEEN INFLUENCED BY HIS FAMILY'S MILITARY VOCATION AND THE HEROIC ATMOSPHERE THAT SURROUNDED HIS CHILDHOOD?

Perhaps, for he later considered life as warfare.

BUT WAS HE A SOLDIER?

No; he chose an intellectual profession.

WHICH?

That of Lawyer.

WAS THIS IN KEEPING WITH HIS CHARACTER?

Yes, on account of the intellectual power required to ask all the questions, and also because if it were not he would not have chosen it.

WHAT DOES THAT MEAN?

That he did not seek easy success, but the real heart of a matter.

WAS HE ALSO ATTRACTED BY POLITICS?

No, his real vocation was for study.

THEN WHY DID HE ENTER POLITICS?

Because circumstances obliged him to, though against his will.

WHAT CIRCUMSTANCES?

The fall of his father's government and the profanation of his memory after his death.

WHAT WAS HIS FATHER?

Head of the Dictator Government, 1923-30.

SO HOW DID JOSÉ ANTONIO'S POLITICAL LIFE BEGIN?

Asking for a seat in parliament to vindicate his father's memory.

THEN WHAT HAPPENED?

Without realizing it, he found himself at the head of a group that followed him.

DID HE THINK OF FOUNDING THE FALANGE THEN?

Perhaps. He thought of founding a political movement incorporating the youth to prevent the collapse of the country which was already speculating about the future.

WHAT DOES "SPECULATING" MEAN?

To foretell, to foresee.

AND WHY WAS THE COUNTRY DOING THIS?

Because, with the fall of the dictatorship, and the Monarchy, the collapse of the Republic which had, in a way, been every man's hope, there reigned in Spain only chaos and disorder.

WHY DID THE REPUBLIC COLLAPSE?

Because, instead of doing constructive work, it confined itself to hurting people's feelings.

EXPLAIN.

It scoffed at religion and this cut the Spaniards to the quick.

SO WHEN CAN WE SAY THAT JOSÉ ANTONIO FULLY ENTERED POLITICS?

A little before October 29, 1933, *when, with a group of university men and some army men, he decided to found the Falange.*

AND WAS HE HAPPY IN HIS NEW LIFE?

Happy, no. He was being forced by circumstances as he inwardly thought.

WHY?

Because, by inclination, he would have lived quietly far from the public eye.

WHAT DOES THIS MEAN?

He would have liked, like all men, to love a woman as she should be loved and share a quiet, sweet, and Christian life with her.

WHY DIDN'T HE?

Because, according to him, "We have been touched by the destiny of war into which we must throw ourselves heart and soul."

SO, WE CAN SAY THAT JOSÉ ANTONIO WAS A HERO?

Yes, for he voluntarily abandoned all the pleasures of life to place that life in the service of a great cause.

WAS HE BRAVE AND STEADFAST IN WHAT HE DID?

He was brave and calm, without boasting, as the leader of a spiritual movement should be.

WHAT DOES "WITHOUT BOASTING" MEAN?

Without arrogance, presumption.

WOULD THIS NOT HAVE COME FROM HIS MILITARY BACKGROUND?

Again, perhaps, for since his childhood he had learned to prize dignity and honor.

WHEN DID HE DIE?

November 20, 1936, *murdered by the Reds in the prison at Alicante.*

HOW DID HE DIE?

Preparing his soul to give God an account of his life, as a good Christian should, and with our cry, "Spain—arise!"

HOW OLD WAS HE WHEN HE FELL?

Thirty-three, and he died like so many other comrades to whom he had taught that death in the Falange was the only act of service.

WHERE DOES HIS BODY REST?

In the monastery of the Escorial, harmonious and beautiful as the Spain he loved.

20 . . .

Next morning at five o'clock, I paid my rent bill, shook hands with Dolores, her mother, and Lola, and bade them good-by.

The sky was still black. I put my motor in gear and headed toward Madrid. I found the streets on the outskirts of Barcelona bathed in darkness and cluttered with a never-ending procession of rickety, wooden carts drawn by donkeys. Perched atop or walking beside each cart were long files of men, women, and children accompanied by dogs. The carts were heaped high with vegetable produce that they were taking to market.

As darkness waned I climbed slowly into craggy hills that gave way to mountains bathed in blue mist. The air grew so cold that I had to stop my car and put on my topcoat. I ascended a high mountain peak and lo! it was day, full and bright and streaming from behind a high, rocky horizon. Light was pouring into the world like a flood of shining water, but in the plunging valleys far below there were dark islands of mist and cloud. I mounted dizzy peaks and had to slow down to thirty kilometers an hour, for the road slanted and curved while skirting sheer precipices. I passed leaning trucks stacked so high with bales of hay that I thought that they would topple over onto my car.

A brutal sun burst forth from behind jagged, fantastically sculptured rocks and painted the wildest and most savage landscape that I had ever seen. Naked promontories of rubble jutted up into a pale, flat, blue sky that refused to bend at the horizon. An uneasy loneliness settled upon me, for I drove hour after hour and failed to see a single other car. The highway was an empty path stretching through an empty world, belonging only to me, the desolate peaks, the sun-filled sky, and the whirling birds. There were no signs whatever of industrial or farm life and when, later, I did see a rare smokestack, black or red, lost and lonely in the scaly hills, it resembled an exclamation point, emphasizing how far Spain had fallen to the rear of her sister European nations.

I passed vast, high, flat, surrealistically shaped mounds of red laterite whose ancient geological formation brought to mind images of tidal waves, volcanic upheavals of the earth's crust, and the cosmic force of tearing winds—for only actions of so superhuman a nature could have carved out these gigantic sweeps of erosion. The scene was magnificent, but for aesthetic enjoyment only; one could not conceive of its sustaining human life.

Then came brown hills, red lands, russet-gray vineyards, dun-colored olive groves with here and there a flick of green thrusting through. Scrubby trees struggled to grow on gruesome mountain-tops. It was a melancholy world with a spell of sadness haunting it.

Each little village of squat, clay-colored houses was different from the last, yet somehow they were all alike, clinging precariously to the slopes of bleak and crumbly mountains, each having the same general coloring as the niche in which it nestled, partaking of the tint of soil around it. Ofttimes I was almost upon a fairly large town or village and could not see it until I could discern the outlines of its cathedral or town hall, and then, like magic, a whole new world would miraculously disclose itself.

21 . . .

I entered the grim precincts of Guadalajara just as a blood-red sun was setting. I rolled slowly through its narrow, mean streets, giving the place a once-over, admiring the stalwart, scarlet hills, now turning purple and black, that ringed the town like a fortress. It was vulgar-looking and the adjective "beautiful" could never possibly be applied to it. Even though it was nearing twilight and an awful pall of heat hung in the air, the people looked so silent and subdued and the streets were so quiet that you felt that something was wrong. I saw more than what I felt was the usual number of Civil Guards hugging their black machine guns and I had to admit that the Franco regime was not at all shy in its dictatorship; it made no bones of the fact that its rule was based on naked force.

I picked out a retiring, sedate, yet modern-looking hotel just off the main thoroughfare and entered to register. But it took me more than an hour to get my room, for I walked smack into the middle of one of the most typical of Spanish dramas.

At the front desk in the hotel office stood some nine or ten people engaged in a violent verbal battle, shouting, waving arms in passionate gestures, and banging fists upon the top of the desk. Two of the disputants were policemen with shining badges upon their chests. A greasy-faced fat man with a vast, ballooning stomach and a dark, dour pair of eyes was obviously the proprietor; and the woman standing stoutly at his side, all fat bosom and neck and arms, with her palms planted defiantly upon her hips, and with a flamingly indignant face, was, no doubt, his wife. There was an obsequious, hawk-faced man in a blue denim uniform whom I took to be the hotel porter, and the tall, raw-boned woman with the defeated-looking eyes and the white dress was, of course, the hotel maid. Two other men who might have been plain-clothes policemen or guests stood watching grimly in the background. That left a tall, blond young man who stood silently at the side of an olive-skinned young woman who was now declaiming Spanish in a loud and angry voice. Just what the fracas was about I could not tell; but, when the girl had completed her shouted oration, there was an explosion of vehement objections on the part of the proprietor and his wife.

"*No, Señorita!*"

"*Jamás aquí!* Never here!"

"*Nunca!* Never!"

"*Imposible!* Impossible!"

The tall, blond young man detached himself from the group and walked toward the doorway in which I stood, rubbing his hands over his face in a nervous gesture and exclaiming in English: "Good Lord!"

"Are you American?" I asked him.

"No. English," he muttered.

"What's the trouble?"

"I really don't quite know," he sighed. "I don't speak Spanish. Do you?"

"I have only a few words," I told him. "Does the young lady speak English?"

"She's Spanish," he explained, "and she knows no English." He winked at me. "We don't communicate on *that* level," he said cynically. "You see, we're not married and—"

At that moment the proprietor bellowed something about "Gibraltar . . ."

The young Englishman whirled, shouting: "Stop talking to me about Gibraltar! I've nothing to do with Gibraltar! Take that up with my government!"

I had thought that the discussion was about sex, and now it had veered toward politics. The Englishman turned to me, explaining; "They're mad. They're condemning me for keeping Gibraltar."

It was so funny that I laughed out loud, an act which at once drew unfavorable attention to my presence.

A lynx-eyed officer stepped forward, confronted me, and demanded: "*Pasaporte!*"

Since my country had nothing whatever to do with that huge pebble of Gibraltar, I surrendered my passport with a light heart. He glanced through it, then eyed me dirtily, ardently longing to find me guilty of something. He rudely shoved my passport back into my hands and rejoined the verbal war raging at the desk.

"I wouldn't make an issue of it," I advised the young man. "Moral jitters of this sort have been known to happen in London, you know."

"Yes. But we don't insult girls there like they do here," he complained.

"Brother, this is the land of the Virgin," I informed him. "The law is dead against sin here."

The two policemen now seized hold of both of the girl's arms and jerked her violently toward the door. It was the first time I had seen the girl's face; she was pretty in a rough, tartish way—slender, muscular, with brown hair and flashing gray eyes. Her face was livid and she was screaming. The Englishman gallantly stepped forward.

"*Por qué?*" he demanded, blocking the way with his long, outstretched arms.

"*Contrabando!*" the policemen shouted in return, sweeping his arms aside.

The girl was trying desperately to calm the Englishman, fearing that he might get himself into serious trouble if he interfered with the operations of Spanish law. She kept shaking her head at him and repeating: "No, no . . . *Nada, nada* . . . *Quédase tranquilo* . . . *Un momento*. . . . Nothing, nothing . . . Stay quiet . . . a moment . . ."

"They are accusing her of black-market activities," I told the Englishman.

"But that's crazy!" he shouted, beside himself. "She hasn't done anything!"

"*Contrabando!*" the policeman shouted at the girl.

"No! No!" the girl screamed. She lurched out of their grasp and stood in the center of the room. "*No contrabando!*" she shouted. She straddled her legs and clapped her right hand hard upon her dress, seizing hold of her vagina through the cloth. "*Contrabando? Sí, Señor! Sí, sí, sí,*" she repeated harshly. "*Contrabando? Sí, sí . . . Nada más!* Nothing more!"

She had been so brutally direct that she had made herself more naked than if she had ripped off her clothes. The proprietor's wife paled with anger, crossed herself and rolled her black, bulbous eyes toward Heaven. Even the maid shook her head, shocked. The policemen stared in triumph around the room, their facial expressions saying:

"See! What brazen a creature she is!"

The Englishman's face burned red. As the policeman dragged the shouting girl away, I caught a glimpse of a golden medallion of the Virgin about her throat.

"Er . . . Just where did you meet that girl?" I asked him.

"I picked her up in San Sebastián," he confessed. "We've been traveling together ever since. We've put up at one hotel after another. But this is the first time we've had any trouble. I drove up in my car about half an hour ago," he explained. "We registered and no one said anything. We went to our room. Then we were summoned downstairs and confronted with these policemen."

One of the policemen re-entered the room and jabbered to the porter, who took down a key from a board and handed it over.

"They are opening the door of our room," the Englishman said, outraged. "They are going to search our bags."

"Don't they need a warrant for that?" I asked.

"Evidently they don't, here in Spain," he said.

Yet, the religious assumptions here are correct and consistent; if sin is suspected, you certainly have the moral right to seek it out; for how can sin be punished unless it can be found?

"Do you have anything illegal in your bags?" I asked him.

"I've nothing illegal but the girl," he said.

He looked to be about twenty-six or -seven and perhaps this was the first time in all of his short young life that he had ever had a whole, live woman all to himself and he was in trouble about it. But he was manfully standing his ground. I surmised that he had come hopefully from his fogbound, puritanical England, carrying a headful of illusions about a sunny, sensual, liberal, and forgiving Spain. . . .

I approached the desk and at once the hotel owner began explaining his side of the argument. I listened patiently, understanding but little of the rigmarole. I glanced at Franco's photo on a wall above the desk and I was surprised at the severity of the dictator's mien; if the proprietor had selected this particularly icy version of his demigod's face, then it showed that the poor English boy did not have a dog's chance. I registered and the maid escorted me chastely to the door of my room.

I had dinner in a little restaurant on the main street, then wandered about a bit. It seemed that half of the local citizens were on parade, marching slowly to and fro, arm in arm, reaching the end of the street and then turning and retracing the distance that they had covered. They moved quietly, talking in low voices, their eyes glancing at random—men, women, and children. I recalled the brutal faces of those policemen in the hotel office and I understood why these people walked here so aimlessly, hour after hour. There was nothing else for them to do!

I went to my room, took a stiff drink out of a bottle, and settled in bed and began to read Carmen's political catechism, turning to lesson five:

For Girls Ten To Twelve Years of Age—The Concept of Tradition

WHAT DO WE UNDERSTAND BY TRADITION?

The knowledge we have of things past.

WHAT IS ITS USE?

To know what our ancestors did.

WHAT ELSE?

To know what we can do in the future, basing ourselves on what they did.

SO PAST DEEDS CAN BE OF HELP TO US?

Yes, for they do not obey the laws of chance, but historical constants.

WHAT DOES "HISTORICAL CONSTANTS" MEAN?

The permanent reasons a nation acts upon in the world.

ARE ALL HISTORICAL CONSTANTS THE SAME FOR ALL NATIONS?

No, for some have to influence others and others to be influenced.

HAS THIS ALWAYS BEEN SO?

Yes, because it depends on the character and way of life of each people, which is invariable.

IN WHAT CATEGORY IS SPAIN?

Among those who influence others.

HOW DO WE KNOW THIS?

Because history and tradition tell us so.

SO OF WHAT USE IS TRADITION TO US?

It helps us to know that Spain has much to do in the world, since we know by history and tradition that it achieved much in other ages.

WHEN WAS THAT?

At all times from when it provided Rome with writers and rulers, but especially in the age beginning with the Catholic Kings and ending with Philip II.

WHAT DOES A NATION SEEK WHEN IT INFLUENCES OTHERS?

Its historical plenitude or empire.

SO, IF SPAIN ONCE ACHIEVED IMPERIAL PLENITUDE, WILL SHE BE ABLE TO REGAIN IT?

Yes, if she can follow the rule of her historical constants.

WHAT HAPPENS TO A COUNTRY THAT DOES NOT FOLLOW ITS HISTORICAL CONSTANTS?

It loses sight of its destiny and even of the possibility of existence.

WHY?

Because it will be governed by other countries.

SO WHAT MUST SPAIN DO TO FIND THE ROAD OF HISTORICAL DESTINY?

The same as those who succeeded in the age of Spain's historical plenitude.

IN THE SAME WAY?

No, because times have changed.

SO WHAT MUST BE DONE?

We must try to guess what our ancestors would do if they lived now and do it ourselves.

WHY?

Because tradition, as José Antonio says: ". . . is not a state but a process, and for nations as for men it is difficult to walk backward and return to childhood."

WHAT DOES THAT MEAN?

"That we must look at tradition not to imitate it, but to guess what our great ancestors would have done, were they alive."

WHY?

Because there is no doubt that they found the way for Imperial Spain.

BUT CAN WE TODAY USE THE SAME FORMULAE AS YESTERDAY?

The same formulae but not the same processes.

HOW IS THIS?

Because formulae are the invariable in the characteristics of our country and the processes are what are required by each different age.

22 . . .

Next morning, when I descended to the dining room for breakfast, I saw the Englishman and his Spanish sweetheart seated peacefully at a table.

"May I join you?" I asked him, nodding to the young lady, who had large, dark rings under her restless gray eyes.

"Please do," he said, motioning to a chair.

I sat and ordered coffee.

"Looks like things came out all right," I commented with a smile. "What happened? Did they take her to jail?"

"No," he laughed. "They were suspicious about us and they were fishing. Their denouncing us for sleeping together was a false alarm. They thought that we were black marketeers. But they had no evidence and could find none. You see, the laws here are tricky. I've found that every law can be used for four or five different things. An accusation here for any one thing can serve as a cloak for something else. They wanted to look into our bags, but they began by accusing us of breaking moral laws. When they saw that that wouldn't stick, they switched to the real aim. . . . Oh, they went through our things, all right. God knows what they were really looking for. Then they wanted to know if I had been in Spain before, if I had taken part in the Civil War—"

"But you were too young for that," I said.

"Of course," he said. "They just wanted to look us over. We hadn't violated any law; they got us before we had a chance to. We hadn't been to bed. But they refused to let her sleep in my room. I had to engage a separate room for her. So, this morning, about one or thereabouts, I went to her room and spent the night. No one was looking or watching. Now, everybody's happy."

"And you promised to return the Rock of Gibraltar?" I asked him, laughing.

"Not so that you could notice it," he said.

23 . . .

There was no vast, black, girting belt of tumbling industrial suburbs circling Madrid that one had to traverse before entering the city proper—sooty, smoky suburbs such as too often mar the approach to great world capitals. From Guadalajara one streaked over a smooth macadam highway past barren and dusty stretches of red and yellow clay and then suddenly one saw tall apartment buildings of reinforced concrete, new, glistening structures shaped modernistically, all angles and clean, plunging lines, six and seven stories high, their façades tan, yellow, blue—running the gamut of pastel shades.

The sun, a seething disk of brass, blazed brutally down from a sky shorn of all clouds. It was the kind of sky that made one thoughtful; I had never seen a sky whose infinite immensity so dominated the finiteness of human dwellings. I cruised through magnificent, tree-guarded, flower-bordered boulevards that were lined with roomy mansions whose metal shutters were already closed—it was nearing noon—against the dry and searing heat. The tires of my car made a soft, whirring hum that seemed to blend with the air of an arrogantly restrained bourgeois Madrid.

This city surpassed Barcelona in the sumptuousness and splendor of its imposing ministries, its quiet, gleaming museums, its bubbling fountains, and its proud, ornate monuments, but, as in Barcelona, I had to exercise caution to keep from running down chickens, goats, and sheep in the center of the city just a few blocks from some of the world's most luxurious hotels. I passed four slovenly-dressed young men sauntering abreast down the middle of one of the main, busy streets caroling flamenco songs at the top of their tremulous voices to the accompaniment of a twanging guitar, and I was surprised because no one else was surprised.

Shoeshine boys, those inevitable heralds of endemic poverty, clogged the sidewalks. I could see no sign whatever of factories, of mills, of industrial activity. I discovered later that Madrid had no real *raison d'être*, that it had been designated as the capital centuries earlier merely because of its central location. It was not really a city at all, but an enforced conglomeration of bureaus of the Army, the Church, the State, and the Falange—an administrative unit out from which the main arteries of the nation fanned to distant hamlets, like the spokes of a wheel radiating out from its hub.

24 . . .

That evening I settled in a dingy pension and, next day, directly after lunch, I waited in the British-American Club to keep an appointment with a young American bullfighter, Harry Whitney, who had promised to allow me to accompany a team of bullfighters scheduled to perform before an audience of peasants in a village near Madrid.

Whitney was a singular man, a blue-eyed, blond, six-foot Texan of twenty-eight years of age. He had a grave manner, a firm, almost tight mouth, and a diffident air that concealed a volatile reserve of emotion. In his dark suit, he looked more like a student of divinity than a killer of bulls.

"You'll see the real thing this afternoon," he told me. "Let's get rolling and pick up the others."

An opportunity to act as a chauffeur to bullfighters was more than I had hoped for. Whitney directed me through narrow streets to an apartment building on the outskirts of the city, where four Spaniards were waiting upon the sidewalk beside huge, clumsy bundles of bullfighting gear. Having two cars at our disposal, it was decided to pile the bullfighting equipment into one car so that the bullfighters could ride with me. Whitney introduced me to the men.

The team was composed of father and son, both well-known matadors. There were two banderilleros. Whitney was going along to substitute for one of the others should an accident occur. There was no picador; small villages could not afford to engage them. They were an affable, polite lot, deferential yet poised toward a visiting stranger. They were dressed in casual sport clothes and each had a medallion of the Virgin dangling in the V of his open shirt collar.

We rolled into parched and dusty country, our destination being Morata de Tajuña, a village some twenty-seven kilometers distant. Almost at once we were in a range of bald mountains. There was not a single tree, no colors except dull tones of brown, gray, white —even the scrubby grass was a faded yellow. Buzzards circled slowly in the still, hot sky. The air was so dry that it seared the mucous membrane of the nostrils.

"Do you mind talking about yourself?" I asked Whitney, who sat beside me.

"Not at all," he said.

"You're a university man?" I asked him.

"Yes. I spent two years at Brown. I graduated from Syracuse in journalism," he informed me.

"You're single?"

"Yes."

"War veteran?"

"Yes. I was a bomber pilot."

"Were you on many missions?"

"Yes. Mostly over Germany."

"Why did you come to Spain?"

"To learn bullfighting," he told me.

"Now, Whitney, just lean back and tell me why you fight bulls," I said.

It was an exacting demand, but I felt that Whitney was intelligent and could take it. As we rolled slowly over the treacherous, twisting road, I observed Whitney out of the corners of my eyes and could see him reacting strongly. He brushed his right hand over his wavy, blond hair and said in a low voice:

"Only a few people really understand bullfighting. Hemingway has described the technical side of it, but not the emotional. . . . There's one man who knows what it's all about. He's Juan Belmonte—"

"I've read him," I said. "You think he's right?"

"Definitely."

"What do you feel out there in the ring?" I asked him.

"When I'm out there facing a charging bull and hearing that crowd yelling: '*Ole!*', I could stand still and let that bull gore me—"

"Stand still and *let* it happen?"

"Yes," he said emphatically. "I become sort of drunk with it. I feel the bull in my power. That's how many bullfighters get killed."

"Some people think that bullfighting is akin to ballet dancing," I told him.

Whitney bent double with laugher, then stared off, amused.

"A ballet dancer would be killed in thirty seconds in a bullring," he said. "I don't know why ballet dancers wear tight-fitting costumes, but we bullfighters wear tight-fitting uniforms for protection. They are made of tough silk. Now, silk won't keep a bull from goring you, but many times the bull's horn will glance off and not penetrate. . . . Listen, we bullfighters do not seek to move gracefully. Our movements in the bullring are dictated by the bull and the bull only. The essence of the bullfight is not in moving around, but in standing still. And that's a hard thing to do. When you're holding that muleta and facing a bull, your instinct prompts you to run. And if you do, you're dead, for the bull can outrun you. You must plant your feet in the sand and face death. The slow movements in the ring are designed *not* to attract the attention of the bull. . . ."

"With whom does the spectator identify when he's watching a bullfight?" I asked him.

"There are two sets of identifications," he told me. "One is with the bull and the other is with the matador. It's only when the spectator can make the two identifications at once that the bullfight is really experienced—"

"You are acting *for* the spectators?" I asked.

"In a way, yes."

"Has it ever occurred to you that your bullfight costume is very similar to the vestments of a priest?" I asked him.

"You're getting close to it," he said, groping for words. "The bullfight has the intensity of religious emotion. You offer your life to the bull. Without that, there is no bullfight."

"Tell me a little about the world that produces bullfighters," I urged him.

"You're getting at the heart of it," Whitney said. "If you think that what goes on in the bullring is awful, then what happens before one gets into the bullring is indescribable. Novels have romanticized the lives of bullfighters. Their lives are sheer misery; most of those who want to fight bulls never reach the bullring. They starve. They live from hand to mouth. They are not supposed to touch women or liquor. This is not to help you in fighting the bull; it is to keep you in condition to recuperate when you are gored. And make no mistake, you will be gored. I was gored soon after I started fighting and I'm glad it happened, for now I know what it feels like."

"How many times have you fought bulls?"

"I've had sixteen fights; I've killed twenty-six bulls," he said. "I'm beginning, you know."

"Do bulls dislike red?" I asked him.

"Bulls are color blind," he told me. "They'll charge the nearest moving object."

"How many bullfighters are there in Spain?" I asked him. "What is the setup?"

"There are about thirty-five hundred bullfights each year in Spain," he related. "We have about nine hundred eighty bullfighters and we belong to a bullfighters' union which has as its duty the protection of the bullfighters' interests and the promotion of bullfighting.

"Now, here is what makes bullfighting hard as a profession. Of the nine hundred eighty bullfighters, there are about sixty famous ones. Naturally, the public wants to see these famous ones continuously in action. But, if each of the nine hundred eighty bullfighters got their fair share of the thirty-five hundred bullfights, they would fight about three and a half times a year. But what really happens? The sixty famous bullfighters fight eighteen hundred times, which leaves seventeen hundred bullfights to be scattered among nine hundred twenty bullfighters. A young man aspiring to be a bullfighter, no matter how zealously he is trying to toss his life away, has almost got to starve to do so."

"How did you, an American, become a bullfighter?" I asked him at last.

He looked at me and smiled bitterly.

"My life has been hard," he said. "I've had many disappointments. I didn't care what happened to me. So I decided to fight bulls."

"Who is really the wild beast in the ring?" I asked him.

"It's the audience," he confessed. "Bulls don't kill bullfighters. It's the public clamoring for danger. More and more, when you're in the ring, you're not fighting the bull; you're trying to live up to the legend the public has built up about you. They ask for risks and they boo you when you refuse to take them. When the bullfighter believes in his legend and tries to obey the crowd, he's on his way to the graveyard."

"Why does the public clamor for blood?" I asked him.

"I try not to think about that," he said softly.

"By the way, are you religious, Whitney?" I asked.

"No," he answered.

"What do your Spanish colleagues think of your lack of religion?"

"At first they couldn't believe it," he told me. "But when they found that I'd share their lives, they accepted it. They think I'm a little boy who'll finally grow up someday; and, of course, when I grow up, they think I'll naturally be Catholic."

We came to a stop in the middle of a village square covered with yellow sand. At once hundreds of astonished peasants poured, shouting and screaming, out of their homes, cafés, and bars to stare at us. Amidst these naïve yokels I became something that I had never been before, an object that was neither human nor animal, my dark skin and city clothes attracting more attention than even the bullfighters. I was stared at with a kind of fearful, blank, absorbed curiosity that one reserves for the unheard-of, the unnatural, the fantastic. The squat, big-breasted, broad-hipped young women seemed especially struck by me, gazing as though hypnotized at my face, nudging their friends in the ribs with their elbows.

The sandy village square had obviously been built some centuries before with but one thought in mind: bulls. For that square was really only a kind of crude, permanent bullring. Numerous thick, hand-hewn beams of heavy hardwood had been driven like stakes down through the yellow sand and into the clay, forming a rough blockade on the square's four sides, obscuring the dingy façades of the meat markets, wine shops, grocery stores, and even the delicate Gothic entrance of the local church. The heavy beams had been spaced some eighteen inches or so apart so that the body of a normal-sized man could easily squeeze through, but the spaces were small enough to keep out the body of a bull.

In the afternoon heat, colored pennants hung limp from the façade of the city hall and the fronts of stores and houses were decked out in gay bunting. Flies as big as the thumb buzzed and sang everywhere, alighting on the bloody bullfighting capes, trying to suck nourishment from the dried blood clots. Franco's Civil Guards, now an organic part of the Spanish landscape, were planted at intervals with their efficient machine guns. As we unloaded the bullfighting equipment, barefooted boys stood entranced, their mouths opened wide.

Almost everybody was wearing black or green or red paper hats. Little girls stalked to and fro in their starched dresses, waving wooden rattles that made a throbbing sound. Little boys blew whistles, setting off a hurricane of noise. The older men sat on café terraces playing cards or dominoes or drinking beer. The women, dressed in black, sat in seats high above the bullring, fanning themselves, waiting for the commencement of the excitement of blood and death. Amidst all of this strode the men of the Church, carrying their unquestioned authority and power proudly, huge silver crosses bobbing on their black-robed chests. And from a spot high on the front of the city hall a gigantic photo of the ever-watching Franco, now somewhat benign of visage, surveyed his quaint domain.

We entered a café to wash the dust out of our throats; I drank beer, but the bullfighters sipped only a little water, observing a tradition that stipulated that they could not eat or drink until after they had killed their bulls. The blaring music of a band made us rise and rush out. Musicians clad in dark blue were marching into the bullring and children followed them, clapping their hands, laughing, rolling their eyes, and cutting capers with their naked feet in the sand.

The time had come for the bullfighters to don their complicated suits of lights and I was honored by being invited to watch them. Whitney warned me in a whisper: "This is a serious moment. Just sit, look, and say nothing."

A "dressing room" had been set aside for them on the first floor of the city hall. The suits of lights were elaborate, traditional affairs. Five men were dressing and they had to pause frequently to help one another, for it was almost impossible for them to dress alone, so heavy and tight-fitting was the gear. They stripped down to their underwear and I saw that their bodies were a mass of mangled tissue, scars and gashes from previous gorings. First, they struggled into narrow-legged trousers of raw silk brocaded with gold and adorned with tassels. Next they buttoned pleated and ruffled white shirts and tied little black bowties. Then came pink silk stockings, two pairs of them, one being put on over the other in the hope that a bull's horn would glide harmlessly off the leg. . . .

"You'll notice," Harry whispered to me, "that we follow a strict routine in dressing. We always put on our suits of clothes in the order that you have observed."

"Why?"

"Custom," he said.

"What happens if a bullfighter is wounded?" I asked him. "You are laced and strapped like a knight of the Middle Ages," I told him. "How on earth could a doctor get at a wound with all that regalia strapped to the body?"

"A doctor'd have to cut this stuff off of us if we were wounded," he said. "If he tried to undress us, we would bleed to death before he could get to the wound. . . ."

It took them more than an hour to dress and, when they were finished, they were forced to move about with stiff, almost slow movements, so bound and buckled were they. Then, from out of a box, they took a flat package done up in crumpled, brown wrapping paper; they untied it and spread out a two-flapped photo which, when perched upon a table, proved to be a colored image of the Virgin. One by one, they all, excepting Whitney, went and knelt before it, closing their eyes and praying silently. They crossed themselves, then rose. Without a word being uttered, they gathered up their capes, muletas, and swords and marched directly toward the bullring. I ran to the balcony to see them enter.

It was not an emotional bullfight, but some odd and revealing things did occur. The bulls were not good and they had to be run and played long and violently to get them to lower their heads, for there were no picadors to punish the humps of muscle in the bulls' powerful necks.

The first bull bounded into the ring to wild cheers. He was an unruly beast, often refusing to charge and, when he did charge, he did so at the wrong time, hooking viciously. When the matador finally killed him, hundreds of men and boys squeezed through the spaces in the stockade and swarmed onto the sand of the ring and converged upon the dead bull's carcass. Then something happened that made my lips part in total astonishment. The crowd went straight to the dead bull's testicles and began kicking them, stomping them, spitting at them, grinding them under their heels, while their eyes held a glazed and excited look of sadism. They mutilated the testicles of the dead bull for more than ten minutes, until the dead bull's carcass was hauled away.

And the same strange, sadistic ceremony was inflicted by the excited crowd upon the second dead bull's testicles—there were only three bulls killed that afternoon—and they did not cease until the dead bull's carcass had been taken from them. One would have to be psychologically blind to miss the meaning of that. They went straight to the real object on that dead bull's body that the bull had symbolized for them and poured out the hate and frustration and bewilderment of their troubled and confused consciousnesses.

I was later told that in some backward villages the men and the women smeared their faces and bodies with the blood of the dead bull, hoping thereby to gain potency or be cured of various diseases, particularly tuberculosis. In many backward areas the meat of the ceremoniously slain bull commanded a higher price than that of ordinary beef.

I went to my pension for a nap, but could not sleep. I lay in bed and studied the Falangist political catechism, reading lesson ten for girls between the ages of twelve and fourteen:

The Moral Revolution

WHY MUST THERE BE A MORAL REVOLUTION?

Because political and economic revolution would be useless without it.

WHY?

Because there can be no reform without man being reformed.

HOW SO?

Because men make revolutions and no one can effectively serve what he neither knows nor loves.

WHAT THEN DOES THE FALANGE UNDERSTAND BY MORAL REVOLUTION?

The new understanding man must be given so that he can serve efficiently and with discipline the cause of his country.

HOW WILL THIS UNDERSTANDING BE GRASPED?

By knowing Falangist truths.

ONCE THEY ARE KNOWN, HOW CAN THEY BE SERVED?

By voluntarily subjecting one's life to discipline and obedience.

THEN WHAT WILL FOLLOW?

We shall reach the conviction that "in each of our acts, in the most familiar of our acts, in the most humble of our daily tasks, we are serving on a par with our own modest individual destiny, the destiny of Spain and Europe and the world, the total harmonious destiny of Creation."

WITHIN THIS MORAL REVOLUTION WILL NOT THERE BE SOME WHO GIVE THEMSELVES MORE COMPLETELY TO THE SERVICE OF THEIR COUNTRY?

Yes, the Falangists.

WHO ARE THEY?

As has been said, those who voluntarily join the Falange and acquire a "way of life" for the rest of their lives.

THE UNDERGROUND CHRIST

25 . . .

Q. *Are these doctrines [Protestantism] not worse in a certain sense, than those of the pagans?*

A. *You are right; many pagan doctrines are far less impious.*

Q. *Are the propagators of Protestantism trying to spread Socialism and Communism?*

A. *That is the sole reason for all their painstaking efforts. Protestantism is nothing but a vague voice, a negation of the true religion; this is why it suits them best for the purpose of covering up their designs whose aim is nothing else but the destruction of society.*

Catechism on Protestantism, by
Juan Perrone, S.J., Barcelona, 1950

The average Spaniard knows nothing of Protestantism; does not know what a Protestant is; has never, to his knowledge, met one; and would stare with more bewilderment than hostility if he heard someone declare that he was Protestant. And even the Spanish intellectual feels confused and uneasy when the subject of Protestantism is mentioned.

The official Spanish attitude toward Protestantism is, however, a completely different matter. That attitude is reflected in the daily practices and policies of the Church and State. The officials of the

Spanish Church and State know what Protestantism is; they have dealt with Protestants; and they are intimately acquainted with the philosophy and attitude toward life behind Protestantism. Protestantism, according to the Catholic Church, is rank heresy, a mortal sin, and, since the State of Spain is buttressed and supported by the Church, each government official, being naturally a devout Catholic, feels that it is his bounden duty to abhor, defeat, and banish Protestantism when and wherever he meets it.

I was born a Protestant. I lived a Protestant childhood. But I feel more or less toward that religion as Protestants in Spain feel toward Catholicism. What I felt most keenly in Spain was the needless, unnatural, and utterly barbarous nature of the psychological suffering that the Spanish Protestant was doomed to undergo at the hands of the Church and State officials and his Catholic neighbors. For that exquisite suffering and emotional torture, I have a spontaneous and profound sympathy.

I am an American Negro with a background of psychological suffering stemming from my previous position as a member of a persecuted racial minority. What drew my attention to the emotional plight of the Protestants in Spain was the undeniable and uncanny psychological affinities that they held in common with American Negroes, Jews, and other oppressed minorities. It is another proof, if any is needed today, that the main and decisive aspects of human reactions are conditioned and are not inborn.

Indeed, the quickest and simplest way to introduce this subject to the reader would be to tell him that I shall describe some of the facets of psychological problems and the emotional sufferings of a group of *white Negroes* whom I met in Spain, the assumption being that Negroes are Negroes because they are *treated* as Negroes.

As dusk was falling one evening, friends of mine, L. and Z., directed me to drive out along a road leading to a small town two hundred kilometers distant from Madrid. We were going to meet a woman who had a story to tell. Upon our arrival we stopped at a café and Z. made a phone call and it was decided that my woman informant would meet us in a small park bordering a river. It was a hot night and the air was heavy. A wan moon shone in a blue-black sky. We arrived before the mysterious woman and had a dinner of sorts, sitting at tables under the trees eating fried-fish sandwiches and olives out of paper bags and gurgling tepid, foamy beer from bottles.

"Look," I said to Z., "our meeting this lady in an outdoor spot like this—does that mean that she's afraid of being followed or something?"

"It's for her protection," Z. told me.

"Is she being watched all the time?" I asked.

"Why don't you determine that after you have heard her story?" Z. suggested.

I smiled and fell silent. This rendezvous under the trees, far from eavesdroppers and microphones, reminded me of accounts of Russian revolutionaries I had read—revolutionaries who had plotted the downfall of the Czar before the 1917 upheaval. . . .

We finished our picnicking meal and waited. L. and Z. did not seem inclined to talk and I felt that it was not prudent to press them. Occasionally a dark shadow would glide past our table and I began to play a game, wondering what shadow would finally come forward and announce itself. Then, when my attention had wandered, I looked up and saw a buxom, middle-aged woman with a strong and sensitive face standing beside L. She must have passed us several times and then had come forward silently, for I had not heard her approach. All three of us stood. Z., L., and the woman spoke together in Spanish in low tones and then the woman looked at me. Her large, dark eyes reflected fear and apprehension. She sat, stared straight ahead, knotted the fingers of her two hands together so tensely that her knuckles seemed to glow white in the dim moonlight. She was hunched forward, her bodily posture indicating anxiety.

The interview was cumbersome and must have lasted for more than two hours. The woman would speak a few moments, then Z. and L. would interrupt her and convey what she had said to me in English. In her opening sentences she betrayed a terrible nervousness, her finger tips flitting from her chin to her eyes and then to her lips. Midway during her gloomy recital she became calmer and even once or twice managed a wry smile as she related some outlandish incident, glancing at me.

"I'm going to tell you this," she said, "hoping that you can help. But I don't see how you can. Maybe God will help you to help us.

"I come of an old and highly respected Spanish family. We have been Protestants for generations. It's our way of serving God. Other than for our religion, there have never been any stigmas against us in Spain. We have always rendered our military service. We have paid our taxes. We have obeyed the laws of our country. We have helped to enrich our nation. My father was a well-known businessman.

"In my youth I had one great desire. I resolved to give my life to try to redeem my country from Catholicism. I felt called by the Lord to do this. I wanted to see each man and woman free to stand up and acknowledge God for himself.

"In the beginning I used my father's business offices for a place in which to conduct Bible classes for children. But, after a few years, I could no longer use my father's business offices to shelter what I was doing; his business had grown so large that he needed all of the space.

"I was determined that that would not stop me. It was then that I conceived the idea of going into a small village and continuing my work. I was naïve enough to think that I could work in such surroundings without fear of detection. I sought out the poorest families that I could find and asked the parents of those families if I could teach the Bible to their children. Many agreed. Little by little, and over a long period of time, I gathered a class of fifty-eight children of both sexes who came together once a week in a Protestant's home. I gave them religious instructions; I made them learn many Bible verses by heart; I taught them to sing evangelical hymns. Whenever it was possible, I gave them warm food and clothing, for many were in dire need.

"Everything went along smoothly until the local authorities took notice of my activities. One day the police came and told me that I had to stop my classes. I told them that I was violating no law, that I was doing no harm, that I was helping to keep the children off the streets, and that I was training and guiding them so that they could lead morally pure lives. They would not listen to my explanations; they told me that they had received instructions to put a stop to what I was doing. When I pressed them to tell me just who it was who wanted my classes stopped, they would not do so.

"I decided to be careful. As much as I was loath to do so, I stopped my Bible class in that village and moved to another one. I rented a small room in a building owned by a Protestant couple and recommenced my teaching of the Bible to children. Always I found that my neighbors were more than glad to send their children to me. Surprisingly, things went well for almost four years.

"Then one afternoon, about four o'clock, while a Bible class was in session, two policemen descended upon us. They first dismissed the children and sent them home. Next they arrested the wife of the man from whom I rented the room. Then they arrested me.

"They had a paddy wagon—you know, one of those long, black cars with windows in the sides and with the doors locked in the rear—backed up to the door of the house and they made us get into it. The wagon was filled with men and women, many of whom were crying and cursing. We stood jammed between girls who were undoubtedly prostitutes. The men jostled us and called us names. It was the first time in my life that I was so close to such people. My religious beliefs had led me to strange places.

"At the station we demanded to see somebody in charge. Other prisoners were able to talk to the officials, to ask for lawyers, but my friend and I were not allowed to communicate with anybody. No doubt the officials had been told to hold us and say nothing to us. What made matters worse was that the other prisoners kept asking us what we had done, and we knew that it was better to keep our mouths shut for the time being.

"They put us into a dark cell that had only concrete benches for us to sit and sleep on. The man who locked us in asked us what we had done, and we said nothing. We were afraid to express ourselves.

You see, people *do* and *will* ask Protestants about their beliefs, but if and when you try to explain, you can be accused of carrying on a fight against Catholicism, which is our official religion, and you can be punished for it; they call it sedition.

"That night we got on our knees and prayed out loud; we called on God to witness that we had done nothing wrong; we asked God to forgive our enemies. The guards came to the bars and listened and they were amazed. They had never heard anything like it in all their lives.

"Later they took my friend from the cell and kept her for hours. Later she told me that the police had questioned her relentlessly about me. They asked her why she had rented the room to me. They wanted to know if she knew what I was teaching the children. They demanded if she had ever heard me say anything against the Virgin. . . .

"She came back to the cell and we sat up the rest of the night, praying. We could hear footsteps going to and fro in the darkness. When morning came the guards began asking us all over again to tell them what we had done. Many of the guards now crowded around to listen. This time I felt that I should not refuse to talk. Slowly, I told them that we had been teaching the Bible to children. That puzzled them, for they did not know what the Bible was. I told them that the Bible was the sacred Scriptures that God had given to man, and they were silent and stared at me. As they left the bars of our cell, I heard one of them say:

" 'Who's safe under Franco?'

"Next day we were taken from our cell and loaded again in the paddy wagon and taken to a big prison. No one had asked me if I was guilty or not. No record had been taken of our being arrested. No official had so much as spoken to me. In this big prison we were taken far down into the cellars where hundreds of women prisoners were kept. . . . Now, you are not going to believe what I'm going to tell you, but it's true. Many of those women prisoners had their tiny children with them. Some had as many as three children with them there in prison. I asked why children were in the prison and I was told that the mothers had had no one to leave the children with. If I had not seen this with my own eyes, I would not have thought it possible.

"Our cell was dark and unheated. The food was bad, but we did not mind that. We prayed and sang hymns to keep up our spirits. The other prisoners were terribly curious about us, but, as I told you, we had to be very careful about what we said to them. It was always possible that some of them were informers. . . .

"Sunday morning came and a young, rosy-cheeked priest came in. He was laughing and jolly and he called out loudly for everybody to come to mass. My friend was worried and I had to comfort her. We both knew now that we were dealing with the Catholic Church itself.

"All the cell doors were unlocked and everybody went out except my friend and me. We knelt and began praying out loud, witnessing for our faith. The young priest came to the bars and asked us what we were doing. I stood up and told him that we were Protestants. He laughed and said that that was all right, but that we would have to come to mass anyway. We told him that we could not.

"The news spread. Something like seventeen prison officials now gathered about our cell, asking all manner of questions. And when they heard that we were Protestants, they were astonished, for they did not think that people were being imprisoned for their religious beliefs. They began to question us about our beliefs and we answered the best that we could.

"The young priest left. We were finally excused from going to mass. Our cell door was locked and we knelt again and continued our prayers, praying out loud. We asked God to give us strength to withstand our punishment, begging divine aid.

"Everybody knew now that we were prisoners because of our religion. The women, when they returned from mass, came and looked at us curiously. They were not angry with us; they were just bewildered. It was something completely new to them. They asked us what kind of religion we believed in. We told them. What else could we do? We knew that we were risking being called seditious by explaining our religion. We spoke to them about the Gospels and Jesus Christ and they stood about and talked in whispers, abashed. They had never heard of such things before; they had never heard about Protestants. They became very sympathetic and offered us some of their food. . . .

"That evening the prison officials sent for my friend again. I thought that now it would not be very long before they sent for me. But nothing happened. I heard later, through one of the guards, that my friend had been questioned, fined five hundred pesetas, and let go. But I still remained in my cell.

"I demanded to be taken before my accusers, but the guards only laughed and shook their heads.

"It was not until three days later that a guard came, unlocked my cell door, and took me upstairs.

"I found myself facing a judge. The guard shut the door of the courtroom. The judge and I were in there alone. There was no public to witness what happened. I had no lawyer. There was no one to take notes of what was said.

"I asked the judge if he had been appointed to try my case, but he would not answer. He had before him a big pile of papers. And, from the questions he asked me, it was evident that he knew of every religious activity in which I had been engaged for years; he knew of every Bible class I had ever taught. . . . Their system of spying was good and complete.

" 'How much money do you earn teaching the Bible?' he asked me.

" 'I don't earn any money,' I told him.

"He was astonished.

" 'You are rich then?' he asked me.

" 'No,' I said.

" 'Don't foreigners send you money?' he asked.

" 'No,' I said.

" 'Then how do you live?' he asked me.

" 'We Protestants pay tithes,' I told him.

" 'What's that?' he asked me.

"I explained to him that all of us gave one-tenth of what we earned to the church to carry on our work. He shook his head and could not understand it.

" 'I never heard of such a thing,' he said.

" 'It's true,' I said.

" 'Don't you know that you are doing wrong?' he asked me.

" 'I'm doing no wrong in trying to save the children of the streets for God,' I said. 'The laws of Spain do not forbid worship.'

"His face grew red. I knew that he did not wish to discuss that with me. He looked at me for a long time and then at his papers. Finally he said: 'You are a capable woman. I don't see why you are in this trouble.'

" 'I did not ask to be brought to this prison,' I told him.

"Then came the strange part of the interview. The judge looked at me sternly and asked: 'Do you teach children to hate the Virgin?'

" 'No! No! Indeed, no!' I told him.

" 'Are you sure?'

" 'I am sure,' I said.

" 'All right,' he said. 'I'll find out." He stood and pointed his finger at me. 'If you have not been telling me the truth, it will go hard for you.'

" 'With God's help, I speak the truth,' I told him.

"I was told to leave the chamber; and, as I was leaving, I met the children to whom I'd taught the Bible entering the chamber. I stopped. It was clear to me that the judge was going to question those children about what I had taught them. I protested.

" 'Children ought not be questioned unless their parents are present,' I told him.

" 'You shut up!' he shouted at me.

"A guard took me into another room. I could hear the judge's voice, but I could not hear what he was saying. I sat and shut my eyes and prayed that the children would remember well what I had taught them. (I learned later that my little pupils stood by me. They recited their Bible lessons well; they quoted chapter and verse!)

"When the children were released, the judge called me in again.

I asked him what had the children told him and he would not answer. It was plain that he was distressed; he had been assigned to find me guilty, and, so far, he had not found any grounds upon which to hold me.

" 'You ought to respect the wishes of the community!' he told me sternly.

" 'I owe a duty to God,' I told him.

"You must understand that I was never formally charged with anything. I was never booked. I was never really tried. I was simply picked up, lodged in prison and held to suit the convenience of the bishops and priests.

"They finally let me go, warning me not to teach the Bible again. But my case is not over. They told me to be in readiness to be called before the judge again at any time. That, of course, was rank intimidation. They wanted me to live in so much fear that I'd never teach the Bible again. There will never be a formal charge against me; I'll never be tried in public; no newspaper will ever be able to report what the judge will say to me. And there will be no legal grounds for my next arrest, if it ever comes. Yet I can be arrested at any moment and taken back to jail and held there indefinitely."

The woman who told me that story was no violent person. As she finished talking, her fingers were moving nervously, knotting and unknotting her handkerchief. She was the kind of woman who walked the streets of America and England every day, free and unafraid. Her only crime was that she was a Protestant and that she lived in Spain.

That evening I picked up the Falangist catechism and read lesson eight for girls between the ages of twelve and fourteen:

The Falangist Concept of the State

WHAT IS THE FALANGIST CONCEPTION OF THE STATE?

As a totalitarian instrument in the service of the country's destiny.

HOW WILL THE CONSTRUCTION OF THIS NEW STATE BE ACHIEVED?

Through political revolution.

WHAT WILL THE POLITICAL REVOLUTION CONSIST OF?

In place of a liberal state following the doctrines of Rousseau, there will be a National-Syndicalist state following everlasting truths.

WHO WAS ROUSSEAU AND WHAT DID HE DO?

He was a Genevan philosopher who affirmed in his philosophy that, among other things, truth did not exist.

HOW COULD HE SAY THIS?

Because he believed that the body of men who formed a nation had a spirit superior to the individual spirit of each, a spirit capable of deciding at any given moment what was the truth.

WHAT DOES THAT MEAN?

That, for Rousseau, truth was not a permanent category of reason, but, at every moment, a decision of the will.

CAN YOU MAKE THAT CLEARER?

For example—that God existed not by being God, but only if there was a majority which said that He did exist. But, if the majority said that God did not exist, then life must be lived as if there were no God.

WHAT WERE THE CONSEQUENCES OF THIS PHILOSOPHY?

The rise of liberal states and the appearance of universal suffrage as a means of finding the opinion of the majority.

WHAT IS UNIVERSAL SUFFRAGE?

The opportunity given to men so that each may manifest his wish by placing a slip of paper, called a vote, in a special box.

WHY IS THIS DONE?

To find out, as already said, if the majority, that is, the greatest number of people, want any one thing.

WHAT WAS THE CONSEQUENCE OF UNIVERSAL SUFFRAGE?

The appearance of political parties.

WHAT ARE THEY?

As all men did not want the same things, they gathered together in different groups, each group having the same opinions, and these groups were called parties.

WHAT HARM DID THIS DO?

It created division among men and also struggles to see which party could obtain the most votes and so rule the others.

BUT DID NOT THE LIBERAL STATE DIRECT AND MANAGE THE INTERPARTY STRUGGLES?

No. The liberal state, according to its doctrines, could not direct interparty strife nor even manage it in the service of the country.

WHY?

Because, according to Rousseau, only what the majority decided by vote had any right over the state, the country, and even God.

WHAT THEN DID THE STATE DO?

Stood by as a mere spectator, awaiting the outcome of the ballot, even if that were to be its own destruction and that of the country.

DO YOU NOT NOW SEE THE FUNDAMENTAL FLAW IN THE LIBERAL STATE?

Yes; it does not serve anything, or believe in anything, and leaves everything to fortuitous voting.

WHAT DOES "FORTUITOUS" MEAN?

Something that is not permanent, that is subject to change, that can be or not be.

CAN A STATE SUBJECTED TO CHANGE GIVE US THE SECURITY THAT SPAIN WILL STRIVE FOR IN HER HISTORIC DESTINY, THE ONLY JUSTIFICATION OF HER EXISTENCE?

No, because such a state does not even believe in the existence of Spain.

WHAT MUST THE FALANGE DO TO REMEDY THIS?

In place of the liberal state, it must have one that will serve the everlasting truths.

WHAT ARE THE EVERLASTING TRUTHS?

Anything touching what cannot change, such as the existence of God, of the Motherland as an historical entity, justice, etc.

WHAT WILL THE STATE CREATED BY THE FALANGE BE?

As we have said, a totalitarian state which does not put the everlasting truths under discussion, but believes in them and serves them.

WHAT IS A TOTALITARIAN STATE IN PRINCIPLE?

One which does not admit the existence of universal suffrage, nor of political parties, one which seeks the justification of its existence in its own historical or vital theories and which orientates the whole machinery of the state toward serving these theories.

ARE ALL TOTALITARIAN STATES GOOD?

No, only those that serve doctrines of eternal and universal truth.

WHAT KIND OF STATE WILL THE FALANGE CREATE?

One which believes in everlasting truths, which orientates the machinery of state toward serving these truths, casting out as pernicious universal suffrage and political parties.

WHY WILL OUR STATE BE CALLED TOTALITARIAN?

Because everything in it, man, the country, the economy, and the state itself will be in the service of the everlasting truths in which it believes.

HOW WILL THIS BE DONE?

By co-ordinating each man's activities with the service each must give the country, given man as the bearer of eternal values.

WHAT DOES THAT MEAN?

That the totalitarian Falangist State will not use man as if he were an indispensable part of the aggrandizement of the Motherland, glorious as that may be.

WHY NOT?

Because it turns into a tyrannical state.

WHAT IS A TYRANNICAL STATE?

One that sets no store by the ethical value of man, only by his contribution toward the ends of the State.

HOW THEN WILL THE FALANGIST STATE USE MAN?

Taking into account, as we have just said, that he has a destiny to fulfill before God equal to that of the state.

HOW CAN THEY BOTH BE BLENDED?

Starting with the natural units where man spends his life, such as the family, the municipality, and the syndicate [*trade union*] *and blending his own duties with those he owes to the state.*

SEX, FLAMENCO, AND PROSTITUTION

26 . . .

IN SPAIN sex has been converted into a medium of exchange for almost all kinds of commodities and services to a degree that cannot be found in any other European country.

Partly fortuitously and partly determinedly, an amazing concatenation of fantastic circumstances—religious, social, economic, familial, cultural—has fostered and abetted the creation of a well-functioning system of prostitution of women on almost all levels of Spanish life. Madrid alone, according to spokesmen of the Catholic hierarchy itself, has more than one hundred thousand prostitutes, forty thousand of whom are not registered with the police or health authorities. Barcelona and Seville literally crawl with hungry women willing to grant access to their bodies for bread or its equivalent.

These trapped and unfortunate women have been referred to as a "wall of flesh" and that wall is everywhere: in bars, cafés, pensions, hotels, sidewalks, churches, parks, etc. Almost all of these women are deeply religious and almost all of them have children to feed. A large portion of them are sunk in illiteracy. Some practice prostitution professionally, some part time; some operate on their own, others have pimps. White slavery between Spain and the bristling brothels of North Africa is a wide-scale, well-organized, and genially conducted business—prostitution being perhaps the biggest business in the Mediterranean world. The unbelievably low wage rates for domestic workers are enough to convince any girl with any capacity for reflection that it is by far preferable to merchandise her body than to be an ill-clad, half-starved slave to some spoiled, bourgeois Spanish wench.

The first and foremost factor in this set of circumstances is that painful and muscular contraction in the empty belly known as hunger, a hunger that is chronic throughout the nation. Spaniards simply do not get enough to eat. (And those who do manage to eat do not know how to eat; their diet is lopsided with starch and oil. Bicarbonate of soda vies with salt and pepper on the restaurant tables of Spain.) Undernourishment is universal, blazoning itself in the tense eyes of children, announcing itself on the wan cheeks of young women—the foundations of this hunger resting solidly upon a surplus of more than two and one-half million farmhands, a scarcity of water almost everywhere, a deficiency of fertilizers, a soil worn out by a system of one-crop farming and ruined by erosion, primitive methods of agriculture, a lack of power and transport, and a landscape of rock and rubble.

Back of this indigenous poverty and supporting it is a naïvely pagan attitude toward life that is the opposite of the practical: a love of ritual and ceremony; a delight in color and movement and sound and harmony; an extolling of sheer emotion as the veritable end of human striving; a deification of tradition that lifts them out of the world that is shared by most of Western mankind; a continuous lisping about greatness, honor, glory, and bravery; a dull doting on the surface aspect of things; an infantile insistence upon one's own feelings as the only guide and rule of living; a training that has conditioned them to expect to sustain their lives by being overlords to the "morally" less pure, to the "spiritually" inferior; all of which finds its ultimate sanction and justification in the practices and canons of Spanish Catholicism.

Growing out of this curious intertwining of archaic cultural values and endemic poverty is still another facet that anchors prostitution in the social structure: a religion whose outlook upon the universe almost legitimizes prostitution: the Spanish Catholic concept of sin. Sin exists, so declares this concept. Prostitution is sin, and proof of sin. So prostitution exists. To account for prostitution in economic or political terms is to be guilty of more sin, that is, flirting with liberal thought which, in itself, is a mortal sin. Therefore this universal prostitution is not something to be grappled with in terms of social or economic engineering; it is not something to be dismayed about or even astonished at; it is not a blight to be eradicated; it is simply an indication that the work of salvation is not yet complete, and that a more strenuous effort must be made to call men to God (and women, too!). And, of course, a prostitute can at any time enter a church and gain absolution.

In the life of Spain as a whole there is a strange lack that contributes to this: the concept of the citizen does not exist in the Spanish mind and the reality of the citizen does not exist in Spanish life—that free, sovereign, responsible, self-moving man or woman whose inspired functions created the Western industrial world; that solitary, individual impulse that built vast, powerful, lay, public-spirited philanthropic enterprises which assume and play so dominant and reformist a role in American life. He who falls by the wayside in Spain is lost, is only an object of private or Church charity or compassion, and highly placed intellectual Spaniards have been known to rationalize this situation by boasting to strangers that, if Spanish streets swarm with numerous beggars, it is but proof of the kindness of Spanish hearts that overflow with almsgiving.

Shoring up and maintaining this situation is a most curious blending of disparate traits in the personalities of Spanish men, a mixture of cynicism and sentimentality toward women. It begins in childhood in the Spanish family. No people on earth so pet and spoil their young as do the Spanish. Hence, if a woman in later years sells her body to feed her hungry children, that in itself is almost a justification of what she is doing. *Para los niños* (for the children) is a slogan among Spanish prostitutes that is almost as prevalent as *Arriba España*! (Spain—Arise!), the slogan of totalitarian-minded Spanish men.

Perhaps their making a cult of the child stems from their feeling for the Virgin and the Child; I don't know. In any case, all Spanish children are, to their families as well as to outsiders, *guapos,* that is, good-lookers. They are pinched, patted, tickled, indulged, stared at, waited on, kissed, fondled, worshiped, dangled, crooned over, hugged and generally made to feel that they are the rightful center of the world. At an extremely early age Spanish children learn to preen, to strut, to feel that they deserve attention, caresses, and admiration; they give and receive drooling compliments at all hours of the day, and the little boy as well as the little girl comes in for more than a normal share of this morbid cuddling. They catch its spirit and, when they grow up and establish families of their own, they pass this sticky maudlinism on to their children in terms of social heredity.

Consequently, the girls quickly develop traits of wild jealousy; they cultivate tantrums of protest, practice the imperious policy of being the sole objects of amorous solicitation. They learn to bedeck themselves with flowers, earrings (I've seen earrings six inches long!), develop the arts of gesturing sensually with their arms, shoulders, and fingers; they master the violent, sexual contortions of flamenco dancing and singing; in short, being a woman in Spain means being mistress of all the tricks of sexual seduction and almost nothing else.

Spanish women have evolved a manner of staring at men with long, intense, bold looks. They expect to be publicly admired in a way that would make an American woman uncomfortable. Yet they expect and demand more gallant attention than would an American or French or English woman, an expectation that has been drilled into them since infancy.

But if the Spanish woman stares at you, the Spanish man all but converts the streets and cafés of Spanish cities and towns into bedrooms. The Spanish male learns early to divide all women into two general categories: one group of women are those with husbands, children, and a home; or they are young women of good families, yes, young women whose hymen rings are technically intact. These are the good women and you bow low to them and tenderly kiss their hands, murmuring compliments the while.

The other group of women has been placed on earth by God, just as He placed rabbits, foxes, lions, etc., to be hunted and had.

Still another buttressing aspect of this sexual atmosphere must be mentioned. I, for one, feel it naïve in our Freudian, twentieth-century world even to allude to the bruited sexual lives of priests and nuns. I do not know nor am I interested in whether they have sexual lives or not. I hope that they do, for their own sake; and I'm sure that God does not mind. But while in Spain I found an amazing degree of preoccupation on the part of the ordinary men and women with the legend of the supposedly torrid sexual lives of the men of the Church. It was a kind of sexual projection of the common populace upon the priesthood. I heard whispers of priests keeping mistresses; in clubs and bars I was shown many little wooden carvings of priests, carvings that displayed, under the religious habit, the genitals, indicating that there existed a tremendous sexual jealousy and tension on the part of the laymen for the rumored sexual prerogatives of the men of the Church. It does not matter whether these allegations about the priesthood are true or not; what does matter is that the laymen are preoccupied with them. Their reasoning seems to be: if they can do it and get away with it, so can I.

27 . . .

One morning an English acquaintance phoned me at my pension and said: "The Spanish government authorities know that you are here. You have written against the present regime. You had better go over to the Ministry of Information and talk to them, let them know what you are doing here."

"You think it's important that I go?"

"Well, yes, your prior political background being what it is."

"I can't conceal my background; in fact, I don't wish to," I said.

"Good. Then just tell them that. The main thing is to let them know that you are not sneaking in, that you are not trying to hide."

I was graciously received at the Ministry of Information by a tall, swarthy gentleman who gratuitously accorded me the title of "doctor."

"We had heard that you were in Spain, Dr. Wright," he said in an impeccable Oxford accent.

"I have long wanted to see Spain," I told him. "But, after all the war bitterness, I had been a little hesitant about coming. I had not been for Franco. And I'm not a Catholic. My purpose for being in Spain now is not primarily political. I want to see how the people live from day to day, what they're thinking and feeling."

"That's quite all right," he said, laughing easily. "We like people to come forward and have their say, no matter what their ideas are. Now, just what aspects of life in Spain are of interest to you?"

"At the moment I'd like to see some flamenco dancers and singers," I said. "Also I'd like to see some gypsies."

"That's easily arranged," he said at once. "I'm going to give you a letter to our tourist department; they'll take care of everything. And, please, Dr. Wright, feel free to come and go in Spain as you like."

At the tourist department I learned that a room had been reserved for me in the Parador (Wayside Inn) San Francisco in Granada for five days and that I should leave the following day.

I had long heard of the engaging manner in which Spaniards fraternized on trains and I decided to make the trip to Granada by rail. Next afternoon I stood in a queue for two hours at the railroad station to buy a second-class ticket. The stone floor was dirty; the people around me were dour, drably dressed, silent, shifting uneasily from foot to foot, their eyes avoiding the muzzles of the machine guns on the forearms of the Civil Guards. One unshaven man tried to edge his way to the top of the line and immediately a tirade of frenzied protest broke out.

That night I rode south in a second-class compartment in which sat five women, a baby, and, besides myself, two other men—the eight of us being jammed into a space that the French railways would have reserved for four people. Flies half dead from the night's cold crawled over the dirty upholstery. The floor was soiled and gritty and the stink from the lavatory drifted throughout the coach. The train labored through the mountains, puffing as though each puff would be its last.

My traveling companions were a diversified lot: sitting next to the window was a mustached, fastidious, elderly man who turned out later to be a country doctor and who kept aloof from everybody; a husky young man, evidently a manual worker, sat next to me. Among the women was a pretty girl who rode with her coat draped over her knees, obviously to protect her virginity. Another young woman, plain and slightly stupid, was traveling with her mother. Then there was the young mother who held her baby upon her lap—a pudgy monster that had just learned to say a few words. The most interesting and intelligent of the women sat almost opposite me; she was about forty, wore eyeglasses, and seemed to spend her time studying the other occupants of the compartment, including me, with an amused and ironic air, but with no trace of condescension; indeed, she seemed to possess a capacity of entertaining herself with what was at hand. I was no doubt a great oddity to her, for my eyes caught her looking at me with great wonder more than once. Was she a businesswoman, a professional woman, a housewife?

We men were polite and reserved toward one another, but the antics of the baby provided a means for the women to unbend and talk.

"*Qué guapa!*" sounded endlessly as they touched, smiled and patted.

Fatigued, I settled into my seat, and dozed. Some time later I was awakened by the train's jerking motion, the *clack-clack-clack* of the wheels over steel rails, the soft sound of rhythmic handclapping, and the melancholy, quavering lilts of flamenco singing. I sat up and stared. The lights had been dimmed. The baby was sleeping in its mother's arms. The five women were singing and I felt enclosed in a warm, cozy dream. Smiling, I leaned forward and nodded affirmatively to show my appreciation. The two men slept or pretended to. The women saw that I loved their singing and they smiled.

"*Le gusta á usted el flamenco?*" the woman who wore eyeglasses asked me.

"*Sí, sí, mucho, mucho,*" I answered with such glee that they paused in their singing and laughed.

When they had finished, I called feelingly: "*Más flamenco!*"

"*Señor Flamenco!*" the woman wearing eyeglasses said.

"*Señora Flamenco,*" I said, bowing.

The names stuck. The women howled with laughter, pointing to me and saying: "*Señor Flamenco!*" and then to the woman with the eyeglasses, saying: "*Señora Flamenco!*"

Through the black night the train rattled up and down the mountainsides and the women sang, their trembling voices and quivering throats evoking sad, accusative moods, celebrating death, lonely love, futile yearning. Exhausted, they leaned back and stared with nostalgic eyes, resigned to disappointment and sorrow.

"*Usted de Nueva York? Americano?*" Señora Flamenco asked me.

"*Si, yo Americano. Casa en Paris,*" I stammered.

"*Familia?*" she asked.

"*Sí, ma femme y dos niños,*" I said, mixing languages. "*Dos muchachas.*"

"Oh! Ah!"

They exclaimed as though I was the first man they had ever met who had a wife and two children.

"*Fotografías?*" they chorused.

I had no photos of my family with me and their faces fell.

"*Le gusta á usted España?*" Señora Flamenco asked me.

"*Sí, Señora. Mucho,*" I said.

"*Por qué?*" she asked me in a gently ironic tone.

There had been strange echoes behind her voice. I had to be careful; I did not know who she was.

"*Mucho flamenco en España,*" I stammered.

That I had narrowed down my reactions to Spain to a love of

their sad songs struck them as extremely funny and they laughed.

"*La vida muy mala en España,*" they said.

Though we had practically no words in common, we had succeeded in communicating.

Señora Flamenco rose and took down her suitcase from the rack above her head and opened it; she found a little booklet and handed it to me. It was a collection of flamenco songs in both English and Spanish.

"*Para Usted,*" she said.

"No, no," I protested.

"*Sí, sí,*" she insisted.

"*Cuánto?*" I asked.

"*Nada,*" she said.

"*Muchas gracias,*" I said.

I did not like the idea of accepting a book from her without some form of restitution.

"*Usted, Señora . . . ?*" I asked.

She opened her purse and handed me her card, then she burst into song. I followed the words in the booklet:

> Tell the Lord Mayor,
> Tell the Magistrate,
> That due to Luis Candelas
> I am dying of love.
> Tell them he is a scoundrel,
> Tell them that he's a thief,
> And that I allowed him
> With pleasure to break my heart.
> I want this love song
> To pass from mouth to mouth
> Just as if I were crazy. . . .

Later they sang:

> Follies and always follies,
> I must sing about follies
> Until with the help of follies
> I shall make you fall in love. . . .

After the wedding night
A beautiful girl had a toothache
And an old maid was saying:
"If I could only suffer from that pain!"

Later the elderly doctor, who slept in a seat next to the window, roused himself and began performing a strange ritual. He took a bottle of alcohol and a wad of absorbent cotton from his little black medical bag and, dampening the cotton, he began swabbing his hands carefully, sterilizing himself. Afterward, he opened a paper bag containing sandwiches and began munching. I looked at my watch; it was three o'clock in the morning.

"*Agua . . . Agua . . .*" The little baby had awakened and was demanding attention.

The mother put a nippled bottle of water into the infant's spasmodic mouth and it suckled greedily. The train jolted and shook, whistling mournfully in the night. Everybody now unwrapped packages of food and there unfolded one of the most moving ceremonies I had ever seen. No one touched his food until all the varieties of sandwiches and fruit had been spread upon their laps. Then they offered their food, their eyes beseeching others to avail themselves of what was proffered. It was as though they felt that to eat before someone else had partaken of their food implied that they would never eat again. I stared at their wan faces, their tired eyes, and I could feel that poverty, loneliness, and despair had forged this compulsion to be mindful of others.

I started violently, feeling hot liquid splashing me. The baby across the aisle had tilted back its little head and, from its tiny mouth, a hot stream of sour vomit was gushing up, spattering my legs and shoes. I leaped out of the way, my face registering horror. The mother stared at me with stricken eyes. The women rushed forward with newspapers and began mopping me clean of the baby's swill, then they carefully spread newspapers over the pools of vomit on the floor.

"*Oh, perdone, Señor,*" the young mother cried, leaning abjectly forward, her wide-open, moist eyes pleading.

"*Nada,*" I breathed, actually managing a smile.

I cleaned myself in the reeking lavatory and, when I returned, the women had finished eating and had resumed their flamenco singing. The doctor had completed his snack and was sterilizing himself again. He looked disdainfully at my crumpled suit, as though saying:

"That's what you get for fraternizing with women."

The women slept, heads resting on others' hips, knees drawn up and touching others' backs, arms flung out in unconscious abandon upon others' laps, their bodies swaying as the train groaned through the black Andalusian mountains. The pungent odor of vomit hung in the air; all about me was a yeasty stickiness.

I took out my notebook and began to jot down my impressions; I had been scribbling for some time when I glanced up. Señora Flamenco was staring at me with an open mouth. I felt guilty, for I could see that she knew that I was making notes of what I had observed. I braced myself for a negative reaction. But, no. She smiled and nodded her head with an air of understanding.

"*Es usted un hombre muy inteligente!*" she whispered. "*Escritor?*"

"Sh," I sounded, placing my finger over my lips and looking significantly at her sleeping sisters. "*Sí.*"

"*Comprendo,*" she whispered. She touched my knee with her hand to show that she approved.

"*La vida es muy mala.*" She sighed and closed her eyes.

The doctor ran up the train curtains and daylight revealed scarred mountains. The compartment awakened, yawned, stretched.

Señora Flamenco was holding a handkerchief to her eyes.

"*Daño a los ojos?*" I asked her.

She lowered the handkerchief and pointed to her eyes, from which a yellowish matter oozed.

"*Médico,*" I said, motioning toward the doctor.

The doctor glared at me and shrugged. He was not interested in the woman's ailment. I had a vial of eyewash in my briefcase—a solution of parts of novocaine and adrenalin suspended in distilled water. I offered it to Señora Flamenco, but she was too frightened to use it. She stared questioningly at the doctor, wanting his approval. The doctor took the vial from my fingers and examined the label.

"*Es usted médico?*" he asked me abruptly.

"*No, Señor,*" I said.

He returned the bottle and shrugged his shoulders.

I put two drops of the medicine in each of my eyes.

"*Bueno,*" I told her.

"*Sí,*" she said.

She threw back her head and I stood and doctored her eyes. They cleared at once. The fumigated doctor gaped in amazement. Señora Flamenco examined her eyes in her purse mirror.

"Dr. Flamenco!" she cried with joy.

Everybody in the compartment, including the disdainful doctor, burst into a loud and long laugh.

When I was ready to get off the train in Granada, I felt that I had known them all of my life.

28 . . .

The Parador was one of a number of such establishments maintained by the Spanish government for the convenience of tourists. Located in picturesque settings, they were tastefully furnished, well-staffed, and expertly run. The management was expecting me and, an hour later, I was in bed. I was sleep starved.

That afternoon I ventured out. The sky was a high deep blue, the sun blindingly bright. The horizon was a ring of purple mountains. Olive groves, orange trees, hedges, flowers, and winding walks made a landscape that was so beautiful as to have an air of the unreal. Peasant women sat hunched in the sun making lace with their fingers; old men stood at benches fabricating inlaid wooden boxes. It was a distinctly feudal atmosphere better suited to the days of the Moorish kings who once ruled here some five hundred years ago than to our nervous, atomic twentieth century.

I wandered over the ruins of Alhambra and Generalife, which lay but a block from the Parador, and walked through the palace, the fortress, and the summer gardens, then among the vast brick battlements erected centuries earlier by the Moors. Washington Irving had been charmed by this monstrous pile of dead glory and had woven romantic tales about it. These relics represented the terminal point of the influence of the East and Africa in Europe. Since the vanquishing of the Moors by Ferdinand and Isabel in 1492, the tide of history had reversed itself and Europe, with a long and bloody explosion, had hurled itself upon the masses of mankind in Asia and Africa and the then unknown Americas. . . .

The crumbling Moorish monuments stretched over acres. What massive and brutal simplicity, what long straight lines! The moldering clues left by a race of an alien temperament tried vainly to speak, to explain. Through the pathos of distance one felt that that vanished race must have been of a titanically childlike disposition, for it had sought to fill all space with a kind of visual dream that blotted out the real reality of the world.

I entered gardens built and arranged so that, wherever the eye roved, clusters of sparkling images caressed the senses. Bubbling fountains filled the air with lisping waters; endless hedges of laurel exuded subtle perfumes; the depths of sleeping pools were ravaged by clouds; cascading waterfalls fell with such steadied and trickling momentum that their musical cadences made you feel, through empathy, the aesthetic moods of the men who had created them; groves of orange and lemon gleamed darkly; and, beyond tall thickets of noble cypress, were banks upon banks of brooding flowers, some stretching away toward verdant valleys, others lifting skyward. It was a paradise, but a static one—a paradise whose vitality was only skin-deep.

A Catholic cathedral, built by Charles V, was housed in the ruins of this once pagan shrine, and it was odd to observe the successive layers of civilization lapping one over the other; in Granada one could see out-croppings of Gothic, Greek, Roman, Jewish, Moorish, and Christian ruins. But the most engrossing sight was the architectural depiction of the passive Moslem dream being shattered by the psychological dynamics of death and resurrection of the Christian Cross. What vengeful methods the old-time Catholics had! It was not reverence for the past that had stayed their hands from destroying the pagan temples; they had erected their Christian cathedrals on top of them, thereby symbolically straddling the neck of the beaten enemy for as long as stone and marble could endure, heralding and flaunting their victories down the centuries.

I glanced at the shaded arbors, the sunlit patios, the sumptuous courts and their proud sculptures, the fragile Moorish tilework of blue and gold, then drifted off, surfeited. My twentieth-century hunger could not be sated here. These moss-covered ruins were far less interesting to me than those landscapes of subjective ruins that strew our world today—ruins that were harder to detect and much more difficult to appreciate.

I descended past the rotting piles of Alhambra and Generalife and returned to the Parador. Tired, I stretched out on the bed and thumbed through the Falange catechism, reading lesson six for girls between the ages of twelve and fourteen:

Historic Mission

WHAT IS THE POLITICAL SIGNIFICANCE OF THE FUNDAMENTAL CONCEPTS OF OUR DOCTRINE?

Spain's historic mission, orientated toward the universal.

WHAT DOES THAT MEAN?

That a nation that feels it is the bearer of a special destiny in history can have no other end but the projection of its personality over the world.

HOW CAN THIS BE ACHIEVED?

By implanting in all the population the political and social formulae that give reality to Falangist doctrine.

HOW?

By means of the revolution.

WHY IS REVOLUTION NECESSARY TO ACHIEVE INFLUENCE OVER THE WORLD?

Because an inflence such as the Falange desires cannot be based on the unfairness of life among so many Spaniards.

WHAT ELSE?

Because a state must be created which will serve the ends of the Motherland.

AND FOR WHAT OTHER REASON?

Because men must have a system of ethics which will enable them to know and serve the ends of their Motherland.

SO, WHAT WILL BE THE NATURE OF OUR REVOLUTION?

Political, economic, and moral.

ONCE THE REVOLUTION IS PAST, WHAT WILL THEN BE SPAIN'S HISTORIC MISSION?

One of leadership among the nations of the world.

HOW WILL THIS BE?

Because empires will then not be like the old ones, the predominance of one nation above all others.

WHAT WILL IT BE?

The domination by one group of nations—united by ideological and historical ties—over another group of nations with different ideas.

WHAT WILL OUR LEADERSHIP CONSIST OF?

Being the head or axis of the group of nations to which we belong.

WHY US AND NOT ANOTHER NATION?

Because it falls to us historically, since our influence will be over Portugal and Latin America, which Spain civilized.

WHY WILL IT BE THAT GROUP OF NATIONS?

Because these nations, on account of their Spanish origin, have been those nations in this world that have most strongly upheld the superiority of eternal values over the materialistic and liberal concept of life held by some nations grouped together on the opposite side.

SO THIS HISTORIC MISSION IS IDEOLOGICAL AS WELL AS TERRITORIAL?

Yes, though to fulfill it we need certain territorial recoveries which hinder our power of rule.

WHAT DOES THAT MEAN?

Recovery means demanding something that is justly and lawfully ours, that is, while we do not, for example, seek our geographical integration by seizing Gibraltar, this presumes that it is because the British are stronger than we are and, for the time being, exert considerable influence in the world.

HAVE WE TO RECOVER ANY OTHER LANDS FOR SPAIN?

Yes, some possessions in North Africa which, by geographical position, assure our country's independence.

SHALL WE THEN NEED ALL THE LANDS THAT WERE OURS AT THE TIME OF THE SPANISH EMPIRE?

No; territorially, we need only those necessary to maintain our independence and our strength.

HOW WILL THE PEOPLES OF AMERICA JOIN IN THIS COMMON DESTINY?

As the independent nations they are, but united to us by religion, culture, blood—stronger claims than the soil.

HOW THEN SHALL WE ACHIEVE THE NECESSARY RECOVERIES?

By treaties or by conquests, because, in principle, to gain an empire you have to conquer it.

WHY?

Because that is a way of showing strength and there is the old motto of the J.O.N.S. which says: "Do not halt until you have conquered."

WHAT THEN WILL SPAIN NEED TO BE ABLE TO ATTAIN HER HISTORIC DESTINY?

Great inner strength, assured by economic independence, an increasing population, a high standard of education and a great Land, Sea, and Air Force.

29 . . .

That evening I took a taxi and invaded the precincts of gypsy town. Blocks before I arrived I could hear the stomping of heels on tile floors, the thumping of guitars, the clicking of castanets, and the high-pitched and quavering bellows of flamenco. The night was warm, the sky filled with fiery stars. We climbed a steep mountain and the taxi stopped amid a throng of gypsies.

Gypsy town was situated upon a mountainside and I passed rows of caves dug out of hard rock. In these spacious cavities scores of gypsy families had made their homes. Legend had it that these gypsies were the most favored of all the gypsies in Spain, for it was reputed that their ancestors had aided Ferdinand and Isabel to drive out the Moors. They earned their living by giving singing and dancing exhibitions, among other things, for tourists. The front rooms of their cave homes had been converted into small dancehalls where a gypsy family or clan would, for a price, assemble and entertain you an hour.

For the sake of prudence, I chose a cave having a number of European clientele and went in. An exhibition was being organized, that is, a levy was being collected from those who had entered. When the traffic had been taken for all it would bear, an old, evil-looking woman began clapping her hands, the diamonds on her withered fingers flashing. As the audience, which sat in chairs along the wall, grew quiet, the old woman assembled her brood.

Back of the woman and along the whitewashed walls were photographs of gypsy ancestors and a few prints of Jesus preaching to multitudes. I was informed later that they practiced a kind of ancestor-worship religion, that they could not marry out of the tribe, and that you had better keep your hand firmly upon your pocketbook while listening to or looking at their "culture." These were tribal people living under urban conditions; their religion had made them reject the people around them and those people had, in turn, rejected them. They had thus been reduced to beggary, singing and dancing in order to eat and have a cave roof over their heads. If ever there had been anything romantic about these gypsies, it had long since been swallowed up in commercialism.

Three young men entered in tight-fitting black trousers, black hats, high-heeled shoes, with guitars slung under their arms. About twenty-five females, ranging in ages from eight to fifty, stationed themselves about the floor. Pink carnations were tucked into their jet-black hair; from their ears dangled gold loops; and they wore cheap cotton dresses that had loud, splashing patterns of color. Red-lipped, rouged, their faces were tired and damp in the night's heat; now and then one of them yawned.

The old witch clapped her hands; the guitars strummed; and the girls plunged into wild whirlings, their arms lifted and their castanets clacking, their cotton dresses rising and floating out at the level of their hips, their black hair flying about their faces, and the cave was suddenly filled with the scent of unwashed bodies and cheap perfume. Abruptly the dancers broke and crowded along the walls, leaving one lone girl in the center of the floor. A young man laid aside his guitar and joined her. Their dance was a wild sexuality lifted to the plane of orgiastic intensity. The man approached and then veered from the spinning girl, evading her while the girl, red lips pursed, her eyes half closed, her arms flung above her head, stood still in the center of the floor and stomped her heels madly, wringing and twisting her buttocks as though she were in the grip of reflex muscular movements only. Then she gritted her teeth in a grimace, clutched the hem of her dress with both hands and put her fists upon her hips, disclosing her thighs and legs. She advanced across the room, stomping and writhing to the beat of the music, her face carrying an expression of one about to fall in a swoon. She then threw back her head, placed her palms upon her trembling buttocks and stomped back across the room to the pound of the music. The man approached the girl and they danced around each other, their heads tilted backward, their eyes looking into each other's.

The Germans, Swiss, Americans, Englishmen gazed open-mouthed at an exhibition of sexual animality their world had taught them to repress.

With sweat streaming off their faces, the girl and the man concluded and a child who looked to be about eight years old came into the center of the room, her castanets clicking. She had a thin, haunting face and her long, straight black hair fell down to her waist. The music and clapping blared forth and the little tot whirled, twisted her tiny hips and rolled her eyes sensually. She too induced on her lips that expression of savage sexuality; she must have been copying it, for I was sure that she could not really feel what she was portraying. She had a charm, a grace, and freshness that the older women lacked, yet there was something pathetic about a child expressing sexual emotion far beyond its capacity to experience.

The pale white faces that looked on were shocked, but entranced.

30 . . .

Granada's one hundred and fifty thousand inhabitants were so tourist conscious that I was repelled. It was almost impossible to see the city for the hordes of chiselers swarming in bars, cafés, and even cathedrals. Accordingly, I hastened the time of my departure, booking train reservations for Madrid, which meant that I had only forty-eight hours more of time. I strolled through ancient monasteries, visited the most arrogantly dreamlike cathedral I had ever seen and paid my respects to the lead coffins of Ferdinand and Isabel, then tried to digest the food in the city's restaurants.

Next evening I picked up the telephone in my room at the Parador and asked the girl at the switchboard to dial the number that I had found on Señora Flamenco's visiting card. I waited, hearing the phone ring.

"*Dígame,*" came a woman's voice over the wire.

"*Yo, Señor Flamenco,*" I said and paused.

There was silence, then a gale of laughter erupted at the other end of the wire.

"*Un momento!*" a woman spoke urgently.

I knew no Spanish and she knew no French or English; I guessed that she was trying to solve the problem of language when she told me to wait.

I caught echoes of excited feminine voices, doors slamming, and running footsteps. I held the receiver for five minutes.

"Hello!" came a panting voice. "I speak Engleesh. . . ."

"Oh, yes? This is the man who met Señora on the train—"

"Wait a meenute. I tell her," the voice said.

I heard giggling, then: "She wants you to come to dinner. She wants her friends to meet you. I'll be there to help you talk."

"Sure. What time?"

"Is nine all right?"

"Yes."

A little before nine o'clock, I bought two bottles of red wine and a bouquet of flowers and took a taxi to Señora Flamenco's home, which was in a dark, narrow street just behind the city's main business section. Señora Flamenco, flanked by two other women, stood smiling at the edge of the sidewalk.

"Señor Flamenco!" the women chorused, laughing delightedly.

We shook hands all around and I extended to Señora Flamenco the bouquet of flowers. Her face assumed an expression of mock anger and she shook her forefinger in my face, scolding me roundly.

"She says that you must not do that," one girl said in English.

Chuckling, we entered a tenement doorway and mounted dark stairs. Señora Flamenco's second-floor apartment was sparsely furnished, cramped, but neat, every detail proclaiming pride and poverty. I was led into a combination living-dining room that was so tiny that only one person could pass between the table and the wall. On the ceiling a bare, weak electric bulb glowed. The room's only window was open and the discordant sounds of night traffic were wafted up to us.

Señora Flamenco's English-speaking friend, Marie, was shy, blonde; she was a stenographer and she smiled nervously whenever I looked at her. She seemed to be in her early twenties.

"*Mí, Lita,*" Señora Flamenco told me.

"Ricardo," I said, pointing to myself.

Sharing Lita's apartment was a young girl who aspired to be a dancer, Lucile; she was stately, tall, had an unearthly beautiful face, coal-black hair and eyes. Lita's aged mother-in-law (who was ill and in bed) occupied another room, which accounted for the apartment's three bedrooms.

Marie's bookish English proved too elementary to permit of much communication. Lita now related to her friends how she had met me on the train, how she had caught me making notes about our traveling companions.

"What are you?" she asked me through Marie.

"I'm a writer," I said.

"You are writing about Spain?"

"Yes."

Lita stood and stared, then solemnly lifted her joined palms toward the ceiling.

"You love freedom?" she asked me.

"I do, with all of my heart," I told her.

"You will tell the people in America about us?"

"I'll try; I'll do my best."

"What will you tell them?" she wanted to know.

"I shall tell them that the people of Spain are suffering," I said.

When Marie had conveyed that information, there was a long silence. Lita stared at me, then rose and walked seemingly aimlessly around the table; suddenly she covered her face with her hands and hurried from the room, weeping.

"She has suffered much," Marie said.

We were silent. Lita returned and began arranging the flowers in vases, with stony eyes.

"Has Lita a husband?" I asked Marie.

"No. He's dead," she said.

Lita had understood my question; she turned and pointed a forefinger and said: "Boom!"

"The Civil War?" I asked.

"Yes."

"He fought for the Republic?"

"Yes. Of course."

"You have no children?"

"No. But I support my dead husband's mother."

"How is life here?"

"Bad . . . Hard, very hard. We eat, that's all. We eat a little."

Lita busied herself placing bread, butter, cold meat cuts, and bottles of wine upon the table, her brooding black eyes filled, they seemed, with far-off memories. Marie sat and stared at me. Lucile stood looking out of the window into the black, noisy night. The heavy atmosphere that hung in the room made me feel that perhaps it had been wrong of me to come. Then a miracle happened. Lita turned to me and opened her mouth; her eyes were blank, hollow; her throat quivered and I could see a bluish vein throbbing in her throat; and out poured a stream of pure, drenching, melancholy song. The others came to attention, looked at me with moist eyes, and joined Lita's singing.

When the last tremor of song had died, we sat and joked about how to make oneself understood without words. I pantomimed what I wanted to say and they were willing to take time to imagine, to guess, and, in the end, to understand; and they were patiently determined to make others know and feel what they thought and felt. Around midnight, as we ate and drank, we imitated the miaow of the cat, the hoot of the owl, the bark of the dog, the whinny of the horse, the low of the cow, the crow of the rooster, and the results made us laugh for long minutes.

Speaking through Marie, I asked Lucile: "What kind of dancing do you do?"

"Flamenco," she answered. "*Le gusta a usted?*"

"*Sí, mucho,*" I said encouragingly.

At Lita's urging, Lucile rose and found a bit of space at the far end of the rom and, as Lita and Marie sang and clapped their hands, the girl began a sensual dance that made a kind of animal heat invade the room. I watched her, enthralled. When she finished, I applauded. Lita, however, was pointing an accusing finger at me and saying:

"*Lucile, hombre peligroso!*"

Marie and Lita spilled over with laughter and Lucile's virginal cheeks reddened with shame. I covered my face with my hands to atone for the light that had been in my eyes when I had watched her dance.

The doorbell rang.

"Roberto," Lita whispered.

A young man of about nineteen entered carrying a huge book that turned out to be a Spanish-French dictionary. He was shabbily dressed, shy, subdued, and again I marveled at how strong and self-possessed the women of Spain were in comparison to their men. Roberto was a student and a nephew of Lita. They told him that I loved flamenco and at once he sat and broke into song while the others clapped their hands. He sang of the death of a soldier and there was silence when he finished.

Lita rose suddenly and stood over me, her face a mask of brutal hardness.

"Franco!" she croaked with fury. "*Comprende?*"

"*Sí, Señora,*" I said.

"*Hombre malo,*" she said.

She lifted her arms and her thin white hands made a fluttering movement and her mouth imitated the roar of plane engines; through her rounded lips came:

"BOOOOOOM! BOOOOOOM!"

"*La guerre,*" I said.

"*Sí, Señor,*" she said. "*Libertad terminada . . . La mitad de la gente española no come,*" she hissed. "Liberty is finished. Half of the people of Spain are hungry."

I nodded, struck by the bitter intensity of her passion.

"We have no hope," she told me through Marie.

I sat and brooded. They sang again and baptized me in their sorrow. I was glad that we could not talk freely, for words would have profaned what they communicated to me of their hurt and dejection.

Lita set out a big bottle of liqueur and we began to sip it.

"Roberto, what do you wish to be?" I asked the boy, speaking through Marie.

"*Médico,*" he said shyly.

"*Bueno,*" I said, patting his shoulder.

He shook his head and smiled bitterly.

"No money," he said trying to use his school English. He pushed out his feet and showed me his tattered shoes, then spread his hands in a gesture of despair.

Poverty in Spain was self-effacing, ashamed of itself. Out of another heavy, awkward silence, Lucile turned to me and asked: "*Le gusta los toros?*"

"*Mucho,*" I said, pantomiming my love of bullfighting by waving an imaginary cape.

Lita clapped her hands and laughed. Lucile got to her feet and took a lace shawl from her head and dangled it in front of me, imitating a matador.

"Ha! Ha!" Lucile prompted me.

Amid screams of laughter, I got on all fours and glared at the shawl. Lucile shook it; my head bobbed as my eyes followed the shawl's movements.

"Ha! Ha!" Lucile prompted me again.

I lowered my head and charged and the shawl floated away.

"*Ole!*" they cried.

I was still on all fours, looking about for the shawl; I turned and found it. Lucile, proud, disdainful, jiggled the cloth before me.

"Ha! Ha!" she said, her black eyes flashing contempt for danger.

I eyed the shawl and charged again, hooking my imaginary horns viciously, trying to gore or snare the shawl, but it went away.

"*Ole!*" they sang.

Lucile now stood close to me, dangling the shawl near my eyes; rising and falling on her heels and toes, grunting: "Ha! Ha!"

I saw the shawl, but I also saw Lucile's trembling blue dress.

"Ha! Ha!" Lucile goaded me again.

I charged, not for the shawl but at Lucile, my head gently colliding with her pelvis. The girl's eyes registered shock; she dropped the shawl and stepped backward. The room exploded with laughter. Pawing the floor with my hind legs, I bellowed:

"RRRRROOOAAR!"

Lita screamed and fell out of her chair to the floor, where she lay squirming in a spasm of laughter. Marie yelled and clapped her hands over her gaping mouth, her eyes round with moral consternation. The room was filled with yelling. Roberto leaned his head on the cluttered top of the table and laughed so strenuously that spittle drooled from a corner of his mouth. Lucile's black eyes were two pools of astonishment.

"*Usted niño!*" Lita yelled at me.

I rose and turned to Marie and said: "Tell Lucile that bulls gore sometimes."

Marie transmitted this to the girl, who continued to gape at me with incredulous eyes. I extended my hand compassionately to Lucile.

"*No fait mala?*" I asked her, mixing languages.

"No," she breathed, staring as though in a trance.

Poor virgin! Maybe she was thinking that I should marry her now? Lita led the dazed girl from the room and we continued laughing. A few moments later Lita returned with Lucile, who had now recovered from her goring and gave me a ghost of a forgiving smile.

I glanced at my watch; it was six o'clock in the morning; the night had fled. Gray dawn stood at the open window.

"I've got to catch a train at eight o'clock," I told them.

They were silent and sad. I prepared to leave. Lita spoke to Marie, who told me: "We want to come to the train with you."

"Wonderful," I said.

We drank coffee, then went down into the quiet, empty streets, crowded into a taxi, and, singing softly, rolled to the Parador, where I got my bags. At the station we sat upon an outdoor bench. Lita closed her eyes and began humming flamenco. Roberto and I walked to and fro, puffing cigarettes. The sun was strong now and lines of weariness showed on our faces.

I returned to the bench and tried to talk to Lita, but she motioned me to silence by placing her finger upon her lips. Again she closed her eyes and lifted her voice in song. Lucile and Marie joined her. People stared at us and smiled. In Spain song was a special language with special privileges. I stood before the singing women, conquered by their sorrow.

The train puffed up and stopped. I shook hands all around, then climbed aboard. I opened a window and looked down into their naked, pleading eyes and I knew that this love that they were demonstrating was not for me alone; it was an appeal to that world that they had never seen and whose reality they had almost grown to doubt. I represented that world to them. . . . I took out my fountain pen and waved gently toward them.

"*Para usted*," I whispered to them. I put my hand upon my heart.

They nodded their understanding with charged and misty eyes. The train bell tolled. The train moved and I waved my hand as long as I could see them and, as the train picked up speed, they sang louder. Then they were gone, both the sight and sound of them, and I could hear only the melancholy grinding of steel upon steel. But they were in my heart, standing there, pleading. . . . I turned wearily and heavily to my seat in the coach.

31 . . .

Being near North Africa, I decided to make a quick trip to Tangier to take advantage of the free-money market, then visit Seville and return to Madrid. I boarded a dirty, hot train that puffed and groaned toward Algeciras. A milky-white and sometimes bluish haze obscured the low-lying mountains. Irrigated terraces rose in tiers that held vineyards and olive groves. The faraway mountain ridges resembled the scaly backs of prehistoric dinosaurs basking in the sun.

Toward noon working-class Spaniards took out big, wicked-looking pocketknives to eat their lunches. Opposite me sat an old, withered woman with a toothless mouth. She opened her lunch, extracted a hunk of bread, a slab of raw, smoked ham, then pulled from her purse a shiny pocketknife which she opened by flicking a button. She sliced off a piece of bread, which she carried to her mouth with the blade of the knife, then chipped off bits of ham which she ate in the same fashion, chewing slowly. I had the feeling that she was so old that she was eating more from habit than hunger. She paused, took a swig from her bottle of red wine, swished it about in her hollow cheeks, then swallowed. Having eaten, she licked the knife blade clean and laid it carefully beside her upon the seat, stored away the leftovers, stoppered the wine bottle, and took out an apple. She peeled the fruit slowly with the pocketknife and cast the peelings between my legs and under my seat with a kind of sublime absent-mindedness, her eyes fastened unseeingly upon the passing mountain landscape.

At Algeciras I boarded the ferry for Tangier, slept one night in a Tangier hotel, and, next morning, attended to my money errand. That afternoon when the ferry docked at Gibraltar, I taxied to the port to make connections for Algeciras. It was then that I witnessed yet another example of the hardy daring of the Spanish woman. Swarming under the shed that served as a waiting room were some three hundred women who had just completed their day's work for the British on Gibraltar; they were now on their way home, that is, to Algeciras.

These women were dressed in a most remarkable fashion; though it was not raining and the temperature stood somewhere in the nineties, most of them wore glistening black rubber boots that came up to their knees. They attracted my attention because they were engaged in a frantic activity the nature of which I could not, at first, determine. I seated myself on a bench among them and smoked a cigarette, trying to appear as unconcerned as possible, yet letting my eyes stray over the unfolding of a fantastic ritual. I seemed to be looking at a factory in full operation as the women feverishly opened packages: soap, cigarettes, perfume, cold cream, lengths of cloth, lotion, Kotex, fountain pens, packets of pudding powder. . . . Ah, these women were smugglers!

Until now there had been a buzzing of conversation, then not a word was heard. I saw them looking furtively at me, whispering among themselves. A stout woman came to me and asked: "*Usted Americano?*"

"*Sí, Señora,*" I said.

She thought a moment, then murmured: "*Bueno.*"

She joined her sisters and spoke to them; what she told them released a storm of activity. Of course, they were still on British soil and British officials did not care; it was the duty of the Spanish customs officials to catch these smugglers and it was the task of these tough-looking working women to outwit them.

The picture before me now became quite clear. These women were working against time to secrete these items about their persons. Right before my eyes I saw a consumptive-looking woman grow into a fat Spanish matron as she lifted her skirt shamelessly and stored merchandise into the nooks and crannies of her body. Before she could hide an item, she had to take off its Cellophane wrapper ever so carefully, fold it and put it into her purse so that the article could be rewrapped once it was safe on Spanish soil.

One young woman took a small article out of her purse; it flashed like a piece of jewelry, gold or silver. She handed it to an old woman accomplice who proceeded to take the chignon from the back of the young woman's head. The old woman then tucked the bit of jewelry deep into the tresses of the chignon and then pinned the chignon neatly back into place on the mass of the young woman's rich, dark-brown head of hair.

"*Gracias,*" said the young woman, patting her magnificent crown of luxuriant locks.

"*Nada,*" the old woman breathed.

Another woman was pulling a pair of rubber boots onto her naked feet and legs; she opened a bag of coffee and poured the contents into the top of the boot. I counted ten pounds of coffee sliding into each booth. (I wondered just how much of the coffee drunk in Spain was flavored with rubber and sweaty foot odors.)

In port at Algeciras about one woman out of every ten was stopped and hauled away to be searched by women police matrons. Even so, it must have been a highly lucrative business and was undoubtedly efficiently organized and sponsored and protected from somewhere high above.

32 . . .

Next morning I boarded a bus for Seville and arrived during the sultry afternoon. I was in the capital of Andalusia, the city whose cathedral held the body of Christopher Columbus. Though rich in oranges, sugar beets, olives, wheat, rice, the impression of poverty was so all-pervading, touching so many levels of life that, after an hour, poverty seemed to be the normal lot of man; I had to make an effort to remember that people lived better lives elsewhere.

On my own in this city of four hundred thousand people and being without my car, I sank wearily into a chair in the shade of an outdoor café fronting the Alameda de Hercules, a bare, sandy park patronized mainly by working-class people. Unemployment must have been right, for scores of ragged men lounged against walls in the sun, staring bleakly.

Yet the physical appearance of the city resembled a garden; tall, spreading trees shaded almost every front yard; the approach to homes was frequently through vine-covered arches; most houses were painted in pastel shades of tan, blue, yellow, and cream. The façades of many buildings were done in brilliant mosaic tile designs deriving without doubt from the influence of the Moors; beyond iron-grill fences were artistically arranged patios that were Alhambra-like in their static but lovely beauty.

A man with a shoeshine box approached me and, with elaborate gestures, asked to clean my shoes. I let him.

"You speak English? French?" I asked him.

He pointed to his mouth and ears, implying that he was deaf and dumb. When he had finished my shoes, he scribbled upon a bit of paper and handed it to me.

"*Un momento, Señor,*" it read.

"*Sí, sí,*" I nodded.

He scurried off and returned a quarter of an hour later with a young man whose right arm was withered.

"I son," the young man said in an original brand of English. "He father," he continued, pointing to the deaf and dumb man. "What you wan'?"

"I'm looking for a pension. Can you help me?"

"*Sí, sí.* You wait. I go. I come queek. No?"

"*Sí, sí,*" I said, settling back. An hour later he reappeared, his withered right arm, which was shorter than his left, bouncing up and down excitedly as he neared me.

"You find something?" I asked him.

"I t'eenk so," he said.

"How much a day?" I asked.

He took out a fifty peseta bill and said: "Feety."

He said it too pat; no doubt he was getting a rake-off, but I was willing to settle for fifty if I liked the room.

"Okay, let's see this place," I said, rising.

"Yes, meester," he cried, happy, bobbing along at my side.

It was a private house facing a square in a working-class neighborhood and that decided me to accept it. There were four women in the two-story house: Señora F., a plump, tanned, raven-haired, bulbous-eyed woman of about thirty; she had a restrained and studied manner, but was thoughtful and kind. Her assistant, M., a young woman in her late twenties, actually ran the establishment; she had a pale, ascetic face and was very nervous. The third woman was Señora F.'s mother, a stout, baffled, ailing woman who rose late in the day and went to bed early. The fourth female was a tall, stupid scarecrow who thought that anyone who did not understand or speak Spanish was deaf, and she always lifted her voice when she spoke to me. She did the heavy work. The little pension was quiet, clean, with many a crucifix in the hallways and one over each bed.

Settled in my room, I became aware of a strange sound that I could not, for the life of me, define. It was a quiet chorus of high-pitched emissions of complaint, like the squeaky chirping of newly-hatched birds: *peep-peep-peep.* . . . Vainly I searched my balcony for birds' nests. The piping sounds continued. Yes, they were coming from behind a locked door in my room that gave onto the dining room. Then, over and above the soft squirts of whistling sound came the murmuring voices of women speaking Spanish. The more I listened, the more intrigued I became. Finally I decided to investigate on the pretext of asking where I could post a letter.

Leaving my room, I walked down a corridor and entered the dining room and stood still, my eyes riveted upon a strange scene. About twelve baby chicks were on top of the dining-room table pecking away at pellets of meal-like grain. About the table were grouped the four women of the house, lisping endearments, doting, smiling. Señora F. saw me and beckoned me closer.

"*Bonita!*" she crooned, picking up a chick and kissing it.

"*Sí,*" I said, feeling that I should agree. She had spent some years in Paris and I could speak to her in French. "*Mais, où habitent les petits poussins?*"

"*Sur le toit,*" she said. She snapped her fingers and made a clicking sound with her tongue. "*Nous pouvons les manger à partir de six mois.*"

A cup had been turned upside down in a saucer and from its edges the tiny fluffy chicks were drinking, poking their sharp, pearly beaks into the water and then lifting their bald heads and making mincing, scissorlike chewings to swallow. Well, if chickens were allowed to eat on the dining-room table, maybe pigs slept in the kitchen? What went on in this pension? Ah, but I could not then even imagine what other fleshy and sinister doings transpired in that house. I finally did discover them, but by accident, so wonderfully well were they cloaked by sugary words, crucifixes, pious miens, and signs of the cross. . . .

After mailing my alibi letter, I wandered the sizzlingly hot night streets. A tent of black sky sagged low over the city's rooftops and its burden of burning stars gleamed like glowing holes. Tree leaves glistened wetly, drooping and motionless in the still air. The scent of burning olive oil stood in the streets like a solid wall. People had come outdoors to escape the heat of their concrete houses and the narrow streets were cluttered with chairs. Under the weak blobs of yellow light shed by street lamps groups of scrawny children clapped their hands in complicated rhythms that reminded me of the children's games I had seen in the African jungle. So congested was the working-class quarter that one had only to poke one's head out of one's window and one was looking into the bedroom or kitchen of one's neighbor.

I paused in front of a kiosk, looking for English-language newspapers.

"Do you carry the Paris *Tribune*?" I asked an old lady inside the kiosk.

Her eyes went blank; my English was Greek to her.

"You know damn well you can't find the *Tribune* down here!" a voice boomed behind me.

I whirled and saw a grinning white face.

"Hi," I said. "Are you American?"

"I sure am," he said. "You're at the bottom of nowhere, guy. Nobody reads English here. Tourist?"

"Sort of," I said.

He was a tall, blond fellow with a hard, bullet-shaped head and face. There was a hint of something evasive about him, yet his thin lips seemed to hold about ten different kinds of smiles. I had the feeling that he would have smiled even had he been angry or afraid.

"How did you get lost down here?" I asked him.

"Oh, I'm on business here," he said. "How long are you here for?"

"Just a day or so; that's all."

"Having a good time?"

"Can't say I am. I just got in."

"You can't miss a good time here," he informed me significantly.

"Yeah?"

"What are you looking for? What do you want to see?" he asked me.

"I got the flamenco bug," I confessed.

He leaned his back against a parked car and roared with laughter.

"That's about all that they've got here," he said. "Where're you staying?"

"In a pension, a couple of blocks away."

"Meet me here at eleven o'clock and I'll show you enough flamenco to last you a lifetime," he said.

"You know this place well, then?"

"I know it."

"Okay. It's a deal. Here at eleven tonight."

"Sure thing, boy," he said.

"Your name?"

"S. Yours?"

"Ricardo."

"So long."

"So long."

Well, I would see some flamenco. . . . He seemed to know his way around Seville. Maybe a businessman? Yet he did not quite look like one. Perhaps one of those GI's who had stayed behind in Europe after the war and had drifted into Spain? Maybe. In fact, I could not, in terms of profession, place the fellow.

33 . . .

At eleven that evening I made my way to the kiosk where S. was waiting in his shirt sleeves.

"Ready for flamenco?" he asked me teasingly.

"Guess so. Where do we go?"

"Not far; right down the street," he said, leading the way.

We entered a curtained door over which a neon sign proclaimed: EL CISNE.

"A friend of mine runs this," he said.

It was a tiny night club, and about thirty girls, all more or less young, were doing a whirling dance to the music of a small orchestra. S. went directly to a table and we sat and ordered a bottle of white wine. I noticed that almost every girl dancing on the floor looked at S. and nodded or smiled.

"You're sure popular," I told him.

"You said it," he said, grinning cryptically.

The dancing was beautiful; the girls wore brilliantly colored, heavily starched cotton dresses whose hems had been threaded with ribbons of various colors. As they whirled, their skirts flared straight out, floating at the level of their hips, revealing their bare, shapely legs, and, when they reversed their whirling, the dresses wrapped around their bodies, clinging. The girls stomped their heels on the floor and tossed their heads in wild disdain, their red lips sultry, their black eyes somnolent, their nimble fingers tapping castanets, their shoulders moving fetchingly, enticingly. . . .

"What do these girls earn a night for dancing?" I asked S.

"About seventy cents," he said.

"Then they work on the side?"

"Yeah, sure. They sleep for a hundred pesetas a throw."

"I've never in my life seen so many young and pretty girls on the sexual market at such cheap prices," I said.

"I'm trying to solve that," he said, grinning, his eyes narrowing.

"What do you mean?" I asked.

"Forget it," he said, laughing. His hand swept toward the dancing girls. "This is only a fraction of the women available in Seville," he explained with the air of a veteran dealer in women. "I have a list of available women in this city and that list is over three yards long, and covers every section of the city. And, boy, that list is *selective*."

I wanted to ask him how he had gotten that list together, but I inhibited myself. We drank wine and watched the girls flinging their arms and legs. The dance stopped and several girls came to our table. S. spoke to them in Spanish, then he took out a notebook and began jotting down information. What was this man doing? One of the girls spoke to me in Spanish.

"*No comprendo*," I said. I asked S, "What did she say?"

"She wants to know if you are going to take her to North Africa," he told me, laughing.

I laughed too, but I was puzzled.

"What does she mean?"

"She thinks that you are the boss," S. said.

He looked at me with a smiling, ironical expression. (I did not know then that he was wondering how long it would take me to catch on to what he was doing!)

Four girls were at our table now. The orchestra played and they wriggled their shoulders, rolled their eyes, and snapped their fingers. Most of them were in their twenties. And they kept looking expectantly at me.

"I you go Africa," a young girl said to me.

S. bent over with laughter, enjoying my bewilderment.

"But I'm not an African," I told S. "Tell her that I'm an American."

S. laughed the harder, slapping his thighs.

"This is rich!" he said.

"What's the joke," I demanded, nettled.

"Brother, you would never have thought that this would happen to you," he told me.

"But what's happening to me?"

"Look, I'm organizing these girls to take them to Africa next week," he explained. "They think that you are the boss. You see, you are *dark*."

Good God! I stared at him, and then at the doting girls.

"You are a big man," S. teased me.

"But—w-what are you going to do with the girls in Africa?" I asked him stammeringly.

"What the hell do you think? I'm going to put them to work in houses," he snapped, still laughing.

It hit me like a ton of rock. *White slavery . . . !* And S. must have thought that my expression was the funniest he had ever seen on a human face, for he roared.

"Jesus!" he yelled. "Boy, these girls'll do *anything* on earth for you. They think you're the *boss* from Africa. Look, don't be upset. I knew that they would fall for it, see? I knew that when I saw you tonight. You don't look like a sailor. So I wanted to see how they would receive you."

"They think I'm the one they would work for in Africa?" I asked.

"They think you own the cathouses in Casablanca," he guffawed.

I stared at the white slaver and, at the same time, tried to appreciate his strange brand of humor.

"White slavery?" I asked him haltingly, leaning forward and speaking into his ear.

He looked at me mockingly.

"No. Not white slavery," he chuckled. "Olive-skinned slavery."

I looked at the girls again. They were fresh, young, happy, pretty, healthy. . . .

"But . . ." I tried to speak.

"What's the matter with you?" he asked me, clapping me on the shoulder, bending double with laughter.

"You mean that they *want* to work in the *whorehouses* in Africa?" I asked.

"They are *dying* to go," he told me. "I got the pick of thousands of women to make up my quota. That's why they were eying you; they thought that you were the black boss from Africa." He went off into another long laugh.

I managed a sick smile.

"You smuggle them out of the country?"

"Hell, no! They travel on the train and ferry. I buy their tickets."

"No knockout drops in their drinks, hunh?"

"Listen, I can't sleep for the women in Seville begging me to take them to Africa." He looked at me with a derisive smile. "Knockout drops? Novelists write that shit."

I was glad that I had not told him that I was a novelist. I was doing a quick laundering job on the moral notions in my brain and the moral feelings of my body. This was white slavery, and how simple and open and jolly it was! The women and girls were begging to go; they were hungry.

"Look, there are plenty of women in North Africa," I said. "Why do you have to ship these there?"

"They are white," he said.

"They want *white* women?"

"*That's* it."

"Racial revenge in bed, hunh?" I asked him.

"They *pay*," he said.

That settled it.

"Do they make much money?" I asked him.

"Two years' work over there and a girl can buy a house in Seville," he said.

"Is there any girl here who has been there?" I asked.

He looked around, then summoned a girl with that hissing sound that Spaniards always use to call someone—a sound that I had grown to hate. A girl, still seemingly in her twenties, came over. She was flashily dressed and had several gold bracelets dangling on her arms.

"She's one of our graduates," he said, laughing.

I offered the girl a glass of wine and she smiled and murmured: "*Gracias.*"

She did not look any the worse for wear, but, of course, I could only see her face.

The flamenco road led in many directions, and this was one of them. Well, given the conditions, the moral attitude of the Church toward sex, the poverty, the ignorance, this was bound to be. It was all socially determined. The Church could call it sin, but it was something far more awful than that. Crush, inhibit, deny the impulses of man, thwart his instincts, and those instincts would find a devious way out, a way to freedom, and the instincts of women too would find a way.

"How many of these girls can read and write?" I asked.

"Oh, about three out of ten," he said.

"Just how is business?" I asked him, grinning.

"It's good," he said soberly. "It's damn good."

Later we left El Cisne and paid a visit to another night club, the Congo, then to still another, the Citroën, and, in each place, S. interviewed and signed up girls to work in the whorehouses of North Africa.

At two o'clock in the morning I pleaded fatigue and went to my pension. I was too tired to sleep. I lay in bed staring in the hot darkness, not wanting to accept how men lived their lives on this earth. I tossed and turned on the warm sheet. Suddenly I was alert.

A car had stopped down in the street in front of the house. I heard the front door of the house open and close. Footsteps mounted the stairs and there was the soft buzz of whispered voices. Then silence. Some roomer coming in late, as I did, perhaps. . . .

About twenty minutes later I heard another car stop in front of the house; I listened to the front door opening and closing again, then once more footsteps sounded on the stairs and more whispered conversations. What's going on?

Half an hour later still another car came to the front door. This time I bounded out of bed and went to the window and gently opened the shutters. Looking down, I saw a man pay off a taxi driver and vanish with a girl into the front door of the building.

Was it possible? I did not want to presume. I waited; minutes passed. Yes; there was another taxi. It slowed and stopped below me and a man and a girl got out.

There was no doubt about it. It was not quite a whorehouse; it was a house of assignation. I still stood at the window. I saw a man and a girl leave. A moment later yet another taxi came. . . . Spain seemed one vast brothel. And those four women were so quiet, charming, respectable. I turned toward my bed and became aware of the crucifix on the wall and I blinked. I lay down. Business was going on around, over, and under me. I drifted into an uneasy sleep.

34 . . .

Have I sounded harsh in my speaking of the women of Spain? It has not been my intention to slur or slight them.

The Spanish women are undoubtedly the most electrically beautiful of all the women in all the world. A Spanish woman is all solid woman and nothing else. Stalwart, they bear the burdens of their poor nation and with but few complaints. They bind up their men's wounds, cater night and day to their childish passions and needs. Against impossible odds, they administer the routine of millions of bleak, hungry, and ignorant families; indeed, it is because of the dutiful presence of Spanish women alone that the hovels that shelter those families can be called home. In short, the women of Spain make her a nation.

The daily striving and suffering of Spanish women make what little structure there is to Spanish society, knitting together in a web of care and love what would otherwise be a landscape of senseless anarchy. They are a proud women, a sweet women, a forgiving women, a compassionate women, women of easy laughter and easy tears. The mighty maternal instinct of the Spanish woman is the anchor of responsibility that holds the ship of Spanish life steady while the Spanish man babbles abstract nonsense in the countless smoky coffee houses.

They are a lithe-limbed women who whirl and clack their castanets and stomp their heels and make of an otherwise dull nation an exciting and human spectacle; women who plow the fields; who wash clothes in country streams; who drive the oxen-drawn carts; who satisfy their men and nurse their babies; and who, at the beginning and the end of the day, creep forward and kneel humbly before the weeping and jeweled Virgins in the dim and drafty cathedrals; long-suffering and enduring women who follow their hot-eyed men into war and peace when they understand nothing of the causes of war and peace; desperately practical women who sleep with strange men for food while their babies coo or cry in nearby cribs; undernourished, skinny women who flee the chill of their concrete houses to sit on curbstones and mend tattered clothing in the sun's wan light; despairing women who send lunch boxes to their daughters who work in the whorehouses; old lonely women who weep at the memory of their sons and daughters who have gone off to seek their destinies in the cold, strange world; silly women who sleep half the day and pay their maids five dollars a month and who primp themselves long and lovingly before their mirrors so that they can walk arm in arm with five other women down the Ramblas and not impair their respectability; Lesbian women living their quiet, secluded lives within the shadows of cathedrals where they go to confess and make their atonements; blind women who sit on street corners in rain or sun and sell lottery tickets; bold-eyed women who begin staring at you ten feet away and whose eyes hold yours until you are abreast of them; women who ask men to their beds without a flicker of shame; shy little women who swab the tile floors on their knees and whose frightened eyes beseech you not to soil the floor that they have so meticulously cleaned; beautiful, rouged, jeweled women drinking cognac in bars who will tell you with a sweet, sad smile that they cannot read or write; ugly women with black and blue marks on their arms from the embrace of drunken sailors; hard-faced women who are willing to escape loneliness by cooking, working, whoring, and dying for a man; frail, dry little women who sell candies and sunflower seed and almonds and who sometimes die while sitting in their little wooden stalls; fat and frightened women who, when they see the black hearse drawn by two magnificent black horses with purple plumes on their heads, cross themselves and throw a kiss from their index fingers to the Virgin of their devotion; tall, long-limbed women who stride down the street, lifting up their big feet and planting them down with the assurance of men; solemn, vindictive women who stand gossiping in the middle of the street with elbows akimbo; young, devout women who have husbands who are hopelessly ill and who stifle their deepest physical needs while their hair whitens before they are thirty—yes, all of those and more are the women of Spain, the heart of Spain. Spanish men have built a State, but they have never built a society, and the only society that there is in Spain is in the hearts and minds and habits and love and devotion of its women. . . .

P.S.

Since the above observations were written, the following news item appeared on March 12, 1956, in the European edition of the New York *Herald Tribune*:

SPANISH BROTHELS TO CLOSE

Madrid, March 12 (A.P.).—The government has allowed brothel keepers three months to close, under threat of heavy fines and prison sentences. Prostitution has been "tolerated" in Spain, and known prostitutes were given special identity cards and forced to pass medical inspection every ten days. A decree published in yesterday's official bulletin also ordered the closing within three months of "houses of tolerance," even though they don't keep prostitutes on the premises and only rent rooms.

The above is typical of the moral approach induced by shame and self-consciousness stemming from world opinion. The Spanish mentality, branding prostitution as sin, is incapable of dealing with it as a social problem—a social problem born of economic conditions buttressed by a political system. Such an approach implies flirting with liberal ideas, and liberal ideas are a mortal sin. Concepts of social causation smack of "dangerous thoughts."

The closing of brothels will, of course, but scatter a vast horde of hungry women through the population, making a desperate problem even more desperate, and converting many respectable buildings into centers of illicit sex trade.

THE WORLD OF PAGAN POWER

35 . . .

I FELT that I had bitten off a large enough chunk of Spanish reality to engage my thoughts and reflections for the time being. Accordingly, after a few days' rest in Madrid, I pointed the nose of my car northward and rolled to Paris.

Before going into Spain my ideas about its problems had been mainly political. I had had a vague notion that I was going to be deeply concerned about comparing the economic conditions under Franco with those that had prevailed before and under the Republic. But my journey and the nature of the reality that I had seen had provoked other and different questions in my mind, questions that went far beyond mere economic and political considerations. No neat, simple dialectical diagnosis of class relations could clarify the reality that had flooded in upon me.

Frankly, I had not been prepared for what I had encountered. Yet I could not feel that the fault was mine. I had diligently waded through scores of volumes by eminent Spanish authorities and scholars to provide myself with some background against which I could measure and inform the reality that I would discover. But the more I had probed and looked and listened, the more obvious it became to me that my trek to Barcelona, Madrid, Granada, and Seville had not been a voyage that I could by any means describe as having taken me through the precincts of the Western world.

Though Spain was geographically a part of Europe, it had had just enough Western aspects of life to make me feel a little at home. But it was not the West. Well, what then was it?

That was the question that plagued me and I grew slowly to feel than an answer to that question was much more important than a long poring over economic statistics or my trying to understand the diabolical gyrations of the Falange, the State, the Army, and the Church, for it was now clear that these Spanish organs of power had been shaped by, and were drawing their vitality from, some deep irrational core that made up the heart of Spanish reality.

To be a functioning and organic part of something is to be almost unconscious of it. I was a part, intimate and inseparable, of the Western world, but I seldom had had to account for my Westernness, had rarely found myself in situations which had challenged me to do so. (Even in Asia and Africa I had always known where my world ended and where theirs began. But Spain was baffling; it looked and seemed Western, but it did not act or feel Western.)

Since I now felt most strongly, in fact, *knew* that Spain was not a Western nation, what then did being Western mean? (And what about the Republic? The Civil War? The Anarchists? To my mind those realities now became deeply modified and less important by the non-Western character of the country I had seen.) Was being Western something so absolutely different from Spanish life and civilization as to be of another genus? Or was that difference a mere nuance, an angle of vision, a point of view? It was not my task to define the totality of the contents of Western civilization; I was interested only in that aspect of it that engaged my attention in relation to Spain. I was finally led to believe that that difference lay in the area of the *secular* that Western man, through the centuries and at tragic cost, had won and wrung from his own religious and irrational consciousness. In Spain there was no lay, no secular life. Spain was a holy nation, a sacred state—a state as sacred and as irrational as the sacred state of the Akan in the African jungle. Even the prostitution, the corruption, the economics, the politics had about them a sacred aura. *All was religion in Spain.*

When I arrived at that conclusion, still another and bleaker conclusion thrust itself upon me, became deductively mandatory. The traditions of the Akan African were unwritten, were fragile, and had already been mortally jolted by the brutal and thoughtless impact of the Western world. The African, though thrashing about in a void, was free to create a future, but the pagan traditions of Spain had sustained no such mortal wound. Those traditions were intact today as never before. In fact, they were officially revered and honored; they were the political aims of the State. This was a fact that made me feel that the naked African in the bush would make greater progress during the next fifty years than the proud, tradition-bound Spaniard!

But even this was not the whole story. The nature of Spain's religious area differed markedly from all other religious areas in Western Europe, including Italy. Why? What had happened in Spain? It was too easy to say that Spain had, somehow, missed, slept through a whole period of historical development—a period in which science, art, politics, and human personality had established their own autonomy and justification. In a way that had happened. But that was only one way of describing the real situation. The boundaries of Spanish religiosity went *beyond* the Church. . . .

For a long time my own Westernness proved a veritable stumbling block to my seeing the truth that stared me in the face. The cold fact was: *Spain was not yet even Christian!* It had never been converted, not to Protestantism, not even to *Catholicism* itself! Somehow the pagan streams of influence flowing from the Goths, the Greeks, the Jews, the Romans, the Iberians, and the Moors lingered strongly and vitally on, flourishing under the draperies of the twentieth century. An early and victorious Catholicism, itself burdened with deep traits of a paganism that it had sought vainly to digest, had here in Spain been sucked into the maw of a paganism buried deep in the hearts of the people. And the nature and function of Catholicism had enabled that paganism to remain intact. And today Spanish Catholicism boasted that it was the most perfect and the purest Catholicism in all the world. . . .

I had, of course, read Castro's *The Structure of Spanish History* and Madariaga's *Spain*, both of which, in different ways, were monuments of scholarship and which now and then had hinted at the real underlying truth. But even these recent and authoritative pronouncements did not seem to me to go deeply and boldly enough into the real heart of the question of the Spanish animal. They had, on the whole, both Castro and Madariaga, refrained delicately from calling things by their right names.

I protested to myself for wanting to dump the entire life of a European nation into the lap of the irrational. It just could not be, I argued with myself, that a nook of Europe had completely escaped the secularizing processes that were now rampant even in Asia and Africa. But, in the end, I had had no choice. . . . True, the West had its areas of the irrational; Germany and Italy had only recently been rescued from a bloody Sargasso of the irrational and were still in a period of convalescence. But, in the West as a whole, a substantial margin of the secular, strategically anchored in science, industry, and in daily lives of hundreds of millions of citizens, had been won and it was safe to assume that those margins would not only remain, but would be, and were daily being, enlarged, extended. But whatever of the secular in Spain had ever existed had been blotted out almost totally by the Civil War and the decimation of its free men through death and exile. I did, here and there, encounter a few timorous Spaniards whose outlook longed toward the pragmatically rational and the secular, but they were as chaff before the totalitarian whirlwind. (One of the most intelligent men I talked to in Spain has since been cast into prison!)

I soon discovered, however, and to my own dismay, that calling things by their right names in the area of Spanish reality, an area charged with passion and abounding in the quicksands of subjectivity, was no easy matter. To accept the idiotic assumptions of the Spanish Falange was, of course, out of the question, that is, if one accepted living in an even somewhat rational world. And if I had, which was impossible, embraced, even as a value judgment, the metaphysical assumptions of the Catholic Church in Spain, I would have been forced to endorse the surrealistic nature of the reality of present-day Spain as the normal lot of man, and that was inconceivable. And it would have been less than senseless for me to have tried to judge Spanish reality in terms of Western, twentieth-century concepts, for the historical soil out of which such concepts grew was completely lacking in Spain. On the other hand, to have attempted a psychological approach in a Freudian sense would have implied a much more intimate acquaintance with the daily family lives of the people than I had—an access to case histories and clinical material even. Otherwise my facts would have been forever wide of the theories. In the end I resolved to accept the brute facts and let the theories go.

Why, I finally asked myself, was I worrying about guides, precedents, concepts? Why not take the reality of Spain just as it struck me? Yes, why not? That was what I had begun to do, so why not just keep on doing just that even when talking to Spanish intellectuals and looking at cathedrals and ceremonies? I so decided.

The first thing, though, that I had to be clear about was my own deep non-Catholicness, my undeniable and inescapable Protestant background and conditioning, my irredeemably secular attitude, and, beyond all that, my temperamental inability to accept childlike explanations of a universe which, if it had any ultimate meaning, was surely not the kind of universe that could be represented by pictorial images of a cosmic family whose members were quarreling among themselves.

Yet Spanish religion was a reality. That religion had been called "an opiate of the masses," but I felt that that definition was more negative and tendentious than a true description. The Spanish religion and its effects that I had observed were nobody's opiate. The Spaniards were ruling in the name of their religion and they were capable of killing you in the name of that religion and of writing a book to justify it.

Possessed by that religion, the Spaniards had despoiled entire continents. Could I possibly, though, accept, for purposes of description, what they had done and were still doing in terms of their own actions and *still not accept it?* Could I handle their explanations and at the same time stand outside of them? As difficult as that was, it seemed to me to be the only honest recourse I had. It meant walking a mental tightrope, yet it did not commit me to any creed, let alone theirs, and it left me free, in a fashion, to depict what I saw.

That was my mood and intention when I headed back toward Spain in the late spring of 1955. And it had been my mood all along.

36 . . .

The moment I recrossed the Franco-Spanish frontier—this time at Hendaye and in a pouring rain—I noticed and felt a sharp drop in the material and psychological quality of living. No matter how lushly green the valleys, the Spanish villages were grim and sorry. Along the wet highways trudged peasants bent under heavy burdens: sacks of grain, loads of hay, boxes, etc.; open trucks rattled along filled with men and women standing packed like cattle, the rain lashing their faces. The women's dresses clung to their misshapen bodies; the men's ragged shirts bagged about their shoulders and hips. Then came that immemorial symbol of Spain: an old woman whose head was covered with a dirty cloth hobbled alongside her heaped and donkey-drawn cart. . . .

Quitting San Sebastián, I followed a winding, treacherous mountain road shrouded in fog and rain and ascended toward Azpeitia to see the sanctuary and the birthplace of St. Ignacio de Loyola, the Soldier of Christ and founder of the Society of Jesus. The shrine and retreat lay some kilometers off the main highway amid mountains covered with scraggy pines. At last I saw a soaring dome and I knew that I was on the spot that housed the personal effects of the first man who had made Christianity a militant and deliberate way of life.

It was a vast but compact establishment lifting some four stories into the air. Of course, the actual edifice in which Loyola had first seen the light of day was no longer intact, but a most skillful feat of preserving what little remained of it had been done. Around the few surviving beams, the façade, and a collection of many other minor mementos, the brooding and thorough Jesuits had constructed a jewel of a religious monument.

Owing to the water shortage, the electricity had been cut and a young priest, the first well-nourished and healthy-looking man I had seen since re-entering Spain, showed me the holy relics by the murky beams of a flashlight. A profound calm possessed the shrine. The rooms and hallways were spacious, ornate; most of the floors were of marble; many famous paintings hung on the walls; and everywhere was the soft, cloying scent of cedar. In the dimness I examined glass cases in which were locked fragments of clothing once worn by Loyola, yellowed letters written by him, a sword which he had once used, gilded boxes, etc.; and I could not help but remember the fetish huts that I had seen in West Africa, huts containing the hallowed objects of ancestors.

"These things were actually handled by Loyola himself?" I asked the young priest.

"Yes. The saint touched them," he said in a voice of deep reverence.

These items, therefore, were regarded as holy. Inlaid marble, carved ebony and walnut, silver, gold—in short, the most precious and lovely of earthly materials had been lavished here to make this shrine arresting and memorable, and the maintenance of it had taken precedence over other and more practical projects. If one accepted the premise that this was a gateway to eternal bliss, one had to endorse the manner in which the rich beauty of this shrine contrasted with the squalor and misery that lay about it.

As I wandered through the shadowed rooms I saw young men kneeling and praying with joined hands before tiny chapels framed by flickering candles. It was believed that a magical mana dwelt in the objects to which their prayers appealed and they were therefore attempting to establish a relationship with those objects in order to partake of their blessedness. And these young men were all strappingly healthy. Just how many physically robust and mentally alert young men and women in Spain were huddled in these dim and remote sanctuaries tucked away in secluded settings, sworn not to reproduce themselves, engaged in continual penance, loathing the world, cultivating humility, giving themselves to a Beyond? I asked the young priest how many were in the sanctuary, but he looked off evasively and would not answer.

These suppliant young men were beseeching sanctions for action and thought. The world in which they lived was dark and deceitful and no action deriving from spontaneous impulse and no thought stemming from egotistical interests were acceptable. Justification for action had to bear the stamp of supernatural origin, and only those thoughts born in a body chastened and contrite could be good thoughts.

It would have been stupid to have questioned the sincerity of those young men; they were wholeheartedly, self-sacrificially earnest. Only someone subjectively at war with the religion that those young men were practicing could have doubted them; to the outsider their devotion carried the stamp of the tragically genuine.

But what kind of thought and action could possibly be produced by such distrust of self, such morbid pleading for impersonal justification? Any attitude born of that seeking must perforce be imperiously arrogant and confident, feeling itself allied with the secret and hidden energies of the universe. And all of the world which, for whatever reason, failed to coincide with that attitude's brutal and militant irrationality must seem confessedly evil, an object to be exterminated, banished like the rays of the sun scattering darkness. There was undoubtedly a brand of demonism here, for these young men had become hopelessly entangled in the turbulent and obscure complexes of their own personalities.

It was nearing night when I emerged. The solemn tolling of bells filled the black wet sky. I drove to the nearest village and put up in a chilly hotel room, and, unable to sleep, I wearily took out the Falange catechism and turned to lesson fifteen, for girls between the ages of twelve and fourteen, reading:

The Organization of the Movement

WHY DOES THE MOVEMENT EXIST?

To give life to Falangist doctrine.

HOW IS IT ORGANIZED?

Hierarchically and vertically.

WHAT ARE ITS OFFICES?

By order of importance, first the National Leader, with two accessory bodies to help him in his office.

WHAT ARE THESE BODIES?

The National Council and the Political Junta.

WHAT IS THE NATIONAL COUNCIL?

A Council to which officers of the Falange belong and a number of members chosen by the National Leader to help him in his duties.

WHAT IS THE POLITICAL JUNTA?

A small delegation from the National Council which aids the Leader in a more permanent and direct way.

AFTER THE NATIONAL LEADER, WHO ARE THE MOST IMPORTANT OFFICERS OF THE FALANGE?

First, the President of the Political Junta and then the General Secretary.

THEN WHO?

The General Assistant Secretary and the Departmental Assistant Secretaries.

THEN?

The National Departmental Delegates and Secretaries; the most important are from the Youth Front, the Syndicates, and the Delegate of the Women's Branch.

WHY ARE THEY THE MOST IMPORTANT?

Because they enroll and train the mass.

WHO COMES NEXT IN THE HIERARCHIC ORDER?

The Provincial Leaders and Deputy Leaders, the Provincial Departmental Delegates and Secretaries, the Local Leaders, and the Local Departmental Delegates.

HOW ARE ALL THESE OFFICES FILLED?

The lower ones are directly filled on recommendation from the immediately superior office.

WHO CHOOSES THE NATIONAL LEADER?

He is unchangeable except in case of death or incapacity.

HOW WOULD THAT BE DONE?

In principle the Political Junta he had chosen would appoint the new Leader from its members.

WHO ELSE FORMS A PART OF THE MOVEMENT?

The members.

HOW ARE THEY ENROLLED?

As adherents and militants, in their Local Branches.

WHAT ARE THE ADVANTAGES OF THIS VERTICAL ORGANIZATION?

That of keeping direct control from the National Leader down to the last of the members.

When I finished reading that, I knew that Loyola had not lived in vain, that his spirit went marching on.

37 . . .

Until now I had more or less avoided the intellectuals of Spain, feeling that I did not wish to talk with them until I had become more conversant with some of the reality that made up their lives. The next few days were spent in Madrid examining the emotional landscapes of intelligent and perceptive Spaniards, hearing explanations and justifications of their plight.

My first informant was a well-known journalist whom I met one sunny afternoon in the penthouse of a friend of a friend. We sat upon a terrace under a high blue sky, drinking wine. Señor G. was in his sixties, portly, white-haired, swarthy-skinned, with a pair of dark, tired, tolerant eyes. He had requested beforehand, through our mutual friend, that his name be omitted in what I would write, and I had promised. Though we had been sitting for more than half an hour, I had not ventured to broach the subject of Spanish life, yet we all knew that the question of "What is Spain?" lay at the background of our minds. Señor G. was a jolly man with a mordant sense of humor; suddenly he was serious; he rose, crossed to my chair and clapped me heartily on the back and said in a laughing and yet somehow accusative tone:

"So you have come to see our poor Spain, hunh?"

"Well . . ." I hedged, wanting him to take the lead.

"We *are* poor," he said, striding to and fro, his hands deep in his trouser pockets. "I'm an old journalist; I used to go to poor countries to look at the natives too." He laughed and waved his hand to stifle my protest. He sat and looked at me and nodded his head affirmatively. "I've been in the outside world: New York, London, Paris, Berlin. I know what they think of us. But we Spanish *are* different.

"Let me start by telling you something quite frankly." He spoke in an accent tinged with a slight but agreeable burr. "Don't take us Spaniards too seriously. We aren't worth it. We have created empires with a sleight-of-hand, and then we frittered them away like smoking a cigarette. All the wars we ever fought were fought for the wrong reasons; we have never been able to tell what our real interests were. Every time we have ever had a chance, we grabbed for the shadow and let the substance go. We were great at a time when greatness was easy.

"Yes; everybody today wants to know what makes a Spaniard a Spaniard." He laughed bitterly. "It starts at birth and it starts all wrong. We Spaniards pamper ourselves. We don't really know anything and we are not taught anything. We are just allowed to grow. Our children do not know what real hard work in the schoolroom is. Our teachers are idiots. I'm not exaggerating. Just go into one of our university class rooms and listen. The wonder is that we are not worse off; there is something that saves us from the sheer bottom of nothingness, and it is not our brains.

"The Spaniard is an animal that is spoiled from the cradle. We are made to feel that we are something precious, something that needs no improvement. We are not shy; we are not even self-conscious, and, God knows, we could use a lot of that. We are never humble;

we are never curious. We trapped the truth with our guns centuries ago and we are certain that we have still got the truth.

"The ignorance among us is appalling. Don't be naïve enough to ask for statistics of literacy or even of population here. Barcelona may be bigger than Madrid, but pride won't ever let us admit it. Figures here mean nothing. We break our figures down into statistics relating to regions. The region that we don't like is the less literate one, less literate than our own.

"We don't like external reality. Every time we speak we remake the world over in the way it pleases and suits us. We murder our own language even. Do you know that there are but few literate Spaniards who can speak and write their language properly? They could, if they really wanted to, but they don't feel any need to—"

"Just a moment," I interrupted him. "A few moments ago you mentioned regions. What about this well-known question of nationalism in Spain? The Basques? The Catalans?"

"Our country has different regions with different habits and different traditions," he said. "But that exists in all countries. Your American South is different from the North, but you don't make national issues out of it. Catalonia is different from Andalusia; one is industrial, the other agrarian. Look, forget this national issue in Spain," he said, waving his hand and laughing. "It's a false issue; really, it is. Let me tell you the secret of it. When Spain was a going concern, we were all proud to be Spaniards. But when Spain began losing her empire, when the belly got empty, many parts wanted to withdraw." He chuckled cynically. "It's like a man wanting to leave a woman who is no good for him any more. Every section of Spain tells you how different it is from other sections, how much better it is. One of the deepest traits of Spain is to be anti-Spanish. When all Spaniards shout that they are different from the other Spaniards, that means that they are all alike.

"Most nations must strive and pile up great accomplishments in order to feel as proud and good about themselves as we do. The mere fact that a Spaniard is alive is enough to guarantee him his delusion of nobility."

"But did not sectional differences help to make for bitterness during the Civil War?" I asked him.

He rose and paced the terrace, chuckling and shaking his head negatively.

"There was never very much bitterness about the Civil War in the first place," he said. "Many people were shocked about the ferocity we displayed during the fighting. . . . Do you know that nobody has yet told the real and simple truth about that war?"

"And what is that truth?" I asked, mentally preparing myself for some political revelation.

"We butchered one another and we loved it," he declared. "The Spaniard was at his best in that war. This is what every intelligent Spaniard knows, but he won't admit it publicly. And we are waiting to start another butchering at the first good opportunity. The Spaniards never had a better time of it in their modern history than they had in that war."

I was silent. I had not expected to hear so frank a reaction to Spain by a Spaniard.

"What about Franco?" I asked.

"You know, he's a Jew," he said. "I'm not an anti-Semite, but knowing that he's a Jew is the only way to explain his peculiar mentality. He is a very brave man, personally. But he has no sense of what a nation is, or what a state is, or what a society is. He sits there, playing the Church against the Falange, and the Falange against the Army, and the Army against the people. I don't think that there is anything vindictive or cruel in him. He is more devout than the ordinary Catholic. The worst that I can say about Franco is that he has lunch with the Holy Ghost every day."

The group of us laughed.

"What about the prison population?" I asked. "I'm told that there are fewer political prisoners now than during and right after the war?"

"Why worry about the prison population?" he asked me in a mocking tone. "At least, they eat. The people who are on the outside of prisons don't eat. I'm not trying to be funny. But there are worse things to worry about in Spain than the people in prisons."

He sat and twisted nervously in his seat, smiling, looking off.

"Look, there is one thing that you must know about us, or you'll never understand us. We are barbarians. And only those Spaniards who know that we are barbarians are a bit civilized. The problem here is deep-seated. We need to start all over again—"

"Because of the force of tradition?" I asked.

"Yes. In order to *overcome* tradition."

"How will you do that?"

"Who knows?" he asked with a sigh. "I'm old. I'm out of politics and I'll stay out of it all. But if you want my opinion, I'd say: Start at the cradle and rear a new generation—"

"But will the Church let you do that?" I asked.

"No. And there's the problem," he said.

"What about increasing the rate of industrialization as a means of creating an area of secular life, of neutrality?" I asked.

"The power of the Church is much, much greater than you think," he declared. "They manage to suck all new enterprises into their orbit. For example, the Germans will build a plant in Barcelona. Those Germans are Protestants. The Catholic Church, through the government, does not want those Germans to have a Protestant Church. After much bickering, the government, acting for the Church, grants the request of the German Protestants, but insists *that their chapel must be in the factory and that no Spaniards can be present. . . .*

"They manage to control *everything*," he went on, laughing. "You Americans are trying to change us. Why, we will change *you* before you change *us*.

"Do you know that your GI's here can hold their Protestant services, but *only* for American Protestants? I don't suppose that the government or the Church has anybody standing at the door to see that no Spaniard gets in. But those were the orders that your GI's received from the Spanish government and your people have not protested. You said: 'Yes.'

"We Spaniards are a cunning and stubborn people. You'll see.

Have you noticed that no Americans wearing the uniforms of the Air Force or the American Army are seen on the streets of Spanish cities?"

"Yes, vaguely."

"Do you know why?" he asked me.

"No," I said.

"It has been written into the terms of the treaty we made with you," he told me. "Your boys can only wear their uniforms when they are on their installations, but not in public. Franco and the Falange and the Army and the Church do not want your smartly clad troops mingling with the Spanish people. You'd sow discontent. In France and Italy and England your boys walk about chewing gum and carrying cameras. But our people often never suspect that your boys are here.

"Our people are cowed and asleep. The government does not wish them to be disturbed. The energies of your people go into production; our energies go into watching one another."

"Do the Spanish people want democracy?" I asked him.

"Yes and no," he said. "Those who understand what democracy is want it. But we know very little about democracy. The nature of our Church is anti-democratic. The Falange scorns the ballot.

"In rural areas there is a kind of traditional democracy. But beyond that our conception of democracy is elementary, still crude. We establish equality by taking something away from somebody. For example, if you have nothing and you think that your neighbor is rich, you ruin him; you don't enrich yourself with his wealth; you just ruin him and then both of you are poor and equal." He laughed. "That was part of the impulse behind destroying the churches. They were too ornate, too lavish, too beautiful; they made the poor people feel miserable. . . .

"Of course, you can destroy something only when you believe in it," he explained. "The Spaniard is a magic-minded person. He felt that he had to kill the magic of the Church before he could practice his own—"

"Do Spaniards believe in ghosts?" I asked.

"No; strangely, we do not," he said, laughing. "I'm afraid that that's an English vice."

"How do you account for that among the Spanish?" I asked.

"Well, we don't need ghosts," he said. "We've got 'em visibly everywhere. Our Beyond is right there to the sight and touch, in the cathedrals."

"Your outlook is black," I chided him.

"No, no," he protested laughingly. "I'm just not proud of being a Spaniard, that's all. I'm an old man; I have no false pride. I live with myself and want to be honest with myself."

That man had lived long years abroad; he had come back to his native land and had made a bitter peace. He was out of the fight and felt that his personal state of mind was more important to him that tilting with the windmills of the Falange. And, yet, there was an element of self-hate in his attitude; he was honest, but he had had to pay a price that was akin to having a thorn sticking forever in his heart.

38 . . .

Like the uprooted Asian or African, the intellectual Spaniard, I found, felt self-conscious about how he differed from the other men of Western Europe. Through an American newspaperman I met in the British-American Club, I was introduced to a young Spaniard who, I had been promised, would "talk."

He was about twenty-eight years of age, of average height, black-haired, with a quick and nervous manner. He had an important position with a large pharmaceutical establishment, had visited England and Germany and had spent most of his youth—the years during World War II—at school in Paris. His sojourn in France had put "ideas" into his head; when drinking coffee with him in a café, I asked if Spain had many problems, and he said:

"This place crawls with problems."

"The water shortage, the agrarian problem—?"

"More than that," he cut me off.

"What, in your opinion, is wrong?" I asked.

"Just about everything," he said, sweeping his hands in a wide arc. He leaned forward tensely and spoke through clenched teeth, trying to suppress his fury. "This place needs to be *civilized*! I'm a practicing Catholic, but I don't like this Church in Spain. I'm anti-Church, anti-Franco, anti-Russian, anti-American (I'm sorry, no personal offense meant), anti-British, anti-imperialist, anti-racist, and I'm against anti-Semitism."

I could not suppress an improperly loud laugh.

"Sh," he cautioned me. "Let's don't attract too much attention."

"French logic has bitten deeply into you," I said.

"Maybe," he admitted. "But, look, what Spain is now going through all of Europe will suffer someday in the near future. We in Europe have lived off the rest of mankind for five hundred years. Those people off whom we lived are now awakened and they are tired of it. . . . We Spanish were the first to lose our possessions and we have never gotten over it. That is the heart of what is wrong here. These people have a morbid complex that they are destined by God to save the human race. It's insane. It's Spain that should be saved. But the Spaniard believes in his crazy mission; he can't forget it.

"France and all the rest of the other European countries that have colonies will be in our sad state soon," he predicted. "The West has been spoiled. It is not a healthy thing to train populations for generations in the foolish idea that they are destined only to rule, and that they must do nothing but rule. There's more mental effort in Spain today about how to rebuild the empire than there is about how to pave our streets.

"We are bad losers. Maybe the other European nations, when they have lost (and they will lose), will outdo us in their bitterness. I don't know and can't say. But at the moment, ours is the worst case. I'm sick of hearing: *Arriba España! Gibraltar para España! Todo para la patria!* I don't like the British; I've been in England. But if they gave us Gibraltar, we'd have to ask them to come and help us run it. . . .

"You see, all of these issues are false. We are one hundred years behind the other European nations. While they were working and building, we were dreaming of a Golden Age. Listen, in 1920, my father represented the Ford Motor Company here. When he drove the first Ford into Extremadura, the peasants saw that throbbing, moving mass of steel and became terrified, thinking that the Devil had come. They stoned that car as long as they could see it.

"Go off the main highways and you'll find whole villages without even outdoor toilets. They use the open fields when the urges of nature overtake them.

"I have a girl friend. Do you know that in many rural areas and in some cities and towns, when I walk the streets with her, I do not dare take her arm? I'd be arrested, or there'd be outspoken comments against it. The police would fine me twenty-five pesetas for that. There are Spaniards who call the mere touching of a woman's arm a sin.

"My fiancée and I speak French, and, to avoid being molested by the Spanish when we wish to kiss in public, we speak French very loudly. Since they think that we are French, and since they think that all the French are immoral, they let us commit the immorality of kissing! I swear it's true!"

"What makes for that?" I asked him.

"The Church. The Church in Spain is too oppressive. Day and night the priests yell against sin, that is, sex. What happens? The people become morbidly sex conscious. Our cities and villages have the highest rates of prostitution of any cities and villages of any of the countries of Europe.

"It's simple. Here's how it works. When a poor boy can't touch his girl, dares not kiss her, can't look at her breasts even when they are covered, what does he do? At the first opportunity, he takes her out into a field and has sexual relations with her. The Church has pushed sex so far down into secrecy that everything has become sexual. Go in the spring and summer into Andalusia and look into the open fields and you'll see the Spaniards fornicating like animals —and the Church has made it like that.

"Spain? It's nothing. It's like Greece."

He was a passionately bitter young man.

39 . . .

One afternoon, just after having lunched in one of Madrid's better-known restaurants, luck tossed in my path a young American architect who was engaged in drafting plans for the construction of the new air bases. He had stopped at my table to have a cup of coffee with me. He was a New Yorker, relaxed, poised, breezy, cocky, with a ready flow of words. He was abreast of the latest in fashion and scientific improvements; he was about five feet four inches tall and wore elevated shoes.

"Just how are the Americans and the Spaniards getting along in their collaboration?" I asked. "How are things going in general?"

"We are getting along like two pieces of sandpaper rubbing together," he said with a drawl.

"Is it serious?"

"Not *too* serious," he said, pulling down the corners of his lips. "There's nothing that can't be straightened out in time."

"I've been informed by people who ought to know that these Spaniards are going to change *you* before you change *them.* Is there any chance of that prediction coming true?" I asked.

He sat up and glared at me.

"Nuts!" he said. "Who in hell's been talking to you?"

"Some fairly perceptive Spaniards," I answered.

"Look, these blokes over here are dense and stubborn," he admitted. "But we can handle 'em. We'll change 'em. You watch."

"How *are* you going to change them?" I asked. "Spain has baffled some pretty astute scholars."

"I don't know what the eggheads are talking about." He snuffed out his cigarette and chewed his gum for a bit. "Look, what these people need is a middle class." He nodded philosophically. "A middle class . . ."

"But how are they going to get one?"

"We're going to *give* them one before we get through," he averred.

"That's a tall order," I informed him. "Liberals in Spain have been fighting for that for decades."

"There are many ways of doing that," he said. "These people cannot resist the new stuff that we are bringing in. They try to, but they can't.

"It's logical to do things the way they ought to be done. When we show 'em something new, they denounce it, shake their heads, but a few days later they are doing it and they like it so much that they want to pretend that they thought of how to do it all by themselves."

"But this church here . . . It's deeply entrenched. That hierarchy sits and watches you," I explained.

"We are not planning any frontal attack on any institutions here," he said. "But we've got a way of working in . . ."

"Spill it, brother. I'm all ears."

"Lemme tell you something," he began. "When I was in Japan we had a similar problem. These Spaniards have no more traditions than the Japs had. The Japs were even more backward. But look at the job we did there. When we entered Japan, there was a black market. We were supposed to smash it. But what was that black market? Just a bunch of gooks who wanted to make a dime, and they had never had anything in all of their lives. We didn't smash that black market. We knew that it went on and we wanted it to go on. We winked at it and let it ride. Why? We wanted more dough to get into the hands of people who had never had any.

"Boy, a new class of Japs got rich and changed their minds about everything. Give a man a full belly and he thinks differently. What's wrong here is too much hunger."

"You can't give me any details of just how this will operate?" I asked.

"No, no; no details. But you just watch. I'll give you my word. We'll shake 'em out of it," he swore.

I reflected a bit, recalling the passionate little barber in Barcelona who had preached to me his gospel of being master of his hunger. He had told me that he was the emperor of his misery and that he would not change for anybody or anything.

"Okay, pal," I said. "I wish you luck."

"Just watch," he said. "We're gonna jolt 'em out of this nonsense."

40 . . .

The next Spanish intellectual I met roused so many conflicts, resistances, and confused emotions in me that I can only lay the matter and its negative outcome, for whatever it is worth, before the reader.

He was a doctor, young, well traveled, and, by repute, one of the most renowned physicians in all Spain. He spoke French, English, and German fluently. He was well versed in the latest scientific discoveries of the Western world, had read papers before the royal societies of England, and there was not the slightest doubt of his prestige, probity, and general learning. He had so warm and winning a personality that it was difficult to refuse his requests. Having heard that I was looking at Spanish life, he voluntarily offered to place his time, his car, and his intelligence at my disposal.

"I want to show you Avila, the birthplace of Saint Teresa," he told me.

"Oh, I'd like that," I told him.

"Good. Especially I want to show you the river that Saint Teresa crossed," he said.

"Yes?"

"It was one of her miracles," he explained. "It was a stormy night. Saint Teresa had to go on an urgent errand. It was a life-and-death matter. But the bridge had washed away. There she stood. The torrent raged. It was dark. What was she to do? She had faith. She stepped in and the waters parted. She walked across."

I stared. At first I thought that he was making a subtle joke; but, no; he was absolutely solemn.

"Really?" I asked softly.

"Yes," he said stoutly. "I want to show you that river. Saint Teresa is my patron saint."

I swallowed. Of course, I had read in the Bible of how Moses had smitten the waters of the Red Sea and had, when the waters had receded, walked across on dry land. Also I had read some of the writings of Saint Teresa, but I had never heard of the waters of a river parting for her. And right before me was a renowned doctor vouching for it.

"Er . . . What is there at that river to show that she really crossed it that way?" I finally managed to ask him. There was nothing else that I could ask.

"Nothing," he said. "That's not important. But the waters parted and she walked across. And I believe it." He did not bat an eye.

41 . . .

Señora O., middle-aged, a Spanish citizen by marriage, was a woman of wide experience, having lived in New York, London, Buenos Aires, Paris, Berlin, Rome, etc. She held a well-paying commercial job and had many Spanish connections. She professed to be a liberal. She spoke as follows:

"A friend of mine had a husband who died only a week ago. Now, she lived in one section of the city and her husband was being buried from the church in that quarter. But, for sentimental reasons, the wife wanted the body of her husband to be taken into another quarter of the city.

"Ah . . . Trouble started. The Church authorities said that it would cost her fifteen hundred pesetas for each quarter of the city through which the body of her husband would pass. . . .

"The Church here is an industry.

"It's a strange thing, but if the police in Paris saw what goes on in cafés here in Madrid, they'd raid the places. And these people call the French immoral. I wonder how that started? It couldn't have anything to do with sexual facts. I'm sure of it.

"The Church here will tell you that the people here love God so much that sex has been conquered. But all that you hear about here is sex. When I first came here, I thought that the Spanish had just discovered sex—they talked so much about it, and they still do. Sometimes they act as if they invented sex.

"Even the children are sex conscious in a way that is not known in other countries. If you don't believe it, then just ask a Spanish child of six to talk about sex. They know *everything*. Don't ask me how and where they learn it, but they know. A Spanish child of six could tell a man of twenty-one in New York things that he does not know about sex.

"And night and day they speak about innocence, about the Virgin. I don't understand it. Life is upside down here. You have to be here, live here to get used to it."

42 . . .

Tall, handsome, pleasant, he had the nervous and evasive manner of a man not at peace with himself. You felt that in his past he had had to watch his step and that his had been a life of quiet, bourgeois living mingled with conditions under which he had had sometimes to reach for his gun. Yet you knew that, despite his preference for peace and order, he was brave and had inflexible convictions. As I faced him and listened to him talk, I said to myself: "This man has had to make too many compromises."

He ranked high in the Spanish maritime world and could trace his ancestry back to the exciting days of Cortés. He was proud of Spain, but hastily admitted: "We made a record that is called the Black Legend. . . ." He sighed. "We Spaniards are a strange people; we are problems to ourselves. We mixed up things terribly in history. We could have been the dominant people on earth today if we had had any sense.

"We had no color bar, really. We married the colored peoples. We gave them our culture in a way that no other European nation ever did, and we meant it. But we were greedy; we were after gold. And that ruined us.

"In South America we had a great man, Las Casas, who loved and defended the Indians." He shook his head in wonder, his eyes baffled. "We are still asking ourselves how and why we messed it all up. We needn't have, you know.

"Yet, we were very brave. Who but Cortés would have burned his ships behind him when he did not know what he faced in Mexico?"

"What you say is true," I said. "But weren't those special conditions when compared with those of today?"

He bowed his head and pondered awhile.

"Yes," he admitted. "They were. Spain is and was a Church-State. The world was a Church-world then. The country that was foremost in that world was Spain. We were at the center of the universe."

"And the people you conquered had religions too, didn't they?" I asked.

He blinked, unable to grasp the point of my question. Those people had been "heathens." He did not say so, but he was convinced that they were still "heathens" and that his religion was the only true one, that it had been entrusted to him and his kind by God for safekeeping.

"Politically, what are you?" I asked him.

"I'm a civilized man," he said ruefully. "What *could* my politics be here? I fought for Franco. I'm not ashamed to admit it. I couldn't help it at the time. But I call myself a liberal. I'm Catholic, but I'm liberal. Of course, I can't tell my priest that. They are backward here."

He was silent. He had had to assume a position of psychological independence and it was bothering him. He longed for a Church that would endorse his humanist leanings.

"I just *had* to fight for Franco," he resumed. "I know my Spain. I could not see the Communists' winning. Do you know what I mean? It's not that I'm so much against Communism, but I just don't like *Communists*. Not at all . . . Let me tell you something. . . .

"One Easter Sunday I saw a Communist leader marching in the religious procession, carrying the Virgin on his shoulders. After the parade, I asked him: 'How can you, a Communist, carry the Virgin?'

"He answered: 'But, sir, *this* Virgin is from my own neighborhood!'

"I cannot support that kind of nonsense. That man had sworn that he did not believe in God. Yet there he was carrying the Virgin. How can you fight with men who twist and turn like that?"

"Do you regret your having supported Franco?" I asked.

"I helped Franco because I could not support something *crazy*," he said in despair. "Something *worse* . . . I had no choice."

He sat a long time hunched in dejection. Then he lifted his face to me and smiled bitterly.

"Those people whom the Spanish conquered," I began, "they had virgins in their religions too."

He stared at me with wide eyes.

"I'm only a layman," he said tiredly, sighing. "I only know what I'm told about matters like that."

"Well, those savages had virgin goddesses that served them just as the Virgin here serves you," I said.

He continued his blank stare. I decided to leave that subject. Then he lifted his head.

"Let me tell you something," he began in a tone of hot anger. "I have a son. Just six years old . . . A few days ago he came home from his class and asked me: 'Father, does God live always?'

" 'Yes,' I said.

" 'And does Franco live always?' "

He stared at me for several seconds.

"I'm a Spaniard, a liberal, a pro-Franco man who fought to save Spain from Communism. But I turned pale when my son asked me *if Franco would live always.* I bent down and asked him: 'Why do you ask me that, son?'

" 'That's what my political teacher says, Father.'

"I didn't even know that he had a political teacher until then. I don't want my son to be taught anything that even remotely mixes up Franco with God!" His whole body was stiff with anger. "That is not what I fought for and I don't like it. No matter what or how they teach, they don't have to confuse children about Franco and God!"

He was a decent man outraged by the conditions of his life.

43 . . .

The next subject to answer my question was a great professor of law, one of the highest-ranking legal minds of Spain, an authority on the political situation. He was a short man with a pleasant, schoolteacher's manner. He was terse, objective, pruning his statements of all emotion and committing himself only to that which could be objectively ascertained by someone else.

"How much bitterness lingers on here as a result of the Civil War?" I asked him.

"The Civil War is just about liquidated," he told me.

"What do you mean by that?"

"It's no longer an issue," he explained. "A new generation has grown up. The old wounds are healed. Even families that were arrayed against one another have made peace."

I believed him, yet I remembered Dolores, that tense and proud daughter who carried the responsibility of her family on her shoulders; I remembered that dog, Ronnie, and his neurotic fury in that Barcelona apartment; and I knew that the shadow of that war still darkened the memories of millions of Spaniards, and that only the death of the participants could ever truly liquidate its horrors.

"What is the number of the political prisoners now being held under the Franco regime?" I wanted to know.

"I can't give you an exact figure," he said. "But it is below the number that obtained before the Civil War."

"And what was the number then?"

"About two hundred and forty thousand," he said.

"So the number of those now being held is less than that?"

"Yes."

"What happens to a freed political prisoner?"

"His plight is very bad," he admitted. "He has not had his civil rights restored. He is discriminated against in job hunting."

"When will the freed political prisoner get his civil rights?" I asked.

"No one knows just when that will happen," he said.

"Sir, there is a lot of talk in France and elsewhere about concentration camps in Spain. Do you know anything about that?"

"I know nothing of any concentration camps. And personally I don't think that there are any. That phase is past," he said.

"What about Communism here?" I asked.

"It is roughly estimated that about five per cent of the population is Communist," he said.

"Party members?" I asked, surprised.

"That's the government estimate," he said.

"How is Communism defined here?" I asked.

He smiled and shrugged. He was factual, but his facts felt like mercury in my hands.

"Some social scientists and others have been urging the government to sample public opinion to find out what people are really feeling and thinking in this country," he explained with an apologetic smile.

"In short, the government here really doesn't know just how the people feel?"

"I don't think it does," he said.

"What about the restoration of the monarchy? One reads a lot about this in the press outside of Spain."

"That's a plan," he said cautiously. "I don't think that there will be any restoration of the monarchy until after Franco is dead. The idea of a monarchy serves to organize certain sections of public opinion."

"Sections of the Falange are opposed to a king; is that true?"

"Yes, that is true."

"Just how strong is the Falange?" I asked him.

"Not so very strong," he said. "In recent parades here in Madrid the Falange did not make a good showing."

"Yet students are obliged to belong to it; are they not?"

"Yes," he said.

"I've plowed through one of the Falangist catechisms," I explained. "It is taught, isn't it?"

"Yes," he said. "All university students must belong to the Falange."

"And how much of the Falangist doctrine do they believe, these students?" I asked, feeling that reality was slipping away from me.

"That is what has to be determined," he said. "Sixty per cent of our youth know nothing of the Civil War, so it's hard to say just what they feel."

I sat pondering. Obviously, the government and the Falange were depending upon the adherence of youth to their doctrines, but there was no way to determine just how widespread the adherence was. I suspected that they assumed that deep adherence was small and that was why such a show of force had to be maintained.

"And the Anarchists? What about them?"

"Well, that is really a kind of lay religious category, you know," he said. "They flourish in Catalonia and Andalusia; but they weave in and out of society as a whole."

"How do the Spaniards regard this pact between America and Spain?"

"It is very popular, but each section of the population has its own special reasons for liking it," he explained. "You might say that the Spanish-American alliance is *dangerously* popular." (His tone of voice did not indicate if he approved or disapproved.)

"In what way?"

"Well, each section sees in it something for itself. . . . For instance, the Falange has boasted far and wide that America, in making this pact, has changed its mind, has admitted that she was wrong in the past and that now she repents and wants to join hands with Spain in fighting Russia.

"Some Socialists feel that there is hope for democracy in Spain because of that pact—"

"On what do they base that hope?" I asked.

"On nothing in particular," he said.

"Have the Americans in any way given encouragement to such hopes?" I wanted to know.

"None whatever," he answered. "The Americans have been most correct, abjectly correct in abiding by the terms of the agreement."

"Those terms are severe," I stated.

"Do you think so?" he asked with a knowing smile.

He was hinting that he did not think much of America's knuckling under to Franco.

"But there must be some critics of the pact, aren't there?" I asked.

"Yes," he said thoughtfully. "Some sections of the Church have voiced strong objections."

"This fellow Segura, the Cardinal in Seville, for example?"

"Yes. He spearheaded the opposition," he said. "But he has been more or less silenced. He is a donkey. He is not important now."

"And what other sections are hostile?"

"Not all Socialists like the pact," he informed me. "There are some sections of the population that feel that their hope for freedom has been betrayed by the pact."

"In short, they regard the pact as an endorsement of Franco?"

"Yes. And there is also a vague hope, born of that pact, that Franco will be heaved out and another regime installed. But there is no basis for such a hope."

"Is that hope irrational?" I asked.

"Yes."

"Perhaps that irrational hope indicates the depths of the despair here?" I questioned him leadingly.

He smiled and would not commit himself.

"The pact has actually increased tensions here, then?" I asked in a tone that was half declaration and half question.

"To some degree, yes."

"Would you agree with me if I said that the Spaniard was a deeply emotional man, sir? I'm not speaking in a derogatory sense, I assure you. I'd class myself as an emotional person—only I think I know that I'm emotional."

"The Spaniard acts," he said.

"Yes, yes. We all act. But out of what does the Spaniard act? Look, what I'm trying to get at is this. It's rather delicate. The question I want to ask is: There is poverty here; there are grievances. There's a dictatorship, open and blatant. Now, is there any fear of a serious uprising here—"

"No, no," he said quickly. "Spaniards are a people with a military personality. Remember that. We fought the Moors for seven hundred years. We had no trained men; we just fought in mobs, in individual exploits, each section of the country making its individual contribution.

"Then we had the Inquisition. Then we conquered the Americas. Those were not organized ventures. Each man went out and did what he could, or did what he wanted to. That heritage has come down to us today. But we want no more war, no more fighting for a change. We are tired of that."

"What is the actual situation in relation to the Church and education?" I asked.

"In the primary grades, forty per cent of the education is religious; sixty per cent is in the hands of the State. In the secondary grades, fifty per cent is State and fifty per cent is Church. Large numbers of children of middle-class Catholic families insist upon sending their children to expensive Church schools conducted by the orders. This is the result of a class difference that splits Spanish society in two. The working classes are thus compelled to send their children to State schools."

"What is the national per capita income of a Spaniard?"

"About five thousand pesetas," he said sadly.

"Roughly a hundred dollars a year?"

"Yes."

"How does this compare with what they received in 1936?"

"Inflation has risen seven times since 1936 and has lowered the standard of working-class living," he stated. "Wages today are lower than in 1936. Suffering is general. The worst section is Andalusia. Men work from four to six months of the year. There's no diversification of crops; the agrarian problem plagues us now as it has for centuries."

"Why can't some step be taken toward a solution?"

"Any radical attempt on the part of any government to solve that problem rouses the anger and opposition of the big Andalusian landowners," he stated. "The Republic expropriated many of those vast estates, but Franco gave them back."

"How much industrialization is going on?"

"There is a lot of it," he said. "But it is under the umbrella of monopoly capitalism. Foreign capital coming into the country is limited by law to a twenty-five per cent participation in industrial enterprises. There are some special cases of a fifty-fifty participation of State and foreign money.

"But the simple truth is that most of the money in Spain is in the hands of a few landowners and a few industrialists. The national income of Spain does not permit of industrialization without foreign aid. We are poor; we are in the situation of many colonies," he concluded.

My interview with the lawyer underscored the fact that "facts" in Spain were elusive. Spain was officially Catholic; any dissent provoked punitive measures. Therefore, on the surface, all was peaceful. But what was beneath the surface? The heart of Spain was the Church; overlapping with and fanning out from the Church were the Falange, the government, the Civil Guard, the Army, etc. That all but twenty thousand Protestants and two thousand and five hundred Jews belonged to the Church was taken for granted. It was the kind of setup that would inevitably create an underground. And I had no special talent for snooping into undergrounds. . . . In the end, all I had before me was one fact: totalitarianism. But I was never able to tell just how strong it really was, and because no one knew its strength, I suspected that it was actually very weak.

44 . . .

Through the intercession of friends, I went one evening to interview a young Spanish Jewish businessman. He had entered Spain some five years previously, having come out of Russia by way of Poland by way of Belgium. He had lost all of his family through pogroms and wars and revolutions. He spoke Spanish fluently, without an accent; he was proud of having blended, in terms of external appearance and manner, with the reality of Spain. Tall, swarthy, with a smooth, gliding, almost courtly manner, he looked and acted distinctly Spanish.

We sat together in a quiet corner of the lobby of one of Madrid's most luxurious hotels. Drinks rested on a little table before us. From somewhere in the vast spaciousness the lulling melody of a Viennese waltz wafted to our ears. Jew and Negro, both from backgrounds of persecution, we sat seemingly securely anchored in a twentieth-century world of sanity and comfort.

"Is there any anti-Semitism in Spain?" I asked him.

He looked straight ahead and the fingers of his right hand wandered to his neatly knotted tie, making sure that the folds were straight, acceptable to the world.

"No," he said after a long hesitation.

Was he willing to talk or unable to? He had lived through bloody pogroms and surely he knew what I was asking. Or did he feel that I, a Negro, had no right to invade that dark domain of his heart? His evasiveness nettled me and I opened up broadly.

"Maybe it was all solved back in 1492 when Ferdinand and Isabel drove the Jews from Spain?"

"Yes," he breathed.

My irritation vanished. It was not that he did not wish to talk; it was simply almost impossible for him to talk. All right. I would wait. He cleared his throat.

"You see, there are only two thousand five hundred of us here in Spain," he said.

"And since there are practically no Jews in Spain, there can't be a problem, can there?" I asked.

"That's right." He sounded as though he were forcing the words out of his throat.

"Why did you come to Spain?" I asked.

"I like Spain," he said.

"There's France, England—"

"You see," he sighed, "my people lived here once."

"You mean—"

"My ancestors were here," he told me simply at last. "I speak Spanish from them."

"Oh! After all those centuries?"

"Yes."

I looked at him again. So that was why he had come back! He was a football of history. . . .

"How old are you?" I asked.

"Twenty-nine."

"Can a Jew marry here?" I asked him.

He was silent again. Finally he leaned forward, stared at the figures in the plush carpet and explained: "If a Jewish boy and girl wish to marry here, they must first get a certificate from the priest in their area—a certificate saying that they have never been baptized."

"Is it easy to prove that you were never baptized?" I asked.

"Well, you never can really prove it," he said with a wry smile. "You just convince them."

"Then the Catholic Church has the *negative* right to say if a Jew can marry or not?"

He scratched his head and a hunted look came into his eyes.

"Yes. Without a certificate of nonbaptism, they cannot marry."

"Then, if you get a certificate of nonbaptism, a rabbi can marry you after you have married under Civil Law?"

"Yes."

"But the rabbinical marriage in itself is not valid?"

"No."

"What effect has a certificate of nonbaptism upon a Jew who belongs to the synagogue?" I posed yet another dilemma for him.

He glanced at me as though I were a policeman grilling him for a crime. He sighed.

"It nullifies our religion and makes us confess the omnipotence of Catholicism," he confessed.

"Suppose a Jew wished to marry a Catholic?" I asked.

"He would have to marry in the Catholic Church and pledge that any issue from that marriage would be brought up in the Catholic faith," he explained.

"But what if he insisted upon marrying outside of the Church?"

"A Jew could not marry a Catholic who would not want to be married in the Church and who would not pledge to rear the children as Catholics," he said.

"Then that particular Jew cannot get married?"

"That's it."

"You can't marry as a Jew, and if you do marry, the children are not yours?"

"That's about it."

"There's a lot of Jewish blood in Spain, isn't there?" I asked him.

"Yes," he explained. "We Spanish Jews have carried the Spanish tongue all over the world. They drove us out and we were scattered, but we still speak Spanish. Many Sephardic Jews still bear their Spanish names." He was identifying himself now and his words flowed freely, proudly. "Franco is partly or wholly Jewish. In fact, there is about thirty or forty per cent of Jewish blood in the veins of the Spanish people.

"You see, we Jews either had to leave, or turn Catholic, that is, become *conversos*. I've come back to the country from which my ancestors were driven centuries ago. *I feel that I am Spanish*."

"You *want to be* Spanish," I said.

"I'M SPANISH!" he repeated. "Names like Perez, Franco, etc., are Jewish names. Toledo is a Jewish word. . . ."

A void hung between us.

"I must go," he said suddenly, rising. I longed to talk to him more, to try to follow the logic of his feelings. I walked beside him through the lobby to the sidewalk. We shook hands.

"Can I give you a lift?" he asked me brusquely.

"No, thank you," I said. "My car's over there."

Without another word he spun on his heels and got into a long, shining Jaguar. One second later I heard the motor roar thunderously and he tore away down the night street at a terrifying speed, swerving like a knife blade through the traffic. I knew that he was seething with shame and burning with fury. But shame for what? And fury against whom?

45 . . .

I left Madrid early the following Sunday morning and traveled south through a wall of rain so solid that I could scarcely see the road. I feared plunging into a deep puddle of water and drowning my motor. Then, ahead, I discerned vague outlines of cars stalled in currents that eddied about their fenders. I about-faced and found an early-morning café where I drank coffee and waited for the storm to slacken.

Later the rain abated and I rolled again under a gray sky. The look and feel of Spain assumed a drastically altered aspect after I quit Madrid. The savage mountains grew tamer; the brooding, red hills shed their desolate character and changed to gentle mounds of gray; indeed, with the passing hours, the landscape turned a shy glad green.

The highway dipped, rose, and, like a writhing serpent, seemed at times to coil back upon itself. Then, when I thought that I was free of mountains, another range loomed. To my left a sky of purplish mist began to wax bright. Gradually a red sheen glowed, banishing straggling veils of clouds. I came out of the mountains and traversed yellow-green hills whose contours waved in the deepening light. Moments later I was climbing into more mountains and the east blazed, thrusting up delicate fingers of pink and blue. I climbed a steep peak of mountain and, *bang!* The sun was there, a bare, unwinking eye of hard blue steel which, as I followed the bending road, played a game of hide and seek that nearly blinded me, making me put on my sunglasses.

I began a slow descent and the air, moistened by vegetation, lost its sharp, dry quality and I looked at the first signs of intensive land cultivation that I had seen so far in Spain. I was in the province of Toledo and the dominant activity was agriculture. I rode into Ocoña, a town composed of a decrepit conglomeration of dingy stone houses sheltering some seven thousand people. Peasants filed heavily along muddy, manure-strewn alleyways, going to mass.

I braked my car on slippery clay, got out in front of the Santo Domingo Church, whose soaring yellow walls were scaly with peeling paint. I entered and found mass in progress. Beyond the heads of kneeling penitents was a gilded altar framed with glittering candles. There was silence save for a softly chanting voice. High along both walls were paintings of floating angels below which were rows of shrines, each with its cluster of crouching communicants, their eyes glazed, their lips moving in silent supplication, their rough fingers telling their beads, and, again, I was moved by what was beyond doubt the deep and abject piety of the Spaniards.

These people were not serving God, they were adoring Him, surrendering themselves before what they felt to be the Supreme Consciousness of the universe. To Catholics the hierarchy of Christianity was external, unspeakably beautiful, powerful, and yet miraculously accessible through the intercession of others, and it was inconceivable for them to think of refusing the aid of intermediaries to enable them to receive balm or blessings from that source.

To Protestants this whole process had been psychologically interalized, made a part of their mental functioning. Protestants had to conjure up out of their imagination, their longings, and fears, and with but few or no visual representations, what they felt to be the Supreme Consciousness of the universe for the balm and blessings they needed. Protestants had to make severe demands upon themselves; Catholics submitted to what had already been arranged.

The Protestant, therefore, could be dynamic, could project into his environment his sense of his dignity, could create his sense of God out of the worldliness of the world. Hence, the social systems of America, England, Switzerland, and large parts of Protestant Scandinavia had been transformed by Protestant pressure molding the environment; they had higher standards of living, more health, more literacy, more industry—all stemming from the Protestant's ability to handle the materials of reality.

But the Spanish Catholic remained static, the victim of a spell cast by the external configuration of fetish objects that coerced his imagination and emotions to unchangeableness. He was doomed to apprehend his environment through the fogged and sacred glass of the Church's hierarchy. And the physical area of the Spaniard's life reflected this: low standards of living, illiteracy, no control over material forces, and a charged, confused consciousness that compelled him to seek release from his frustrations in the projected shadows of his own personality. A glance sufficed to reveal how little Spain had altered during the long centuries. . . .

Emerging from the church, I saw at once that that altar and those shrines were the only beautiful images in that town. In Protestant environments the churches were almost always plain and simple, while living conditions carried the adornments; here, living conditions were sodden, dilapidated, and the only beauty resided in the churches.

A bearded, wrinkled beggar wearing filthy rags blocked my path, mumbling. I dropped a few centavos into his clawlike hand and his dull eyes gleamed with a flicker of life and he breathed:

"*Gracias.*"

46 . . .

I drove under an El Greco sky through villages filled with Goya-faced peasants. Signs painted on walls exhorted the population: *Viva Franco! Arriba España! Todo por la patria!*

I entered the flat plain of La Mancha, the domain of the fabled and abortive doings of Don Quixote, and rolled toward Madridejos, where I paused to examine a yellowed stone church over whose ancient doorway was engraved: 1679. The interior was dim and drab; high up on the altar was a life-sized statue of Crucified Christ against a red backdrop. His nudity was draped by a red silk petticoat in the center of which, in the direction of the genitals, was a cluster of silken embroidery. As I left, swarms of boy beggars with feet shod in rotting canvas shoes surrounded me.

"Ceegarettes! Ceegarettes!" they chanted.

In the next town, Puerto Lapice, I entered an ugly brick church whose murky interior was lit by twinkling candles. A priest sat in the confessional box hearing the whispered transgressions of a kneeling girl of about ten years of age. After listening for a moment, he dismissed the child's sins with a wave of his hand and strode to the altar and began lighting candles. I lingered, looking at two powerful, realistic Christ figures. In one Christ sagged from a cross, His eyes lit with dull agony, His parted lips cracked, His tortured body girded by a red silken sash. The other Christ, His face strained, was bent beneath the weight of a gigantic cross. Sweat glistened on His contracted brow and the effect of physical horror and suffering was almost hypnotic. The veins were distended, the neck distorted. The arms, elbows, and knees had been streaked with red paint to create the illusion of skinned and torn flesh. The eyes were those of a dumb animal in the grip of excruciating pain.

I reached Manzanares, a small town dominated by a hideous church that faced the main square. I was besieged by ragged women, many of whom held babies in their arms; they stretched out their dirty palms and chorused a singsong of supplication. The square itself was thronged with unshaven, shabby men, most of whom stared in sullen silence at every move I made. These were the most dispirited Spaniards I had yet seen. Did their unnatural silence mean that they were the masters of their hunger? Or was Franco the master here?

A few kilometers farther I lunched in a charming Parador and my table was adorned with vases of delicate roses. The splendor of this Parador would have awed the peasants of Spain as much as the cathedrals in which they worshiped. Spanish Catholicism was one of the odd fatalities of the world.

In Valdepeñas I found the town square packed with children in dirty cotton rags and, as soon as I alighted, they began a whining begging. One skinny little girl of about seven carried in her arms a child who seemed to be her baby brother. Their faces were pocked with sores and their eyes were large, moist, round, and bloodshot, perhaps from weakness and hunger. Dirty little hands reached out, palms up.

"*Dame dinero, Señor,*" they whispered.

47 . . .

I now weighed my remaining excursions, pondering over Galicia, Asturias, Santiago de Compostela where, legend had it, the body of St. James the apostle was buried. And I recalled that, when I had passed through Saragossa, I had not stopped to see the famed Virgin of the *Pilar* who reigned over the Cathedral of *Nuestra Señora del Pilar* where, according to religious tradition, the Virgin had made a miraculous visitation and selected the spot for the erection of her shrine. Then there were Ibiza, Mallorca, and Málaga. I concluded that, of all these beckoning place names, I would see the *Virgen del Pilar* and the *Semana Santa* (Holy Week) of Seville. Treks to Galicia and Asturias, and even Santiago de Compostela would be but more sorties into religion.

But, luckily, before I set off toward Saragossa and Seville, the magic of Toledo and El Greco lured me irresistibly. And well it might, for Toledo was a vast museum crammed with the past of Spain. Sheltered by a high, luminous sky and situated amidst flashing rivers and somber ravines, Toledo had narrow, cobblestoned streets that darted up and down hillsides. Tourists swarmed everywhere. Most of the public buildings were monuments of history:

Roman, Jewish, Moorish, and the conquering Catholic. The deserted synagogues, victims of the ingenious cruelty of the Inquisition, were pathetic reminders that totalitarianism was no new thing. . . .

The Alcazar, that hoary Moorish castle-fortress in which Charles V had once lived, was interesting not only because of its gloomy immensity, but for the fetish value with which the Falangists had endowed it by their fanatical militancy that branded every non-Falangist an enemy.

Huge sums of money had been appropriated to refurbish this mammoth structure that sprawled over a vast area and lifted some five or six stories into the air. Swarms of workmen were busy plastering the jagged fissures that had been caused by the shells of the fated Republic. The Alcazar was being converted into a shrine of the fallen Falangists, many of whose bodies had been ceremoniously entombed in its massive ramparts. I poked through its dark chambers and saw how the Falangists had fought and died; their guns, their crude cooking utensils were still there.

On one scarred wall was a full-length painting of the commanding Colonel Moscardo who, when his son had been held hostage by the Republicans, had allowed that son to be slain rather than surrender. This display of theatrical heroism was being underscored by harangues of tourist guides who steered American, French, English, and German ladies through monstrous heaps of rubble.

If the Alcazar was a monument to the Falange's psychopathic strivings toward "Destiny in the Universal," then El Greco's "The Burial of Count Orgaz" was a magnificent projection of the same theme in terms of poetic vision purged of Falangist dross. That masterpiece in the St. Thomas Church of Toledo depicted with truer persuasion man's longing for immortality than all the tortured, blood-clotted Christs in the cathedrals of Spain. Lacking any other account of how the men of the Middle Ages felt about life, El Greco's harmony of evanescent images, done in tones of gray, black, and carmine, could serve as a kind of document detailing the nature of the hope that had once animated medieval minds in their more humane aspects.

Swinging back to Madrid, I went to Saragossa, arriving at twilight. The city was dry and dusty from silt blown from the surrounding red hills. Next morning I toured the industrial section of that metropolis of some 350,000 people, then went to see the Virgin of the *Pilar*, a shrine to which the Catholic faithful from the world over came to ask special favors.

The cathedral was a choir of singing stone; rich, ornate, filled with paintings by Goya and Bayeu, etc., it abounded in marble, bronze, alabaster, silks, satins, silver, and gold. The *Virgen del Pilar* was a lavishly decorated statue, doll-like in size and appearance, and rested atop the original column upon which, it was said, the Virgin had made herself manifest. Before it knelt some hundred or more people, young and old, men and women, rich and poor—all worshiping in perfect democracy, the only equality that they would perhaps ever know—their eyes cloudy with desperate hope. Points of candlelight fluttered amid the dim and soaring columns. The falling lances of ghostly light, the faraway domes, the silence, the odor of incense induced a mood of humility and dependence.

On my right a white-jacketed altar boy carried a four-year-old child in his arms toward the statue so that it could kiss the hem of the Virgin's robe. I watched the child grasp a fold of the glittering robe with its chubby fingers and dab it greedily against its mouth several times. Men and women watched with tears in their eyes, crossing themselves. I was informed afterward that only children under seven years of age were allowed that precious privilege. . . .

That night I put up at a hotel and resumed my study of Carmen's political catechism, turning to lesson twelve for girls between the ages of twelve and fourteen:

The Poetic Imperative

WHAT DO WE MEAN BY POETIC IMPERATIVE?

An inward force that always leads us to prefer the beauty of things.

AND BY THE MERE FACT OF CHOOSING THE BEAUTIFUL, THIS PREFERENCE WILL BE MANIFEST?

Yes, for all that is beautiful tends toward perfection and in choosing the beautiful we also choose what is perfect.

BUT IS THE AIM PERFECTION?

Certainly, for what is perfect is just, what is just is good, and what is good is fit and proper.

WHY MUST FALANGISTS OBEY THE POETIC IMPERATIVE TO BE REAL FALANGISTS?

Because the Falange is, in itself, a poetic movement.

HOW SO?

Because poetry is what is continually creating perfection.

WHAT HAS THAT GOT TO DO WITH THE FALANGE?

A great deal, given that the Falange is a movement tending toward perfection and, moreover, is substantially a poetic movement.

WILL YOU EXPLAIN THIS FURTHER?

The Falange does not seek ornament in poetry, but seeks in poetry, or in superior creation, the solution of all its problems.

HOW DO WE KNOW THIS?

Through all José Antonio told us, and through his life, which always obeyed a poetic imperative.

WILL YOU EXPLAIN FURTHER?

For example, his stubborn insistence on fighting against the coarse, the facile, the vulgar; the rigor and precision of his literary style and of the style of his life; his political solutions for Spain's problems; everything in him obeyed a poetic imperative.

CAN YOU GIVE SOME EXAMPLES?

When he said, "Alas for him who cannot be roused by the poetry that destroys the poetry that promises!"

CAN THERE BE DESTRUCTIVE POETRY?

Yes; apparently beautiful creations that travel on the wrong road, such as separatist movements.

HOW CAN THIS BE, IF WE SAID EVERYTHING BEARS IN IT A POETIC SUBSTANCE TENDING TO PERFECTION?

Because it is the negative perfection that destroys the "strong and beautiful wholes."

WHAT THEN SHALL WE DO TO FIGHT POETICALLY AGAINST POETIC SEPARATISTS?

Offer as a solution the poetry which promises, a poetry superior to theirs, which does not ignore the poetic reasons that they too may have.

ON WHAT OCCASIONS DID JOSÉ ANTONIO SPEAK OF THE SUBSTANCE OF THE FALANGE?

When he said, ". . . that the nations have never been moved more than by poets"; when he stated, on founding the Falange, that, ". . . The flag is raised; we shall now defend it joyfully, poetically." When he told us: "The shortest way between two points is the one that goes through the stars."

48 . . .

Upon arriving in Seville for the second time, I could sense at once that I was in for a frantic week. In almost all the shop windows of the city I saw tiny robed figures with tall, pointed hoods that gave me a creepy feeling, for these objects reminded me of the Ku Klux Klan of the Old American South. It must have been from here that the Ku Klux Klan regalia had been copied. Well, I would see to what use the Spaniards had put this costume. Was pillage or penitency the object when one donned such an outlandish dress?

Tourists had flooded the city and no hotel room was available. I went back to my old pension and found the four sedate ladies willing to accept me and still doing their day's work at night. Seville was like an old friend and my first walk into Alameda de Hercules produced my withered-armed scout who welcomed me and assured me that nothing had changed and that the forthcoming week would be wonderful.

I went to the Cathedral Santa de la Sede and studied the stupendous collection of religious relics, seeing, among other things, a thistle that was said to have been taken from the crown of thorns that had been so cruelly pressed by the infidel Romans upon the brow of Christ. I saw also the ivory-carved crucifix that Hermán Cortés had taken with him on his daring expedition to conquer Mexico. Yellow with age, slender, the cross was strangely modernistic in design and the elongated figure of Christ, with contorted features and a look of agony in the dying eyes, reminded me of those El Greco characters whose delicately pointed fingers and long necks and heads were said to be an indication of a straining and longing for Heaven. This was the symbol that the Christian had raised at the head of his warlike hosts.

In 1455 the Pope had divided the world between the Spanish and the Portuguese and those nations had had not only the right, but the moral duty of enslaving those infidels who failed to kneel and kiss the cross and accept Christ as their Redeemer. Yet how was it that four hundred desperate, half-starved white men, with this cross, had conquered millions? True, the white men had been brave and the minds of their red-skinned adversaries had been ridden with superstition, but even that did not explain how a mere handful could subdue millions.

That they had triumphed in the name of a dead God nailed to a cross was undeniably true, but what had that cross meant to them? And what had it meant to the millions whom they had subjugated? If anywhere in the Western world there was an answer to that riddle, it was here in this slow and sleepy city of Seville, here where tradition had remained intact for four centuries, here in this pile of Gothic stone that soared with such fragile majesty toward a blue sky, here in these narrow medieval streets where each store window showed the images of penitents in white, red, and blue robes.

The weather was sunny and bright. Seats along the routes of the religious processions were in the hands of speculators and I had to pay a premium for my chair. More than the usual number of candles were being lighted in the dim and hushed cathedrals. Women were shopping for black lace shawls. Newspapers were filled with photos of Tortured Christs and Weeping Virgins.

While in the center of the city, I saw a fashionably dressed woman walking along barefooted! I blinked, then looked to see if others saw what I saw. No. People were passing her as if her attire, or lack of it, were normal. Back in my pension, I asked Señora F. the meaning of it.

"She was doing penance. Many people pledge to their priest not to wear shoes, or not to eat on certain days, or to walk a certain number of kilometers. It's quite common."

At three o'clock in the afternoon a man clad in snow-white raiment stepped from a gaping doorway. Children grouped about him and stared at his hidden face, for this man was masked and hooded. A round white peaked cap about two and a half feet tall surmounted his head and a white mask covered his face and chest. Two holes, slitted into the material, provided a manner for him to see. The Christian cross blazoned in red on his chest. He adjusted his white hood carefully and rushed off, the children trotting after him in awe and excitement.

Over all the city other robed and hooded men surged out of dingy doorways; religious processions were beginning a ritual that would eventually converge upon the cathedral. I pushed my way through vast crowds to the place where I had bought a chair; en route I passed masses of hooded figures and I had the feeling that a priest would have had but to utter a single word and these disguised men would have leaped gladly to obey that word. I sat down at Plaza San Francisco.

In the distance I heard the thunder of many drums being beaten in unison: *drum-drum; drruuuum-drruuuum-drruuuum. . . .* And to the beat of the drums thousands of feet trampled over cobblestones. Policemen dressed in blue with red-striped pants, with red rims on their peaked caps, passed, armed to the teeth. Why? Then came the dolorous music of what seemed like a million trumpets. The drums and the trumpets made a message like a death march. The procession arrived with floating banners.

First came a contingent of smartly dressed troops with tall, white plumes dangling from their steel helmets and waving in front of their eyes, giving an impression of lofty and disdainful military might. Their chests were covered with loop upon loop of gold braid and yellow tassels. Their faces were hard and stern. Glittering swords swung from their hips. Their high black boots gleamed and they marched with a slow, almost shuffling tread.

White-hooded and masked penitents, members of church organizations known as brotherhoods, came, each carrying a huge candle that was at least four inches in diameter and more than four feet long. The huge candles rested upon the hips of the penitents and the flickering flames danced above their heads, the molten wax streaming and sparkling in the bright sun, spattering in translucent spots on the dark cobblestones—flying white drops that were like semen spraying, jutting from the penises of sexually aroused bulls. On and on the white-robed, white-hooded penitents flowed past and the drums beat: *drum, drum—drruuuum—drruuuum—drruuuum. . . .* Two white-robed, white-hooded little boys were carrying incense vessels of delicately wrought silver which they swung slowly, creating a thin cloud of purple smoke that rose and scented the air with a sweetish smell as of burning sandalwood. In the sunshine the smoke turned a misty blue. Children penitents were now moving past, each holding a burning candle, and the liquid wax dripped and flew like white tears.

A mammoth float bearing a sculptured Virgin heaved into view. Her head was crowned with gold. Her fingers, lifted in mute supplication, were crammed with rings in whose settings were diamonds and pearls. A wilderness of smoking, burning candles surrounded the Virgin, lighting her sorrowful face so that the glass tears pasted on her cheeks glinted in the light of the dying sun. Soldiers marched on each side of the Virgin, guarding her, protecting her; then behind the float came soldiers of the regular Spanish Army, wearing dark brown steel helmets. The rifles on their shoulders had steel bayonets that gleamed balefully. The troops marched with slow and measured steps, their right legs kicking up, their left legs kicking up—they were doing a modified goosestep. The Church, then the armed State to protect the Church . . .

Still another float came. The figures were life-size. Christ, streaked with blood, sagged from a huge cross. The drums beat: *drum,*

drum—drruuuum-drruuuum-drruuuum. . . . A bugle corps with dragging feet followed and the air was rent with a melancholy refrain. In the wake of the Dying Christ came thousands of closely arrayed troops and their dully gleaming bayonets made a forest of steel. It was now twilight and sweet-smelling incense fogged the air.

Tired, I went home. I sat on the edge of my bed and attempted to sort out what I had seen. Those hooded penitents had been protecting the Virgin, and in the Old American South hooded Ku Kluxers had been protecting "the purity of white womanhood." Even if the white South in America had copied their tactics and costumes from here, it did not explain why men loved to march in defense of what they felt was female purity. Some underlying reality more powerful than the glittering Virgin or southern white women had gripped these undeniably primitive minds. They were following some ancient pattern of behavior and were justifying their actions in terms that had nothing whatever to do with that pattern.

Next afternoon I went again to the Plaza San Francisco to watch the processions stream past. The first contingent came silently, without music or drums. Then came long lines of black-hooded, red-robed men, penitents all. Some were barefooted; I could see the bruised and bleeding flesh where the cobblestones had torn the skin of their feet. Some had iron chains bound tightly about their insteps to make themselves suffer as they felt that their God had suffered.

Then came another huge float showing a Dying God under the tender ministrations of the Suffering Virgin. Banks of candles, hundreds of them, flickered and lighted up the tableau of agony. Red carnations and blue irises formed a halo about the float. Black-robed men with cords of white silk tied about their hips followed. The amount of gold and silver that I saw was stupendous.

At times the processions so choked the narrow street that the penitents could not move. The float stopped and came to rest on the cobblestones and I saw workmen dressed in blue denim pushing aside the heavy red velvet cloth that draped the float to get air. Their faces looked bleak and pinched and their heads were covered with pads to enable them to support the float upon their skulls. I counted some forty-odd men under the float. They were paid, I learned later, forty pesetas a day by the Church for this work. One man took a piece of bread out of his pocket and began nibbling it as his chest heaved from the strain of his toil.

There sounded a knocking, a signal that the men should place their heads against the bottom of the float; another knocking signaled them to lift their heads in unison; up went the float on the heads of the workmen; the red velvet cloth was dropped; the bugles sounded; the drums beat; and the float moved on.

Night fell. The endless processions marched. Float after float passed. Dying Gods and Sorrowful Virgins replaced one another. Grim soldiers, armed with weapons of death, guarded and defended their God and their Virgin. They were symbols of the male and the female principles of life. A God died that man might live again, and the Virgin stood eternally ready to give birth to the God that was to die, that is, the Man-God. . . . The idea was how to die, the degree and readiness for death, the emotional willingness to die for one's aim. This was a militant religion of death and suffering, of death and resurrection, each death being linked with a rising from the dead, and each rising from the dead being enthroned in a new generation of men. This was the religion that had enabled the Spaniards to conquer and despoil Mexico and Peru; these were the roots of the Black Legend. . . .

After a restless sleep, I went once again to the plaza to watch the foreshortened rituals and ceremonies of one of the world's most powerful religions pass before my eyes. A vast float showed Christ seated among His twelve disciples; Christ's face was bleak with despair. His disciples, all but Judas, were bowed over with sorrow. This was one of the most powerful and realistic of the floats that had passed and the crowd, with one movement, rose from its seat and crossed itself. Some women threw repeated kisses from their index fingers to the figure of the Doomed God. Next came a Virgin atop another float; she came slowly amidst an army of tall, burning candles that illuminated the many strings of pearls about her white and beautiful throat. Diamonds gleamed on her outstretched fingers, fingers that seemed straining to touch the Doomed God, to touch Him with compassion. Her eyes were cloudy with sorrow; she trailed yard after yard of white embroidered silk. She stood under a white canopy. Incense bearers swung with slow rhythm their vessels of silver, veiling the air, and the multitude rose again, crossed itself, tossing kisses of adoration.

"*Bonita!*" exclaimed a fat woman beside me as she crossed herself and threw a kiss to the Virgin.

The float paused. From above my head a woman burst into song, caroling a *saeta*, a lament for the Dying God and the Grieving Virgin. The singer stood on an iron balcony; she was dressed in the uniform of a domestic servant. She had heard the sound of drums and bugles and had rushed to the balcony. She lifted her voice in a wild and tremulous hymn of despair and bitter triumph. The crowd listened, moved; then it murmured softly in admiration. On and on the woman wept in tones of melody. When her voice died away to a whisper, there was quiet handclapping. The bugles sounded. The drums beat. The float of the Virgin moved on toward other sections of the city where more *saetas* would be sung to her.

It was night again. There came a float showing Christ roped and tied in front of a cruel-faced Roman soldier. Drums beat sad, martial music. . . .

Day after day and night after night the processions flowed on. In the narrow streets of Seville and over the airways of all Spain the *saetas* announced the tidings of death and rebirth, the psychological law of the Christian life. A feeling of helplessness, of desperation, of wild sorrow, of a grief too deep to be appeased clogged the senses. *Tramp, tramp, tramp* went the feet of the marching troops. The cross was held high and on it was the bloody, bruised figure of a Dying Man, nailed there, crucified, his face sunk in the throes of agony and despair. But behind the Dying Man was the Virgin ready to replenish the earth again so that Life could go on.

And in Spain, where I now stood—indeed, here in this city of Seville—Christianity, in order to survive, had had to institute with a bloody war another form of collectivity. Beleaguered by modern ideas, stormed by the forces of social and political progress, Spain had had to withdraw, had had to go back into the past and find some acceptable form of endurable life that could knit its poetic-minded people together again. The anxious freedom of capitalistic, democratic Europe and America could not be sustained by the Spaniard. He had rejected it as being too painful, too inhuman to bear. The tense Western nomads, hungry for personal destiny, and, above all, the murderous rationalism of sacrificial Communism, had been scornfully rejected in favor of an archaic collective consciousness based on family symbols: One Father, One Mother, One Spirit.

Yet, all of it, Christianity and Communism, had come from one (and perhaps) unrepeatable historical accident that had been compounded in Rome from Greek science and love of the human personality, from Jewish notions of a One and Indivisible God, from Roman conceptions of law and order and property, and from a perhaps never-to-be-unraveled amalgamation of Eastern and African religions with their endless gods who were sacrificed and their virgins who gave birth perennially.

In 1492, in the name of God, the Son, and the Holy Ghost, the Catholic king and queen, Ferdinand and Isabel, had driven the Moors from Spain, had liquidated the Jew, and had scattered a handful of willful gypsies (who were supposed to have forged the nails that went into the cross of Christ!) to the winds. The Inquisition, that cold and calculating instrument of God's terror, had whipped the Spaniards into a semblance of outward comformity, yet keeping intact all the muddy residue of an irrational paganism that lurked at the bottom of the Spanish heart, and Spain had been ready with one Will, one Race, one God, and one Aim.

And Spain, despite all the heroic sacrifices of her liberals, of her poets, of her lovers of liberty, had remained stuck right at that point.

Convinced beyond all counterpersuasion that he possesses a metaphysical mandate to chastise all of those whom he considers the "morally moribund," the "spiritually inept," the "biologically botched," the Spaniard would scorn the rich infinities of possibility looming before the eyes of men, he would stifle hearts responding to the call of a high courage, and he would thwart the will's desire for a new wisdom. . . . He would turn back the clock of history and play the role of God to man.

How poor indeed he is. . . .

Set in Linotype Janson
Format by Robert Cheney
Manufactured by The Haddon Craftsmen, Inc.
Published by Harper & Brothers, *New York*